GLOBALIZING SPORT

GLOBALIZING SPORT

HOW ORGANIZATIONS, CORPORATIONS, MEDIA, AND POLITICS ARE CHANGING SPORTS

GEORGE H. SAGE

Paradigm Publishers
Boulder • London

Copyright © 2010 Paradigm Publishers

Published in the United States by Paradigm Publishers, 2845 Wilderness Place, Suite 200, Boulder, CO 80301 USA.

Paradigm Publishers is the trade name of Birkenkamp & Company, LLC, Dean Birkenkamp, President and Publisher.

Library of Congress Cataloging-in-Publication Data

Sage, George Harvey.
  Globalizing sport : how organizations, corporations, media, and politics are changing sports / George H. Sage.
      p. cm.
  Includes bibliographical references and index.
  ISBN 978-1-59451-757-0 (hardcover : alk. paper) —
ISBN 978-1-59451-758-7 (pbk. : alk. paper)
  1. Sports and globalization. 2. Sports—Sociological aspects. I. Title.
  GV706.34.S34 2010
  306.483—dc22

2010015958

Printed and bound in the United States of America on acid-free paper that meets the standards of the American National Standard for Permanence of Paper for Printed Library Materials.

Designed and Typeset by Straight Creek Bookmakers.

14 13 12 11 10 1 2 3 4 5

Dedicated to Liz—

the brightest star in my personal universe

Contents

Preface   *xiii*

1 Global Sport: The Transformation from Local
to National to Global   1
    "Global," "Globalization," "Sport":
      Clarifying the Core Concepts   2
        Is Globalization Something New?   4
        Sport: From Folk Pastimes to Sportification   5
        Is Sport Something New?   6
        Sportification   7
    Political Economic Forces Shaping Globalization   8
        Globalization from Above   9
        Globalization from Below   11
        Sport and Globalization from Above and Below   13
    Cultural Forces Shaping Globalization   13
        Homogenization (Americanization) Perspective   15
        Hybridization Perspective   18
        Polarization Perspective   19
        Homogenization, Hybridization, and Polarization
          Perspectives and Sport   21
    Forms of Globalization and Manifestations in Sport   22
    Segmentation of the Global Sport Industry   23
    Summary   24
    References   25

2 Global Sport Organizations: Governing the World of Sport   29
    Governing Global Sport: Global Sport Organizations   29

From International Sport Initiatives to Global
   Sport Organizations 32
The Olympic Movement and Its Network 34
   International Olympic Committee 34
   Organizing Committee of the Olympic Games 37
   National Olympic Committees 38
   International Sport Federations 39
   Other Organizations Within the Olympic Movement Network 39
Global Issues Confronting the Olympic Movement 41
   Females in the Olympics 41
   The Amateur Issue 42
   Inclusion of Athletes with Special Needs 44
International Sport Federations: GSOs Within the IOC 46
   The Preeminent International Federation: Fédération
      Internationale de Football Association 51
Global Sport Organizations and Solo Sports 53
   Association of Tennis Professionals 54
   Women's Tennis Association 55
   Multiple GSOs for a Sport: Professional Boxing 55
Global Sporting Organizations and International Games 57
Summary 58
Notes 60
References 60

3 GLOBAL MIGRATION OF SPORTS LABOR   **63**
Human Migration: Past and Present 64
The Migration of Sports Labor:
   Sports Workers Throughout the World 66
Sports-Labor Migration Within Nations 67
   Sports-Labor Migration: Intra- and Intercontinental Migration 68
Global Patterns of Migration Among Sports Labor
   in Selected Sports 71
   Sports-Labor Migration and Soccer 71
   Sports-Labor Migration and Basketball 76
   Sports-Labor Migration and Ice Hockey 79
   Sports-Labor Migration and Baseball 81
   Sports-Labor Migration and Intercollegiate Sports 84
   Sports-Labor Migration and the Olympic Games 86
Related Features of Sports Migration 89
   Sports Migrants' Motivations 89
   Recruitment of Sports Labor 91
   Consequences of Sports-Labor Migration 93
Summary 94
Notes 95
References 95

4 THE GLOBAL SPORT INDUSTRY: PRODUCTION AND PROMOTION   100
   The Rise of Factory Manufacturing   102
   The Growth of Commercial Sports   104
   Manufacturing in the Global Economy   106
   Global Sporting Goods Manufacturing: From Humble
      Beginnings to Transnational Corporations   108
         Wilson Sporting Goods   111
         Adidas AG   112
         Reebok International   113
         Mizuno Corporation   115
         Nike, Inc.   116
   Sporting Goods Manufacturing in the Global
      Economy: The Case of Nike   118
         Nike's Asian Factories: Not a Pretty Sight   119
         Nike's Responses to Factory Reports and the Social Movement   121
         *Nike's New Initiatives: A Commitment to Reform
            or a Public Relations Ploy?   123*
   Beyond Sport Production to Sport Promotion   126
         Individual Athlete Endorsements   126
         Event and Team Sponsorships   130
   Summary   133
   Notes   134
   References   134

5 GLOBAL SPORT AND GLOBAL MASS MEDIA   140
   Mass Communication, Mass Media, and Media Sport   140
   Social Roles of the Mass Media   141
   Global Organizations and the Mass Media   142
   Conglomerate Media Ownership   143
   The Global Media Sport Complex   147
   Articulations Between the Mass Media and Sport   149
         Media Technology and Commercial Sport Evolve Together   150
   Overlapping Ownership of Media and Sport Organizations   154
   The Symbiosis Between Television and Sport   157
         Enhancing Sport Revenue via Television   159
         The Market for Broadcast Rights   161
         Transnational Corporate Sport Sponsorships   164
         Media As Public Relations Tool for Global Sport   167
   New Media and Global Sports   168
         The Internet   168
         Video Games   170
         Twitter, Facebook, MySpace, and YouTube   170
         Online Sport Gambling   171
   Media Sport and Deterritorialization of Fans   175
   Global Media Sport and Gender   175

Summary   178
Notes   179
References   180

6 Global Politics and Sport   185
Political Intervention in Sports   186
Sport and the Promotion of Political Ideology   187
Advancing National Unity and Recognition
    Through Sport   188
Sport As an Instrument of International Politics
    and Diplomacy   189
        Promoting Nazism: The 1936 Olympic Games   190
        Promoting Communism: The Soviet Sport System   190
        East Germany and the People's Republic of China:
            Adopting the Soviet Sport Model   191
        The United States: Joining Other Countries in Sport Politics   192
        New and Smaller Nations Adopt the Model   194
Developing Countries and National Unification
    Through Sport   195
        The African Continent and African States   196
National Embarrassments Through Sport   199
Geopolitical Censorship in Sport:
    Nation-Led Boycotts   199
Global Politics Within Sport   200
        The Politics of Gender Inequality in Global Sport   200
        The Politics of Racial Inequality in Global Sport   204
Politics Within the IOC and FIFA   209
        IOC   209
        FIFA   211
Political Dissent at Global Sports Events   212
Summary   214
Notes   215
References   215

7 Global Sport: Future Issues and Trends   219
Global Population Trends and Sport   220
        World Population Growth   221
        Population Composition   222
        Increasing Global Urbanization   224
The Future of Global Sport Organizations   226
        The Olympic Movement: The IOC, the Preeminent GSO   228
Migration of Sport Labor in the Future   238
Global Sport-Industry Production in the Future   240
        Future Labor Issues in Sporting Goods and Equipment   241

Future Technology and Sporting Goods and Equipment   242
The Future of Media Sports   243
   Television Coverage   243
   Television Technology and Sports Viewing   244
   Internet Technology and Sports Spectatorship   245
   Video Technology and Sports Video Games   245
   Sports Blogging   246
Sport Politics and the Future   247
Summary   249
References   250

INDEX   253

ABOUT THE AUTHOR   270

PREFACE

I want to explain four important features about this book. First, this book is *about* global sport. It is not an encyclopedic treatment of global sport. That would require a sprawling, multivolume undertaking. It would also require a writer fluent in at least several languages in order to be knowledgeable about relevant global sports topics in the major non-English languages of the world.

Second, although most regions of the world are given some attention in each chapter of this book, North America and Europe—including the United Kingdom—receive the most. An abundance of literature is available about sport in the nations of these regions, and media coverage of international sports is overwhelming focused on them.

Third, most books published on the topic of global sport are written for readers who are either upper-level undergraduate students or graduate students in sport studies. These books tend to be descriptions of research findings or interpretations and analyses of research on global sport topics. This is reflected in the fact that several of them are edited books, so they are typically not meant to be read from cover to cover but to serve readers who have a particular research interest in one or two of a book's chapters.

Fourth, my goal in writing this book is to provide readers new to the subject of global sports with an understanding of the field's issues and trends. The book is intended for the general reader who is interested in the international sport world but has never come across a book that deals with this subject. It is also directed to college students who may be studying sociology, sport studies, political science, international relations, geography, history, or the like, and have not encountered a book with a focus on global sport. Finally, faculty who wish to supplement their regular course text-book may find a volume devoted to global sport a good addition.

Sport, a seemingly trivial facet of life, is a fundamental cultural activity in every country of the modern world. In short, global sport transcends national boundaries, and it is both a product of and a contributor to the processes of globalization. In various ways sport is a microcosm of world-wide political, economic, and cultural trends. Thus, you have global sport embroiled in international political issues; transnational corporations marketing sport through the production of global sporting events, such as the Olympic Games and World Cup; athletes migrating to various countries seeking the best salaries and benefits; sporting goods and equipment, essential products for sports, manufacturing in low-wage countries.

Perhaps as much as anything else, global sport is big business. Television networks bid billions of dollars for the rights to televise international sporting events. The new medium of the Internet and its various spin-offs have found sport at the cutting edge of global mass communications. Globally elite athletes, such as soccer's David Beckham and Cristiano Ronaldo, as well as others, command multiyear, multi-million-dollar contracts. Global sport icons, like Phil Mickelson and LaBron James, make more money through product endorsements than they do from their sports achievements. Global sport organizations have some of the same characteristics as transnational corporations, with their business in the management and production of sporting events throughout the world.

In writing a book like this, one must rely on the research and writings of others, and the friendship of colleagues helps too. I am indebted to numerous scholars of global sport, many of whom are personal friends. Their good work has been of invaluable assistance to me in preparing this book. Beyond that, I want to express my profound appreciation to long-time colleagues in sport sociology, D. Stanley Eitzen and John W. Loy, for the intellectual inspiration, encouragement, and continued friendship they have provided me over the years.

With the publication of this volume, my name now appears on twenty books (counting multiple editions), either as author, coauthor, or editor. I dedicated my first book to my wife, Liz. The books that followed were dedicated to other members of my extended family. Now, with this twentieth book, I return to the one who has always been there for me, has good-naturedly always granted time for me to write, has been my greatest supporter, and has been my best friend and the love of my life—Liz.

CHAPTER 1

GLOBAL SPORT

THE TRANSFORMATION FROM LOCAL TO NATIONAL TO GLOBAL

> Sport has become a major actor in modern society and is present everywhere. This phenomenon has spread with our world becoming more and more global.
> —Global Sports Forum, Barcelona, Spain, 2008

In the midst of writing this book, I had lunch with a friend whom I had not seen for several months. At one point during our luncheon conversation, my friend asked what I had been doing. When I replied that I was writing a book about global sport, he asked, "What does sport have to do with global?" Having written some 20,000 words on the subject at that point, I wondered how I was going to answer his question with an appropriately brief synopsis. I decided to use a few vignettes that would, hopefully, help him understand the connections between global and sport. After I had articulated five or six global-sport connections, my friend said, "Enough, okay, I get it."

When I returned to my office, I realized that perhaps, as they opened the cover of this book, many readers would have that same question as my friend, so I decided to write the responses I had used at lunch as a way of illustrating the connections between global and sport:

- Athletes from 205 countries participated in the 2008 Beijing Olympic Games.
- Of the 596 athletes on the U.S. Olympic team in Beijing, 33 were foreign-born.
- The World Cup finals are the most widely viewed sporting event in the world, with an estimated 715.1 million people across the globe watching the 2006 tournament final match between Italy and France.
- In 2007 David Beckham, the British soccer star and best-known soccer player in the world, left Real Madrid, a Spanish professional soccer team he had played for since 2003, and signed a five-year contract with Major League Soccer's Los Angeles Galaxy.
- Of the 818 baseball players on Major League Baseball rosters at the beginning of the 2009 season, 229—or 28 percent—were born outside the United States. At the same time, 48 percent of 6,973 minor-league players were born outside the United States.
- At the beginning of the 2008–2009 English Premier League season, over 337 foreign players were registered and eligible to play in the league, representing a total of sixty-six countries.

"Global," "Globalization," "Sport": Clarifying the Core Concepts

I am not going to make this a dreary definitional exercise, but I do want to clarify some points about three words that will appear throughout this book: "global," "globalization," and "sport." In using the word "global," I will be referring to something that relates to, involves, or affects the entire earth—the whole world. In a later chapter I analyze the global migration of athletes, teams, and leagues. In another I identify and examine the creation and development of global sport organizations. Another describes the global sporting goods and equipment industry, focusing especially on the workers who make the products that athletes and teams throughout the world use to play their sports.

The word "globalization" cannot be new to the vocabulary of readers of this book. It is omnipresent in the media as well as in everyday conversations. Googling the word will bring up over 22 million entries. Since the 1990s a substantial academic cottage industry has evolved around globalization: how do we define it? what does it mean? when did it begin? what drives it? and so on. So while there is little debate about what "global" means, such is not the case for "globalization," which has been a matter of intense debate in the fields of business and social science. I will spare the reader the torturous details of that never satisfying dispute, except to share the results of a survey I conducted.

During the six months leading up to writing this chapter, I casually surveyed dozens of people—family, friends, colleagues, even a few strangers (all nonacademics)—asking them how they define, or view, globalization. I recorded their replies on a small notepad I carry around. Upon sifting through their responses, the word "interconnectedness," or a close synonym, appeared most frequently. Interestingly, I found there was close agreement between my respondents and scholars specializing in the study of globalization. For example, two sociologists, D. Stanley Eitzen and Maxine Baca Zinn, authors of *Globalization: The Transformation of Social Worlds,* say, "Globalization refers to the greater interconnectedness among the world's people" (2009, 1).

Grazia Ietto-Gillies, director of the Centre for International Business Studies at London's South Bank University, describes how globalized interconnectedness manifests itself through a variety of transactions and flows, especially the following:

- international trade in goods and services
- foreign direct investment
- portfolio investment
- profits, interests, and dividends from the various types of foreign investment
- interorganizational collaborative partnerships
- movements of people across borders for leisure or business activities or in search of jobs (2003, 140–141)

Manfred Steger, director of the Globalism Research Centre at the Royal Melbourne Institute of Technology, describes globalization as "an unprecedented compression of time and space reflected in the tremendous intensification of social, political, economic, and cultural interconnections and interdependencies on a global scale" (2002, ix). The connectedness underlying globalization involves growing diffusion, increasing interdependence, an expanding number of transnational organizations, and an emerging world culture and consciousness.

A second feature of globalization on which both my respondents and scholars agree is that globalization is a complex phenomenon more in the nature of a process, not a static state of affairs. Jan Aart Scholte, a director at the Centre for the Study of Globalisation and Regionalisation at the

University of Warwick in England, characterizes globalization as "a process (or set of processes) which embodies a transformation in the spatial organization of social relations and transactions" (2005, 17).

As an aside, I noticed age differences in how my respondents interpreted the process of globalization. Those who had reached adulthood before 1960 viewed globalization as an evolving, changing phenomenon. Those who became adults after 1990 viewed globalization as a fact of life, a given; yes, it was a process, but they couldn't imagine a different world. They have always known a globalized planet.

So, while there are numerous definitions and characterizations of globalization, there is no consensus. Nevertheless, there is universal agreement that the processes of globalization are transforming the world toward greater interdependence and integration, in terms of shifting forms of human contact, flows of goods, capital, information, fashion, culture, and consciousness. Like all human processes, it is in a constant state of change and remolding with outcomes for individuals, families, and institutions worldwide (Eitzen and Zinn 2009; Harris 2008; Hebron and Stack 2009).

Is Globalization Something New?

Some think of globalization as a recent development, but its beginnings reach far back in history. Most readers of this volume will have enough knowledge about human history to know that international migration, trade, and communication have been common for many centuries. In one of the most comprehensive accounts of the origins of globalization, Nayan Chanda, director of publications at Yale's Center for the Study of Globalization, asserts that globalization "began thousands of years ago and continues to this day with increasing speed and ease" (2007, frontispiece; see also Dirlik 2007). According to Chanda, it began with a small group of our ancestors hiking out of Africa seeking better food and security. After thousands of years of wandering, they had finally settled and inhabited all the continents. At this point, Chanda claims, traders, preachers, soldiers, and adventurers from the various civilizations connected with one another, thus launching the process of globalization (2007, xiv).

For thousands of years travel, trade, and migration across political boundaries have been common. These cross-boundary interactions have spread cultural influences and disseminated knowledge, inventions, and understanding (including those of science and technology) (Sen 2008, 19). Although cross-boundary connections certainly have antecedents in earlier centuries, only since mid-twentieth century has globality had a prominent, persistent, comprehensive, and central role in the lives of a large proportion of humanity throughout the world. Millions of people currently have direct—even instantaneous—written, auditory, and visual contact with others across the globe several times each day (Scholte 2005). The transformation of human civilization—in terms of social linkages, institutions, culture, and consciousness—has been profound (Lechner and Boli 2008, 2).

An indication of a trend's status is how frequently it appears in mass media stories. Table 1.1 illustrates how the word "globalization" has increased in the public consciousness through its use by the *New York Times*.

Table 1.1 Increase in the Use of the Word "Globalization" by the *New York Times* from 1980 to 2000

Year	Globalization References*
1990	47
1995	58
1997	205
1999	265
2000	505
1980–1984	2
1985–1989	164
1990–1994	213
1995–2000	1,309

*The first set gives the references for a single year; the second set gives the references for five-year blocks.
Source: Amended from Veseth 2002.

Sport: From Folk Pastimes to Sportification

As you recall, at the beginning of this section I said I wanted to clarify some points about the three words that will appear throughout this book: "global," "globalization," "sport." I have done that for the word "global" and have made an initial foray into examining "globalization." But before I continue my discussion about globalization, it seems appropriate to bring "sport" into this mix of concepts. Then I can return to a fuller analysis of globalization, with an emphasis on its relationship to sport.

If you think globalization is a labyrinth of differing views, you have not heard anything yet. The word "sport" overflows with definitions. They extend to the very scholarly and very erudite to the humorous. Several years ago, I was pressing my students for their definitions of "sport," mostly just to wake them up and get them thinking (it was an 8:00 a.m. class!!). I had been receiving some not very profound replies. One student argued that "sport is what's found on the sports pages of a newspaper"; another advanced the notion that "sport is what appears on ESPN." But my favorite—and it cracked up the class—was the student who offered, "I can't define sport, but I know it when I see it." Who can argue with definitions like that? However, for readers interested in a detailed and scholarly essay on this topic, I recommend John W. Loy and Jay Coakley's entry "Sport" in *The Blackwell Encyclopedia of Sociology* (2007, 4643–4645).

The major focus of this volume will be on professional sport. This form of sport has other designations, such as elite sport and world-class sport. I shall give little attention to leisure, youth, and school or collegiate sports.

Is Sport Something New?

Earlier in this chapter, I posed the question about whether the process of globalization is new. My answer was no; in fact, it has been around for centuries. What about sports? Despite overwhelming natural and social barriers that made involvement in games and sporting activities difficult, anthropologists and historians have found that people of all cultures have engaged in a wide variety of playful physical activities for centuries. It was not until the late nineteenth century, however, that conditions became favorable for organized sports to become a popular cultural practice for a large number of citizens. Technological innovations and the accompanying Industrial Revolution were instrumental in stimulating a transformation in social conditions that gave rise to modern sport.

British sport sociologist Joseph Maguire identifies the last quarter of the nineteenth century as a major phase in "the international spread of sport, the establishment of international sports organizations, the growth of competition between national teams, the worldwide acceptance of rules governing specific sports forms and the establishment of global competitions such as the Olympic Games" (1990, 82; see also Vamplew 2006); this was thus the incubation phase of globalization processes in the sports world.

Sportification

The transformation from primarily informal and expressive folk games to the rigidly formal activities of modern sport forms created a process of what several sports scholars have called "sportification." In this view sportification refers to a universal hegemonic shift toward competitive, rationalized, and standardized organization of sporting practices and organizations This concept is also reflected in the "totalization of sport," meaning that international sport has been transformed from sporting events between individuals or teams to events between nation-states that have unequal resources to produce elite athletes and teams.

There seems to be general agreement that the initial phases of sportification appeared in Britain in the seventeenth and eighteenth centuries, in which ancient pastimes such as cricket, horse racing, fox hunting, and boxing began to assume more organized and regulated forms. The nineteenth century witnessed a bonanza of new sports, such as rugby and soccer, and the modernization of older ones, such as tennis and athletics (track and field). Similar trends were taking place in North America and Europe, but with the diffusion of British sport throughout the British Empire and then the world, the founding of the modern Olympic Games, and the creation of international sport federations, by the beginning of the twentieth century a variety of sports, sport organizations, and sporting events had become a global phenomenon.

By the late twentieth century, sport had become a pervasive global part of life, penetrating every level of educational systems and into political, economic, and cultural systems in the form of professional sports. A growing literature examines this trend. In *How Soccer Explains the World: An Unlikely Theory of Globalization* (2005), Franklin Foer analyzes the role of soccer in various countries of the world as a way of exploring the interrelations between that sport and globalization. Sociologist Barry Smart has summarized the outcomes this way: "As modern sport has become global in scope it has largely lost its playful character and its professional practice has become both a global media spectacle and a serious and financially significant global business" (2007, 24).

If you want an object lesson in the connections between global sport and globalization, follow these instructions: Go to your favorite sporting goods store and choose a sport to outfit, such as soccer or basketball. Now, begin with the footwear. Check to find the country in which the shoes were made. Regardless of the brand, they were likely made in China or Vietnam. Then choose the socks and so on, working through all the items of apparel and equipment for that sport. Likely all were made in a low-wage developing country—China, Vietnam, certain Central and South American countries, eastern European countries, and so forth.

Political Economic Forces Shaping Globalization

Now that I have clarified the distinction between "global" and "globalization" and provided an overview of the transformation of informal pastimes and games into a global sportification, it should be clear to the reader that one cannot really examine global sport without taking globalization into account. Indeed, contemporary sport is an integral component of the political economy of globalization. It is as tightly embedded in the fabric of globalization as are the automobile and electronics industries. For that reason I now turn to the forces shaping globalization to provide the reader with an understanding of the infrastructure of the global political economy as a foundation for understanding global sport.

The economic, political, technological, and cultural consequences and trends of globalization comprise a complex of forces that are not easily summarized. Nevertheless, they have produced a mass of literature that attempts to analyze and explain them and their effects. Many endorse the perspective of Joel Bleifuss, editor of *In These Times,* who claims, "We are witnessing an unprecedented transfer of power from people and their governments to global institutions whose allegiance is to abstract free-market principles, and whose favored citizens are soulless corporate entities that have the power to shape and break nations" (2001, 1).

With globalization, economic, political, and cultural processes and forces that operate worldwide affect individual lives. Most analyses of globalization focus on one of its aspects, such as the global economy or global politics. However, some analysts have attempted to articulate the contending forces of globalization more comprehensively by mapping out a topology—a physical and logical structure—of this phenomenon. According to Richard Falk (1999, 2003), professor of international law and practice at Princeton University, the global forces behind globalization have created a bifurcation of consequences that he calls "globalization from above" and "globalization from below," which can serve as conceptual distinctions and be employed to analyze the consequences of globalization. Falk has argued that "the contrast implied by the counterposing of globalization-from-above and -below is at best a convenience that calls our attention to the main configurations of tension currently at work in the world" (1999, 6).

Globalization from Above

The globalization-from-above perspective views the primary consequence of globalization as one in which all regions of the world are being incorporated into a single capitalist system based on neoliberal principles. See Box 1.1 for a description of neoliberalism. In *Low-Wage Capitalism* Fred Goldstein asserts, "What is referred to as 'globalization' is in fact the expanded export of capital and the use of cutthroat trade by giant transnational corporations to pile up huge profits at the expense of the people of the world" (2008, 279). It is a monumental transformation and restructuring of corporations with the outcome being the production of goods and services that are marketed across the entire planet, accompanied by a worldwide media domination of the culture by what is often called corporate globalism.

No single dominant group comprises globalization from above; instead, there is an alliance of factions of the most powerful, wealthy, and influential persons and groups in business, commerce, government, and mass media. Leading that alliance are transnational corporations (TNCs) that manage and control, by political-economic domination and intellectual leadership, and employ most of the world's labor force. With economic power nearly matching that of nation-states, TNCs control much of the world's investment capital, technology, and contact with international markets. Their numbers have soared from about 7,000 in 1970 to over 77,000 by 2008, and the largest 200 TNCs account for over half of the world's industrial output. Predictably, most of them are headquartered in the developed economies. Of the world's one hundred largest corporations, seventy-one are based in Britain, France, Germany, Japan, and the United States (Shapiro 2008).

A major consequence of this system has been a "global assembly line," in which products are manufactured by low-wage workers and sold in the developed countries. A common outcome of this system is that communities, even entire nations, are restrained from enforcing social, labor, and environmental protections in order to attract corporate capital. Equally devastating is the competition among developing countries that desperately seek jobs and investment at any cost, resulting in what some scholars call a race to the bottom, meaning a vicious competition for the lowest-wage workers and poverty-induced immigration.

Box 1.1 What Is Neoliberalism?

Adam Smith, a Scottish economist of the eighteenth century, wrote a book titled *The Wealth of Nations* that became the bible of liberalism. In it he adamantly argued against government intervention in economic matters, against restrictions on manufacturing, against barriers to commerce, and against tariffs. Such a view was considered "liberal" because it encouraged "free" enterprise and promoted competition in economic affairs.

Liberalism was a prevailing view in the industrializing countries until the 1930s, when it came under criticism because many politicians and some economists felt it had led to the worldwide Great Depression. The United States and some European governments modified liberal economics and adopted a position whereby government intervened in the economy to regulate business practices and advance the common good. However, in the latter twentieth century, with the rise of globalization and the development of huge transnational corporations, economic liberalization was reborn, making it new, or "neo"—thus, neoliberalism.

Neoliberalism is a set of political and economic policies that have become global during the last twenty-five years or so. Like Adam Smith's liberalism, neoliberalism is grounded in "freeing" private enterprise from any bonds imposed by governments. The following are foundational principles for neoliberal advocacy: total freedom of movement for capital, goods, and services; greater openness to international trade and investment, as in the North American Free Trade Agreement; abolition of all price controls; deregulation and the privatization of state-owned industries or services; reduction of wages through deunionization of workers; elimination of workers' rights; and cuts in public spending on social services.

All in all, supporters of the neoliberal way promote a global unregulated market as the best way to increase globalized economic growth, which will ultimately benefit people throughout the world. But as one of its skeptics has argued, "It's like Reagan's 'supply-side' and 'trickle-down' economics—but somehow the wealth didn't trickle down very much." So the beneficiaries of neoliberalism are a minority of the world's people.

Another dominant driver of globalization from above is technological innovation in the field of communication and information, together with advances in new technologies, especially computers, communication satellites, fiber optics, and the Internet, which have transformed information and communication throughout the world. "Anyone with a computer can communicate with anyone else in the world that has a computer" has become common shorthand for characterizing global communication. A system of transnational media corporations, mostly American and European, owned and managed by some of the leading advocates for the neoliberal model of globalization are the principal sources of news and information throughout the world (e.g., CNN). Much of the global "information society," with its extraordinary technology, employs incessant repetition of political, economic, and cultural information that is acceptable to and supported by the forces of globalization from above.

Although TNCs are globally influential and powerful, the political world has been turned into a global web of interdependencies shaped less by military supremacy than by intricate political processes involving international institutions, multinational corporations, and citizens' groups that have challenged nation-state sovereignty. This has led some to suggest that there has been a "deterritorialization" of politics and governance, with political globalization merely a secondary force driven fundamentally by economic forces. Those who advance that view point to the neoliberal policies imposed by the so-called "big three" globalization organizations—the World Trade Organization (WTO), International Monetary Fund (IMF), and World Bank. These are powerful complementary forces to globalization from above because they are important institutions for global governance; they also seek to foster transnational trade and provide economic development in underdeveloped countries. Unfortunately, they have virtually no democratic accountability (Eitzen and Zinn 2009; also see Ietto-Gillies 2003, 347–369).

Globalization from Below

Richard Falk's (1999) distinctive alternative to globalization from above he calls globalization from below. For Falk this latter term designates the global forces striving for global economic fairness, political democracy, social rights, and environmental protections, none of which characterizes globalization from above. More recently, Italian sociologist Donatella della Porta has claimed that the globalization-from-below "perspective challenges the power of markets and states and represents a project aimed at restraining the rule of the market and the sovereignty of states, in the name of universal rights—human, political, social, and economic. Globalization from below aims to empower global social movements and provides spaces for the self-organization of civil society" (2007, 49; also see della Porta, et al. 2006). Further, she stresses that the main theme of globalization from below is to bring about enough democratic control over national governments, markets, and corporations to insure a viable future for all people throughout the world.

The forces driving globalization from below are a combination of coalitions, diverse global campaigns, and local struggles that have been brought together by common interests, goals, and an assortment of activist events, such as global extravaganzas like the Battle of Seattle and disruptions at WTO, World Bank, and IMF meetings. While attention has been focused on big international demonstrations, the movement for globalization from below has in fact been planning and linking up in an enormous range of ways that may be less visible than demonstrations, sit-ins, and the like, but that also transcend their limitations (Brecher, Costello, and Smith 2000; see also della Porta 2007).

As globalization expanded and gained momentum in the 1980s and 1990s, its advocates insisted that it would promote worldwide wealth and prosperity. A favorite slogan was, "A globalized world, like rising water, will lift all boats." People around the world were assured that the benefits of globalization would be a blessing for everyone, if they accepted neoliberalism's edicts. Overall, workers throughout the world accepted the wages and conditions of labor that satisfied governments and turned profits for TNCs, but the promises of globalization from above have not "lifted all boats." Instead, they have aggravated old problems for workers throughout the world and created new ones for the global environment (Eitzen and Zinn 2009; Isaak 2005; Madrick 2009).

Globalization from below has emerged out of diverse concerns and experiences. As manufacturing of products has become more globally mobile, labor organizations realize that international capital mobility is not generating mutual benefits for workers in either developed or developing countries; instead, it is leading to competitive wage cutting, thus widening the income gap between the rich and the poor, causing an increase in global poverty, especially among women, who are the major portion of the workforce exploited in global sweatshops.

Social movements on behalf of a globalization from below are flourishing in locations throughout the world. Networking across national borders, they are linking up by means of the Internet, numerous nongovernmental organizations, and social groups. College students have become outraged that products emblazoned with their college's mascots and logos are being made by children and women, many of them forced to work sixty or more hours per week for less than a subsistence wage. There is even a global justice movement, which della Porta describes as a "loose network of organizations … engaged in collective action of various kinds, on the basis of the shared goal of advancing the cause of justice … among and between peoples across the globe" (2007, 6).

The contrast of the fundamental differences between the top-down hierarchical politics of globalization from above and the bottom-up participatory politics of globalization from below is stark. But Richard Falk, the architect of these terms, argues that "this conflict is not a zero-sum rivalry; it is rather one in which the transnational democratic goal is to reconcile global market operations with both the well-being of peoples and the carrying capacity of the earth" (2003, 203; see also Orbie and Tortell 2009).

Sport and Globalization from Above and Below

The relevance of globalization from above and below to contemporary sporting practices will be evident in various ways in all of the chapters that follow. I will make only a couple of brief comments on this issue at this time.

Elite global sport organizations, such as the Olympic Movement, International Cricket Council, and Sony Ericsson Women's Tennis Association Tour are examples of globalization from above because of the social exclusivity of their leadership, limited opportunities for participation in their sports, and high cost of attending their sporting events. The struggles for women's and gay and lesbian rights in sports, sports for the disabled, and workers' rights in factories making sporting goods in developing countries, as well as the creation of the Gay Games, are all examples of globalization from below in sports.

Cultural Forces Shaping Globalization

The previous discussion about globalization from above and below focused on the political economy of globalization. But economic and political perspectives of globalization cannot be examined apart from the cultural sphere, primarily because the economy, polity, and culture are overlapping and fully integrated in modern societies. Cultural global patterns and practices are as relevant as economic and political patterns and practices, when considering the effects of globalization. The multidimensional nature of globalization demands that the interaction of all three of these social institutions be considered.

The word "culture" has no single, specific definition, but it is commonly viewed as referring to that which characterizes a group or society in a place and time. It is the shared, integrated pattern of language, beliefs, attitudes, values, social practices—such as art, music, language, drama, literature, film, TV, clothing, food, and sports—by which individuals communicate, perpetuate, develop, and transmit their knowledge of life to succeeding generations. David Hesmondhalgh, director of the Media Industries Research Centre at the University of Leeds, explains that cultural industries are usually seen as "those institutions ... which are most directly involved in the production of social meaning, including advertising and marketing, broadcasting, film, print and electronic publishing, music industries, video and computer games, and more 'borderline' cases such as fashion, sports and software" (2002, 11).

Manfred Steger provides a clear and concise explanation of what cultural globalization is about and its significance, saying it "refers to the intensification and expansion of cultural flow across the globe.... The exploding network of cultural interconnections and interdependencies in the last decades has led some commentators to suggest that cultural practices lie at the very heart of contemporary globalization" (2003, 68). The cultural flow that Steger mentions is a vast array of goods, services, and images too huge to list, but some examples were given in the previous paragraph.

Beyond what constitutes cultural goods and services, the expansion of international travel, trade, film, TV, and the Internet, to name just a few, have increased the exposure of people throughout the world to foreign cultures. A fundamental question that has arisen about the consequences of cultural globalization among both scholars and the world's citizens is this: Is globalization making people around the world more alike or more different? Globalization's cultural consequences have created a lively academic and public debate, which shows no sign of achieving widespread consensus. However, as the debate has raged over the past twenty years, three major theses have been proposed and fervently defended (el-Ojeili and Hayden 2006; Harris 2008; Hebron and Stack 2009; Holton 2000; Kraidy 2005; Pieterse 2009):

- the homogenization (Americanization) perspective
- the hybridization perspective
- the polarization perspective

Homogenization (Americanization) Perspective

During the rapid globalizing expansion of the 1970s and 1980s, cultural globalization was being driven by a worldwide marketing of Western cultural industries inspired by mass media technology that appeared to cultural analysts to be configuring toward a process of "homogenization" of marketing, consumption, and selling largely represented by an industry headquartered in New York and Hollywood. As globalizing momentum built, a label gradually emerged with widespread credibility as a synonym for homogenization, "Americanization," referring to the consequences of the spread of American cultural products abroad for local cultures, some very visible, others less obvious. So, in its strongest sense, Americanization is seen as a one-way process in which American cultural forms, products, and values are imposed on other societies at the expense of the local culture—a cultural imperialism, as it were.

For example, the influence of American cultural products on other countries' cultures can be seen, according to Steger, in "Amazonian Indians wearing Nike training shoes, denizens of the Southern Sahara purchasing Texaco baseball caps, and Palestinian youth proudly displaying their Chicago Bulls sweatshirts in downtown Ramallah" (2009, 147). Neologisms like "Disneyfication," "McDonaldization," and "Coca-colonization" convey that global cultural power is largely held by the West, or more narrowly by the United States. They imply a homogenization of consumption, marketing, and selling (el-Ojeili and Hayden 2006).

An Americanization perspective was expressed quite explicitly in 1993 by then Canadian prime minister Kim Campbell: "Images of America are so [globally] pervasive ... that it is almost as if instead of the world immigrating to America, America has immigrated to the world, allowing people to aspire to be Americans even in their distant countries" (quoted in Barth 1998, 40). She was expressing a view that was popular worldwide. Indeed, apprehension about this perspective of the Americanizing cultural globalization process is not new; it has been pervasive for the past forty years. Similarly, denouncing American cultural exports as a source of cultural "pollution" has been fashionable as well. There is actually an organization representing over sixty countries called the International Network on Cultural Policy, which is so fearful of U.S. cultural dominance throughout the world that it attempts to formulate policies to restrict worldwide consumer access to American cultural goods.

In a way it is understandable why such a label came into popular usage. The United States does play a prominent role in cultural globalization for a number of reasons: its size, wealth, and homogeneous culture. With over 300 million consumers, the United States is one of the largest markets in the world, exceeded in size and wealth by only the European Union. Although only 4 percent of the world's population live in the United States, it accounts for 25 percent of global economic output, putting the U.S. market in a dominant position.

In terms of number of languages, races, and ethnicities, the United States is one of the most diverse nations in the world, but in terms of the size of linguistic or racial groups, it is relatively homogenous. Around 97 percent of the U.S. population is fluent in the English language, and some 71 percent of the population belongs to one racial group (Caucasian). Contrast that with countries in which no language is spoken as a mother tongue by any segment that accounts for more than 30 percent of the population, such as Nigeria or India. In the United States speaking English opens communication to almost the entire U.S. population, as well as to hundreds of millions of other people around the world who speak English.

Perhaps better than any other product, the McDonald's restaurant chain illustrates how an American firm, started fifty years ago as a walk-up fast-food restaurant selling hamburgers, has not only saturated the United States with its franchises but expanded to over 32,000 locations worldwide, building 800 to 1,200 more every year. In his book *The McDonaldization of Society* (2004), sociologist George Ritzer argues that the business principles of McDonalds have come to dominate not only the United States but, as a result of globalization, the rest of the world. According to Ritzer, the expansion of other businesses and industries beyond their nation's borders will ultimately lead to global uniformity, which will influence local customs and traditions.

The global flows of the current cultural globalization are produced and directed by global media empires with power, wealth, and communication technologies that enable them to dominate communication worldwide. CNN represents the model global television news network. Created as a U.S. cable news network for American viewers, it now connects with over 200 million households in over 210 countries and territories. In Canada, for example, despite the Canadian government's efforts to preserve the national culture, three-fourths of the television watched, four out of five magazines sold on newsstands, and 70 percent of radio content are of foreign origin. Overwhelmingly, the majority of foreign media products in all of these categories are American.

Among the prominent effects of globalization on culture, the intensification of global "pop culture" is the most striking. In the United States the entertainment industry generates more revenue from overseas sales than any other industry, except the commercial aerospace industry. Many say this form of popular culture is transmitting American pop culture around the world at an incredible pace. A brief by the Levin Institute titled "Culture and Globalization" illustrates the global magnitude of U.S. entertainment: "American television shows, much like movies, are broadcasted throughout the world. Popular shows, such as *One Tree Hill, The O.C.*, and *Gossip Girl*, are TV shows about American individuals that tend to deal with 'typically' American subjects, such as prom, cotillion, American high school life, etc. As a result, teenagers from around the world become aware of these rituals and might even begin to integrate certain 'typically American customs' into their lives" (2009, 12).

Although substantial data indicates that the United States does indeed have a dominant presence in globalizing culture, many social analysts reject the notion that such presence is Americanizing the world. The notion that the United States or other highly developed countries have a cultural international highway via which they are pouring their cultural practices, values, products, and services into spongelike developing countries and small developed countries is rejected by scholars who study the effects of globalization, as well as by many thoughtful citizens throughout the world. Indeed, for them cultural globalization is much more diversified, with cultural flows moving in all directions, certainly not from one country—the United States—to the rest of the world. Moreover, they find this multidirectionality a welcome trend because it offers them access to products and services, as well as customs, values, entertainment, and so forth, that they would not otherwise have if they had to rely only on their own nation's influences.

One of the most prolific scholars of globalization, sociologist Roland Robertson, was among the first to reject the cultural-homogenization thesis, arguing that cultural flows frequently strengthen cultural practices. Robertson is credited with coining the word "glocalization," which, according to him, "means the simultaneity—the co-presence—of both universalizing and particularizing tendencies" (1997, 4), which suggests a complex interaction of the global and local characterized by cultural borrowing.

Without discounting Americanization as a description of the consequences of cultural globalization—because it does have some features that sensitize us to the worldwide reach of the United States in globalization processes—this perspective, like other single-word conceptions used to explain extremely complex phenomena, takes an undifferentiated and oversimplified view of global culture. This is exactly the theme of a recent book titled *How "American" Is Globalization?* (Marling 2006).

Hybridization Perspective

A contrasting perspective to homogenization has emerged out of movements protesting against globalization. Called "hybridization," it gives new momentum to the defense of local uniqueness, individuality, and identity (Osterhammel and Petersson 2005). Jan Nederveen Pieterse, professor of global sociology at the University of Illinois, Urbana-Champaign, calls hybridization a perspective belonging "to the fluid end of relations between cultures: the mixing of cultures and not their separateness is emphasized" (2009, 86).

For thousands of years the agricultural practice of hybrid breeding of livestock has been employed to improve a species of animals, making them more adaptable, faster, or stronger, in the case of horses, or more productive, in the case of milk cows, and so forth. Likewise, hybridization has been used to make crops, such as corn, more productive or adaptable to climate or soil conditions. In the case of cultures of the world, hybridization refers to mixing "Asian, African, American, European cultures: hybridization is the making of global culture as a global mélange. As a category, hybridity serves a purpose based on the assumption of *difference* between the categories, forms, beliefs that go into the mixture" (Pieterse 2009, 83). It occurs as a fusion of cultural elements from various cultural practices rather than the predominance of one cultural element over others.

Migration, interracial and interethnic marriage, cross-border employment, and colonization are mechanisms that nurture hybridization. Marwan Kraidy argues that hybridity is the "cultural logic" of globalization because it "entails that traces of other cultures exist in every culture, thus offering foreign media and marketers transcultural wedges for forging affective links between their commodities and local communities" (2005, 148).

Pieterse articulates one of the most persuasive arguments for cultural hybridity by criticizing the homogenization paradigm. The homogenization perspective, he says,

> overlooks the countercurrents—the impact nonwestern cultures have been making on the West. It downplays the ambivalence of the globalizing momentum and ignores the role of local reception of western culture—for example, the indigenization of western elements. It fails to see the influence nonwestern cultures have been exercising on one another. It has no room for crossover culture, as in the development of 'third cultures' such as music. It overrates the homogeneity of western culture and overlooks the fact that many of the standards exported by the

West and its cultural industries themselves turn out to be of culturally mixed character if we examine their cultural lineages. (Pieterse 2009, 75–76)

Australian globalization scholar and author of *Globalism: The New Market Ideology,* Manfred Steger, an advocate for the hybridization hypothesis, suggests that those who are not yet convinced about "cultural hybridity ought to listen to exciting Indian rocksongs, admire the intricacy of Hawaiian pidgin, or enjoy the culinary delights of Cuban-Chinese cuisine" (2002, 76).

Polarization Perspective

A brief historical review is appropriate in order to set a foundation for understanding the third cultural globalization perspective, polarization. The religious wars of nearly a millennium ago—the war declared against Western civilization by Islam based on the Koran and Islamic law and the Crusaders' military campaigns based on Judeo-Christianity—are widely known. Perhaps not so well known is the remaining mutual dislike and mistrust between Islamic believers and their Christian counterparts. In many ways and in many places, conflict and warfare between representatives of these two sides have persisted throughout many centuries, and they continue to the present. The 9/11 attack on the United States and the invasion of Iraq can be seen as two recent manifestations of this phenomenon.

The polarization perspective of globalization suggests that broadly defined Western and non-Western cultures are moving in a dichotomous manner and producing a series of antagonistic fissures between different cultural worlds. It is grounded in the historic conflict and hate, rather than peace and cultural understanding, that the hostility between Islamic and Western/Christian societies has exhibited for centuries. Two of the most influential books advocating the polarizing cultural globalization perspective were both written in the mid-1990s: *Jihad vs. McWorld: How Globalism and Tribalism Are Reshaping the World* and *The Clash of Civilizations and the Remaking of World Order.*

The former, written by Benjamin Barber (1995), argues that two axial principles of our time—tribalism and globalism—are polarizing cultural globalization at every point. The former, tribalism, takes the form of "jihad," meaning adherence to cultural fundamentalism, tradition, and traditional values, sometimes in the form of extreme religious orthodoxy and theocracy. The latter, authored by Samuel Huntington (1998), envisions an impending clash between the Western and non-Western cultures, out of which a new world order will emerge.

Current globalized culture is viewed as a conflict between these two contrasting stereotypes. Examples: Western stereotypes portray Arabs, Islamists, and Muslims as terrorists and uncompromising religious fundamentalists. On the other hand, non-Western stereotypes paint Western societies as immoral and pathologically individualist and competitive. In this way the globalized world is seen in terms of conflict between two contrasting cultural stereotypes.

Barber contends that at the root of the dispute between Western and a non-Western culture is the belief that McWorld, free market, globalized consumerism, materialism, and secularization dominate the jihad non-Western "tribes." This puts the latter in a subordinate and defensive position against the "superior" McWorld, pressing non-Western nations into a commercially homogenous global network and intimidating them into conforming to the Western cultural "enlightened" globalized trends. This, of course, aggravates radical Islamic hostility to Western culture. The cover of Barber's book shows a "jihadist" quaffing a Pepsi, illustrating McWorld's unbeaten entrepreneurial dictum of "finding a need and meeting it."

Huntington suggests a grim polarized view of contemporary cultural globalization. He outlines a future in which the major divisions among humankind, and the dominating source of conflict, will be cultural. Huntington divides the world into "the West and the Rest"—into the Christian West and the non-Western Oriental and Islamic cultures—claiming these are "the flash points for crisis and bloodshed." He argues that a crucial likelihood in coming years will be the clash of civilizations between these ancient fault lines, and he sees culture wars leading perhaps to a global civilizational war. For Huntington, the only deterrent will be "an international order based on civilizations [as] the surest safeguard against world war" (1998, 321).

These two views of the polarization of global culture are more elaborate and nuanced than I have described here. Their heyday, as it were, was the 1990s. However, they are not obsolete. Events of the past decade—9/11 and the continuing terrorist activities of Muslim groups, as well as the invasion of Iraq and threats toward Iran and North Korea for their nuclear programs—have given renewed credibility to the polarization perspective's prophesies of impending worldwide calamity. Indeed, there is a growth industry in recent literature arguing the polarization theme (Bawer 2007; Gabriel 2008; Spencer 2008; Steyn 2008).

Homogenization, Hybridization, and Polarization Perspectives and Sport

Over the past two decades, there has been a lively debate within the sociology of sport over whether sport is contributing to an Americanized—or homogenized—world culture in which American cultural forms are being imposed on other nations at the expense of their domestic cultures. In one of the earliest expositions of this phenomenon, *The Death of Hockey*, Canadian sport-studies scholars Bruce Kidd and John Macfarlane (1972) raised the issue of the Americanization of Canadian sport. In the early 1990s British sport sociologist Joseph Maguire, in a study of American football in England, concluded that "American football has had a fairly significant impact on English society" (1990, 233). Thus, he suggested that the growth of American football in Britain was evidence of a degree of Americanization. Several studies quickly followed. American anthropologist Alan Klein (1991a, 1991b) was one of the first sport-studies scholars to use the word "Americanization" when he included it in the title of his study of baseball in the Dominican Republic. Australians Jim McKay and Toby Miller (1991) pointed to a qualified Americanization of Australian sport. This was almost immediately followed by Canadian sport-studies scholar Bruce Kidd's (1991) calling attention to the powerful American influences on Canadian sport.

Although the debate about the Americanization hypothesis was never fully resolved among sport social scientists, research on this issue has pretty well ceased, except for a recent study by Yair Galily and Ken Sheard about Israeli basketball. They reported that "the influence of the one society, America, over the other, Israel, is predominantly one-way," asserting that "the 'Americanization' of Israeli basketball, we feel, provides a particularly strong example of this one-way influence" (2002, 55).

The prevailing position sport-studies researchers seem to share acknowledges that homogenizing influences—Americanization—do indeed exist, but they are far from creating anything akin to a single world culture. Instead, researchers believe, different forms of hybridization more closely represent global cultural flows, and American norms and sport culture are not just unwittingly embraced by non-Americans. They subscribe to the notion of a global range of local and regional cultural beliefs, values, and lifestyles throughout the world and consider these good trends. UK sports sociologist Alan Bairner, who has one of the most impressive lists of published works about global sport over the past two decades, is quite clear about his position on this topic, declaring, "American sports per se have had remarkably little effect on the rest of the world despite the economic, military, and political preeminence of the United States, particularly since the collapse of the Soviet Union and its empire" (2003, 36; see also Schwarzkopf 2007).

Globalization researcher Roland Robertson's (1992) notion of "glocalization"—complex interaction of the global and local characterized by cultural borrowing—is viewed as applicable to sports. From this perspective, the increasing exposure to foreign cultures typically experienced by people in their daily lives certainly may bring about modifications in local cultures, values, and traditions, but, again, this is a good thing and can benefit both the exporters and importers of cultural products. Research by Jung Woo Lee and Joseph Maguire into the South Korean media coverage of the opening and closing ceremonies of the Athens 2004 Olympic Games found that the media promoted globalization through themes such as global friendship and association; the event was also framed with reference to unitary Korean nationalism. This suggests that interplay between global and national motivations is a central part of the ongoing process of globalization, much like Robertson suggests with his concept of glocalization (Lee and Maguire 2009).

Forms of Globalization and Manifestations in Sport

In this chapter I have emphasized that globalization is a multidimensional force that takes a variety of forms and is related to sport in a variety of ways. Table 1.2 graphically illustrates the global-sport nexus formulated by sport sociologist John W. Loy. His comprehensive list of the different forms of globalization is accompanied by sporting examples for each form.

Table 1.2 Globalization of Sport

Forms of globalization	Sporting examples
Economic globalization	IOC corporate sponsors
Political globalization	IOC host-city bidding
Cultural globalization	Media empires and satellite telecasts of events
Global migration	International professional athletes
Global tourism	Sport ecotourism
Global slavery	Exploited labor for sporting goods
Global terrorism	1972 Munich Olympics massacre
	Beijing's spending $6 billion on security for the 2008 games

Source: Adapted from Loy 2001; see also Loy and Coakley 2007.

Segmentation of the Global Sport Industry

The global sport industry is also composed of an enormously wide variety of organizations. Many other contemporary global industries are large and complex, so analysts frequently employ a conceptual tool called segmentation to organize and clarify the various parts of an industry. Simply put, segmentation is the division of a complex system into parts to make understanding the whole easier. Two sports management scholars, Brenda Pitts and David Stotlar (2007), have formulated what they call a sport-industry segment model (see Figure 1.1).

Figure 1.1 Sporting goods industry segmentation

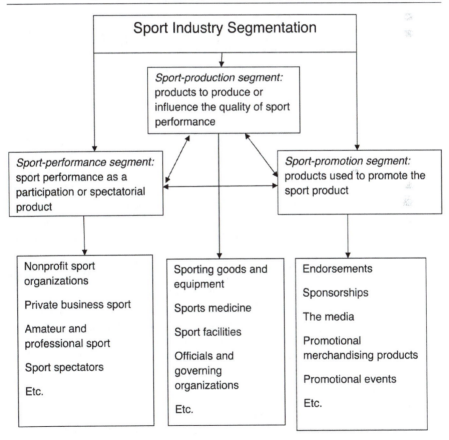

Source: Adapted from Pitts and Stotlar 2007.

This model organizes the sport industry into three segments: sport performance, sport production, and sport promotion. The sport performance segment is concerned with sport as participation, such as nonprofit sport organizations and private-business sport organizations that govern sport participation, amateurs and professionals who play sport, and spectators who attend sports events or view sport via television, video, or the Internet. The sport-production segment includes sporting goods and equipment that are desired, needed, or required to produce or influence the quality of sport performances. The sport-promotion segment involves the promotion of sport products, such as athletes' endorsements, sporting goods sponsorships, media advertising and broadcasting of sports, and marketing sports merchandise.

The sport performance segment of the sport industry is the main subject of Chapters 2 and 3. Following that, Chapter 4 is devoted to sport production and sport promotion through endorsements and sponsorship segments of the global sport industry. Chapter 5 continues the analysis of the sport-promotion segment with the focus on the mass media and sport.

Summary

Despite its frequent use in casual conversations, in the media, and in academic discussions, there is no precise definition of the word "globalization." There is general agreement, however, that it refers to an intensification of political, economic, social, and cultural processes that is evolving and moving the world toward greater interdependence and integration of human contact. There is also agreement that its beginnings reach far back in history.

Sport is not new either, but it is greatly changed from the casual and informal folk games and physical activities that date back many centuries to our present system of global, commercial sports. In the latter nineteenth century, conditions became favorable for the growth and development of organized sports. Some sport scholars contend that we currently have a "totalization of sport," a sportification, as they call it.

The infrastructure for sportification comprises the forces shaping the global political economy. Those forces are the wealth-generating effect of global free markets, free trade, and free movement of capital in conjunction with new information technology—globalization from above. The global assembly line is one of the major consequences of that system. A contending, or an alternative, force of globalization strives for increased governmental democracy, social and worker rights, economic fairness, and environmental protection—globalization from below.

The relevance of these two forces to global sport is manifested in elite global sport organizations; they are examples of globalization from above. The struggles of sports workers, women, and people of color worldwide for equality are examples of globalization from below.

The cultural consequences of globalization have frequently been the subject of academic and public discourse. Over the past two decades, the point of view to engender the liveliest debate has been the claim that U.S. culture is being imposed imperialistically on the rest of the world at the expense of their domestic cultures—Americanization—and American sporting practices and traditions have especially come under criticism for their alleged Americanization of global sport.

References

Bairner, Alan. 2003. Globalization and sport: The nation strikes back. *Phi Kappa Phi Forum* 83: 34–37.

Barber, Benjamin. 1995. *Jihad vs. McWorld: How Globalism and Tribalism Are Reshaping the World*. New York: Ballantine.

Barth, Steve. 1998. Exporting the fantasy. *World Trade* 11, no. 3: 40.

Bawer, Bruce. 2007. *While Europe slept: How radical Islam is destroying the West from within*. Harpswell, ME: Ancor Publishing.

Bleifuss, Joel. 2001. Back to the past. *In These Times*, September 3, 1.

Brecher, Jeremy, Tim Costello, and Brendan Smith. 2000. *Globalization from below: The power of solidarity*. Cambridge, MA: South End Press.

Chanda, Nayan. 2007. *Bound together: How traders, preachers, adventurers, and warriors shaped globalization*. New Haven, CT: Yale University Press.

della Porta, Donatella, ed. 2007. *The global justice movement: Cross-national and transnational perspectives*. Boulder, CO: Paradigm Publishers.

della Porta, Donatella, Massimiliano Andretta, Lorenzo Mosa, and Herbert Reiter. 2006. *Globalization from below: Transnational activists and protest networks*. Minneapolis: University of Minnesota Press.

Dirlik, Arif. 2007. *Global modernity: Modernity in the age of global capitalism*. Boulder, CO: Paradigm Publishers.

Eitzen, D. Stanley, and Maxine Baca Zinn. 2009. *Globalization: The transformation of social worlds*. 2nd ed. Belmont, CA: Wadsworth Cengage Learning.

el-Ojeili, Chamsy, and Patrick Hayden. 2006. *Critical theories of globalization.* New York: Palgrave Macmillan.

Falk, Richard. 1999. *Predatory globalization: A critique.* Malden, MA: Blackwell Publishers.

———. 2003. Globalization-from-below: An innovative politics of resistance. In *Civilizing globalization: A survival guide,* ed. Richard Sandbrook, 191–205. Albany: State University of New York Press.

Foer, Franklin. 2005. *How soccer explains the world: An unlikely theory of globalization.* New York: Harper Perennial.

Gabriel, Brigitte. 2008. *Because they hate: A survivor of Islamic terror warns America.* New York: St. Martin's Griffin.

Galily, Yair, and Ken Sheard. 2002. Cultural imperialism and sport: The Americanization of Israeli basketball. *Culture, Sport, Society* 5, no. 2: 55–78.

Goldstein, Fred. 2008. *Low-wage capitalism.* New York: World View Forum.

Harris, Nathaniel. 2008. *The debate about globalization.* New York: Rosen Central.

Hebron, Lui, and John Stack Jr. 2009. *Globalization: Debunking the myths.* Upper Saddle River, NJ: Pearson Prentice Hall.

Hesmondhalgh, David. 2002. *The culture industries.* Thousand Oaks, CA: Sage.

Holton, Robert. 2000. Globalization's cultural consequences. *The Annals of the American Academy of Political and Social Science* 570, no. 1: 140–152.

———. 2005. *Making globalization.* New York: Palgrave Macmillan.

Huntington, Samuel. 1998. *The clash of civilizations and the remaking of world order.* New York: Simon & Schuster.

Ietto-Gillies, Grazia. 2003. The role and control of multinational corporations in the world economy. In *The Handbook of Globalization,* ed. Jonathan Michie, 139–149. Northhampton, MA: Edward Elgar Publishing, Ltd.

Isaak, Robert A. 2005. *The globalization gap: How the rich get richer and the poor get left further behind.* Upper Saddle River, NJ: Prentice Hall/Financial Times.

Kidd, Bruce. 1991. How do we find our own voices in the "new world order"? A commentary on Americanization. *Sociology of Sport Journal* 8: 178–184.

Kidd, Bruce, and John MacFarlane. 1972. *The death of hockey.* New York: New Press.

Klein, Alan M. 1991a. Sport and culture as contested terrain: Americanization in the Caribbean. *Sociology of Sport Journal* 8: 79–85.

———. 1991b. *Sugarball: The American game, the Dominican dream*. New Haven, CT: Yale University Press.

Kraidy, Marwan M. 2005. *Hybridity, or the cultural logic of globalization*. Philadelphia: Temple University Press.

Lechner, Frank J., and John Boli, eds. 2008. *The globalization reader:* New York: Wiley-Blackwell.

Lee, Jung Woo, and Joseph Maguire. 2009. Global festivals through a national prism. *International Review for the Sociology of Sport* 44, no. 1: 5–24.

Levin Institute. 2009. *Culture and globalization*. New York: Levin Institute. www .globalization101.org/uploads/File/Culture/cultall2009.pdf.

Loy, John W. 2001. Sociology of sport and the new global order: Bridging perspectives and crossing boundaries. Paper presented as the keynote address at the First World Congress of Sociology of Sport, July 20–24, Yonsei University, Seoul, Korea.

Loy, John, and Jay Coakley. 2007. Sport. *The Blackwell Encyclopedia of Sociology*, ed. George Ritzer, 4643–4645. Malden, MA: Blackwell Publishers.

Madrick, Jeff. 2009. Beyond Rubinomics. *The Nation*, January 12–19, 14–18.

Maguire, Joseph. 1990. More than a sporting touchdown: The making of American football in England, 1982–1990. *Sociology of Sport Journal* 7: 213–237.

———. 1999. *Global sport: Identities, societies, civilizations*. Malden, MA: Polity Press.

Marling, William, H. 2006. *How "American" is globalization?* Baltimore: Johns Hopkins University Press.

McKay, Jim, and Toby Miller. 1991. From old boys to men and women of the corporation: The Americanization and commodification of Australian sport. *Sociology of Sport Journal* 8: 86–94.

Orbie, Jan, and Lisa Tortell, eds. 2009. *The European Union and the social dimension of globalization: How the EU influences the world*. New York: Routledge.

Osterhammel, Jurgen, and Niels P. Petersson. 2005. *Globalization: A short history*. New Brunswick, NJ: Princeton University Press.

Pieterse, Jan Nederveen. 2009. *Globalization and culture: Global mélange*. 2nd ed. Lanham, MD: Rowman & Littlefield.

Pitts, Brenda G., and David K. Stotlar. 2007. *Fundamentals of sport marketing*. 3rd ed. Morgantown, WV: Fitness Information Technology.

Ritzer, George. 2004. *The McDonaldization of society*. Rev. new cent. ed. Thousand Oaks, CA: Pine Forge Press.

Robertson, Roland. 1992. *Globalization: Social theory and global culture*. Thousand Oaks, CA: Sage.

————. 1997. Comments on the "global triad" and "glocalization." In *Global-ization and indigenous culture,* ed. N. Inoue, 217–225. Tokyo: Kokugakuin University.

Scholte, Jan Aart. 2005. *Globalization: A critical introduction.* 2nd ed. New York: Macmillan.

Schwarzkopf, Stefan. 2007. Who said "Americanization"? The case of twentieth-century advertising and mass marketing from a British perspective. In *Decen-tering America,* ed. Jessica C. E. Gienow-Hecht, 23–72. New York: Berghahn Books.

Sen, Arartya. 2008. How to judge globalism. In *The globalization reader,* ed. Frank J. Lechner and John Boli, 19–31. 3rd ed. New York: Wiley-Blackwell.

Shapiro, Robert J. 2008. *Futurecast: How superpowers, populations, and globaliza-tion will change the way you live and work.* New York: St. Martin's Press.

Smart, Barry. 2007. Not playing around: Global capitalism, modern sport and consumer culture. In *Globalization and Sport,* ed. Richard Giulianotti and Roland Robertson, 6–27. Malden, MA: Blackwell Publishers.

Spencer, Robert. 2008. *Stealth jihad: How radical Islam is subverting America without guns or bombs.* Washington, D.C.: Regnery Publishing.

Steger, Manfred. 2002. *Globalism: The new market ideology.* Lanham, MD: Rowan & Littlefield.

————. 2003. *Globalization: A very short introduction.* New York: Oxford Uni-versity Press.

————. 2009. Global culture. In *Globalization: The transformation of social worlds,* ed. D. Stanley Eitzen and Maxine Baca Zinn, 147–150. Belmont, CA: Wadsworth Cengage Learning.

Steyn, Mark. 2008. *America alone: The end of the world as we know it.* Washington, D.C.: Regnery Publishing.

Vamplew, Wray. 2006. The development of team sports before 1914. In *Hand-book of the economics of sport,* ed. Wladimir Andreff and Stefan Szymanski, 435–439. Northhampton, MA: Edward Elgar.

Veseth, Michael, ed. 2002. *The New York Times twentieth century in review: The rise of the global economy.* Chicago: Fitzroy Dearborn Publishers.

Chapter 2
Global Sport Organizations

Governing the World of Sport

The global sport economy represents a complex structure [that] ... is arranged and regulated, as well as claimed and contested, by a set of hierarchical organizations at the apex of which are Global Sport Organizations.

—John Forster and Osvaldo Croci, "Sport and Politics: The Question of Legitimacy of International Sport Organizations," 2006

Governing Global Sport: Global Sport Organizations

Sport is often thought of as merely fun and games, isolated and apart from other sectors of our lives. But sport, from the youth leagues to the elite international level, is governed through hierarchically designed organizations much like other social institutions. At the highest level of sport governance is the global sport organization (GSO). GSOs have been characterized as "trans-national authorities who, more than states, manage various multinational sports and thereby affect the options open to participants, spectators, and those who provide the necessary finance.... Each game or sport ... has a different kind of authority, or mix of authorities" (Strange 1996, 96). In their influential book *The Political Economy of Global Sporting Organizations* (2004), Australian scholars John Forster and Nigel Pope pose the question, What exactly makes a GSO? They answer, "Virtually without exception, the GSOs claim a legitimate control over their respective sports or some global sporting event. And often it is both" (2004, 5).

Thomas Hoehn, a specialist in the economics of the entertainment and media sectors, explains that GSOs have broad, sometimes total, "freedom to organize their sport in terms of setting sporting rules, designating a hierarchy of competitions and leagues, selecting athletes for championships, promoting and relegating clubs in leagues, assigning media and sponsorship rights and redistributing money earned from the commercial exploitation of these rights" (2006, 232). Also intermingled with national governments, they are emerging as significant actors in the global economy alongside transnational corporations (TNCs), so they actually constitute what some call a global sport political economy.

GSOs must abide by the laws of nation-states, so the capital investment, revenues, and advertising contracts they enter into locate them within the commercial orbit. Thus, the threads of influence for GSOs extend through sport, politics, economics, and culture, making them unique and difficult to categorize as an organizational type. Some scholars have classified GSOs as a subdivision of international nongovernmental organizations because they are established and controlled by individuals or groups, not by nation-states, and they promote shared interests and values in a specific area, in this case sport (Ronit and Schneider 2000).

GSOs are founded as governing organizations for the advancement of a sport or group of sports—the latter applies to the International Olympic Committee (IOC)—but they typically have broader, more idealistic and humanistic goals as well. In the case of the Olympic Movement, founder Pierre de Coubertin articulated an ideology of "neo-Olympics," which the Olympic Charter describes as "the concerted, organized, universal and permanent action, carried out under the supreme authority of the IOC, of all individuals and entities who are inspired by the values of Olympism," whose goal "is to place sport at the service of the harmonious development of man, with a view to promoting a peaceful society concerned with the preservation of human dignity" (IOC 2007, 11).

Each GSO is a private and autonomous entity, but each functions within networks of sport organizations that are major participants in the establishment of a global sporting culture, with their own particular political economies. John Forster and Canadian political scientist Osvaldo Croci point out, "These networks, each in a different way, are the source of a process of mutual legitimization and hence authority for the GSOs, both inside and outside their own sporting spheres. Such a reciprocal legitimization process rests on the defense and promotion of mutual interests that the GSOs and other sporting organizations could not pursue effectively independently of each other" (2006, 5).

These networks are hierarchically structured, with power and control descending from top to bottom, so a graphical display of a pyramid makes a natural representation of a GSO structure, as Figure 2.1 illustrates. Global networks directed by a GSO exist for all sports. Figure 2.1 shows that subordinate continental, national, and individual organizations exist for each GSO, and each directs lower-level components of organizations within that sport.

Figure 2.1 Model of global network that exists for each GSO

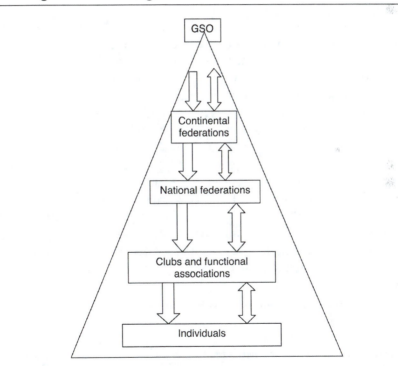

The single pointed arrows indicate that authority proceeds from top to bottom. Double-pointed arrows indicate mutual recognition and acceptance of authority and subordination at the various levels in the pyramid by all the organizations in it (amended from Forster and Croci 2006).

An inherent requirement of a hierarchically structured organization is that certain principles must be recognized and accepted for the stability of the individual and subordinate components of the organization. I have adapted to global sport networks three principles that Forster and Croci (2006) believe to be important for organizations:

- recognition of the GSO structural system as a whole (that is, the membership in, and the position of each member within, the global sport network) by each individual and subordinate organization within that GSO network
- recognition by both continental and national GSO networks of other continental and national GSO networks as independent and coequal
- recognition of the organization at the apex of the global GSO network as the supreme governing body for that sport

Controversies and conflict are inevitable by-products of large organizations, and GSOs constantly contend with them. For GSOs, the first line of response is typically through the exercise of authority inherent in their hierarchical structure, meaning they must be recognized and accepted "as the legitimate, supreme, governing body by all other organizations within the pyramid network at the apex of which they stand" (Forster and Croci 2006, 10). Figure 2.1 illustrates this by the arrows pointing downward from top to bottom. According to Forster and Croci, the legitimacy of GSOs' authority "derives primarily from the process of mutual recognition of organizations belonging to the same pyramid network" (2006, 11); the double-pointed arrows in Figure 2.1 symbolize the process of legitimization.

Most people throughout the world know that GSOs are the governing bodies for the Olympic Games and the World Cup, and many believe that similar GSOs operate for all the sports played internationally. But this is not the case; there are sports without a single ultimate, global governing organization. In general, it is in individual sports, such as boxing and golf, as opposed to team sports, that multiple governing organizations exist.

From International Sport Initiatives to Global Sport Organizations

In Chapter 1 I briefly described the transformation of folk games and pastimes to modern sport. Now I recount the transition from international sport initiatives to full-blown GSOs. Competitive sporting activities stretch back into the deep recesses of history; the first international sporting event—defined as competition between athletes or teams from different countries—has not been definitively established. Indeed, there are several contenders for this designation, but this is not the place for an extended discussion of this dispute.

A tennis match in 1819 between British and French players is sometimes advanced as the first international sport competition. International yacht races had become quite common in the decades leading up to the mid-nineteenth century, and the first international cricket match had taken place between the United States and Canada. Surprisingly, the country of the sport's origin, England, was not involved, although Canada at that time was under the British Crown. In 1881 the International Federation of Gymnastics (IFG) was founded in Belgium with three member countries: Belgium, France, and the Netherlands. Some argue that makes it the oldest governing body of an international sport. With three member nations, the IFG could appropriately be called international, but it certainly was not a GSO.

British sport historian Dennis Brailsford argues that by the mid-nineteenth century, boxing had become the first world sport. He states, "No man now could feel himself to be truly champion without defeating all comers from both sides of the Atlantic. There was no vestige of any international organization behind the sport. There was no national organization at all in the United States, and only the very sketchiest and most intermittent one in Britain; yet fighting had become international and the concept of a world championship had begun to take root" (1988, 139).

These sports events, and others like them, were single-sport competitions. Daniel Bell undertook a study of international *multisport* competitions, defined, as he says, "as competitions between two or more nations competing in two or more sports in the same location at the same time" (2003, 1). Bell acknowledges that the modern Olympic Games can appropriately be considered the pinnacle of international multisport competition, as well as the first global multisport event, but he identifies several precursors to the first modern Olympic Games.

These predecessors to the modern Olympic Games were multisport events, and several used the word "Olympic," but they were not international because athletes and teams came from a single country. According to Bell, a "Cotswold Olympics" began in England in 1612 and continued on an annual basis for over 239 years. In the 1830s an Olympic Festival was held at Chelsea Stadium in England. In the nineteenth century, prior to de Coubertin's modern Olympics, "Olympic Games" were held in Sweden, the "Drehberg Olympics" in Germany, the "Palic Olympics" in Yugoslavia, the "Rondeau Olympic Games" in France, and the "Pappas Olympics" in Greece. It was against this backdrop of multisport competitions, and the use of the word "Olympics" in their names, that Baron Pierre de Coubertin created the modern Olympic Games.

The Olympic Movement and Its Network

International Olympic Committee

In 1894 French aristocrat Baron Pierre de Coubertin founded the first GSO, the International Olympic Committee, which two years later organized the first modern Olympic Games—the first global multisport event (even though it was predominantly European in creation, development, and perspective). Although a number of international sporting events preceded the first modern Olympic Games in Athens, Greece, none of them had the structure and scope of the modern Olympic Movement. De Coubertin's dream was to foster world peace and communication through the revival of the ancient Olympics Games. In his *Mémoires Olympiques* (1979), de Coubertin claimed the Olympics are not simply world championships but the quadrennial festival of universal youth.

John MacAloon (2008), in perhaps the best book about de Coubertin's creation of the modern Olympics, referred to him as "This Great Symbol." Avery Brundage, an American who for twenty years was president of the IOC, claimed that the Olympic Movement was "a religion for which Pierre de Coubertin was the prophet, for Coubertin has kindled a torch that will enlighten the world" (1968, 80).

De Coubertin knew that the undertaking he envisioned would require support and encouragement from a variety of sources. He realized it was a project much too large for one person to bring to fruition. Moreover, he encountered objection and discouragement from many friends and European royalty, when he first expressed his desire to revive the ancient Olympics Games. It was only through a series of clever diplomatic overtures, persuasion, promises, and his social and political connections—as well as his willingness to commit his fortune in pursuit of his goal—that in Paris in 1894, two years before the first Olympic Games, de Coubertin established the structural foundation of the Olympic Movement, the International Olympic Committee—"the cardinals of sport," as its members are often called. The first IOC members were all from Europe or the Americas, with the exception of one from New Zealand.[1]

The IOC was created as a nonprofit organization, and the games were intended to provide sports competition between amateur athletes from different countries—a sporting celebration of the world's best athletes. Commercialism was antithetical to its founding and during the early Olympiads. But since the Olympics acquired the ability to generate large sums of money, the profit-making potential has gradually become a dominating purpose and function, resembling some of the features of transnational corporations. Indeed, the problems resulting from the contradictions between their nonprofit status and their increasing ability to produce substantial amounts of commercial revenues have been given particular attention by several scholars (Forster and Pope 2004).

The IOC serves as an umbrella organization of the Olympic Movement.[2] Its primary responsibility is the organization and supervision of the Olympic Games. From its beginning, the Olympic Movement has been a highly structured GSO, and its supreme authority is the IOC. As designed by de Coubertin, it is an independent committee that selects its own members; however, to initiate the process de Coubertin chose the first thirteen. The IOC president is chosen by IOC members, and assisted by an executive board, several vice presidents, and various IOC commissions (Chappelet and Kübler-Mabbott 2008). Of the current 108 IOC members, twenty-three are honorary members, and Juan Antonio Samaranch is honorary president for life (Guttmann 2002; see also the official website of the Olympic Movement at www.olympic.org). Remarkably, there have only been eight IOC presidents in over 115 years since its founding.[3]

Also remarkably, there were no women on the IOC until 1981, eighty-seven years after the first IOC was formed. As of 2010 there have been twenty-one female IOC members. Of a total IOC membership of 108, 16 active members are women (IOC membership may not exceed 115; it is sometimes less than that because of death, resignation, retirement, and so forth), and three women are honorary members. In 1990, for the first time in the history of the IOC, a woman was elected to its executive board (Flor Isava Fonseca), and in 1997 another woman became an IOC vice president (Anita L. DeFrantz).

The IOC is not just another GSO; it is the preeminent GSO. It is a huge and complex system of sport and sport-related organizations under the banner of the Olympic Movement. Several Olympic scholars have suggested that the Olympic Movement is analogous to the United Nations in its complexity and the essentialness of belonging—to the United Nations for governments and to the Olympic Movement network for sports organizations (Young 2004). The Olympic Movement has also been compared to a transnational corporation. In summarizing the changing nature of the IOC over the century since its founding, Garry Whannel, a media and sport analyst at the University of Bedfordshire, argues that the IOC now manages "a festival of youth rooted in the idealist philosophy, which has become a global spectacle, creating sporting stars, generating advertising revenue, boosting corporate profits, and agency income" (2008, 126). These features place the IOC in that group of alliances of the powerful, wealthy, and influential groups in business and commerce that I described in Chapter 1 as characterizing globalization from above.

Because of the size, scope, and influence of the Olympic Movement, extended expositions of its organizational structure and functions are typically found in books devoted exclusively to that subject. A broad analysis of this "super" GSO follows, and Figure 2.2 provides a model outline of it. I emphasize that the figure is a basic model because to capture all of the Olympic Movement's components would require several pages of boxes and arrows.

Although de Coubertin envisioned the Olympic Games as a global enterprise, at the first Olympics in Athens, Greece, in 1896, only about three hundred athletes from thirteen countries competed in forty-three events in nine different sports. Still, it was claimed to be the largest international participation in any sporting event to that date. By contrast, as the 2008 Beijing Summer Olympics, a total of 11,500 athletes from 205 countries competed in 302 events in twenty-eight sports.

The 2008 Beijing Summer Olympic Games were officially known as the games of the XXIX Olympiad (five Olympic Games were cancelled: the 1916 Summer Games due to World War I and the 1940 and 1944 Winter and Summer Games due to World War II). The figures in the previous paragraph show the enormous growth in participating countries, athletes, and sports in the 112 years of the Summer Olympics. Add to this the Winter Olympic Games, which began in 1924. The XXI Winter Olympics were held in Vancouver, British Columbia, in 2010, and the XXX Summer Olympics will be held in London in 2012. It is obvious that the Olympic Movement is indeed a popular global sports phenomenon (Miller 2008).

The IOC coordinates with organizations that are collectively part of the Olympic Movement. They include the IOC, the Organizing Committee of the Olympic Games (OCOG), the national Olympic committees

Figure 2.2 Model outline of the Olympic network of global sport organizations

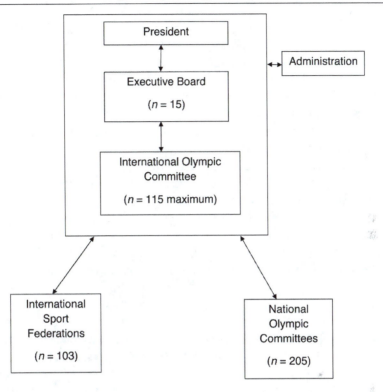

(NOCs), the international sports federations (IFs), and the national associations, clubs, and athletes.

In the following sections I briefly describe the structure and functions of Olympic Movement entities. Moreover, detailed descriptions about these committees and federations can be found on the IOC website.

Organizing Committee of the Olympic Games

When the IOC awards an Olympic Games to a city, an Organizing Committee of the Olympic Games replaces the successful bid committee. The OCOG has full responsibility for planning and executing those Olympic Games, including financing, facilities, staffing, and accommodations. As a consequence, the OCOGs have become enormous administrative agencies employing hundreds of people.

National Olympic Committees

These indispensable components of the Olympic Movement are the individual national constituents in the structural network of the Olympic Movement. Each member nation in the Olympic Movement has a NOC; each takes the name of its country (e.g., U.S. Olympic Committee or German Olympic Committee). As of 2010, there were 205 NOCs ranging from Albania to Zimbabwe, representing both sovereign nations and other geographical areas,

NOCs get their power and authority from the IOC, the sole proprietor and owner of the Olympic Games. Each NOC is responsible for selecting and recommending athletes from its country for participation in the Olympic Games. Also, before a city can compete against those in other countries to host a future Olympics, it first must win the selection process of the NOC in its own country because it is NOCs that nominate cities within their respective nations as candidates to host the Olympic Games. Financial support by the IOC for training and development of Olympic athletes and teams enables NOCs to promote the development of athletes and training of coaches and officials at a national level.

NOC membership often serves as a training ground for promotion to membership on the IOC. Most IOC members are elected after having served on the NOCs of their own countries. It is important to note, however, that they are not delegates from their own countries to the IOC but are officially considered to be representatives *from* the IOC *to* their own countries (IOC 2008).

The Association of the National Olympic Committees (ANOC) coordinates issues and problems of general interest for the more than two hundred NOCs worldwide. ANOC's mission is to make recommendations for promoting the development of the NOCs that are then addressed by the IOC board and other Olympic Movement organizations promoting sports. The complete list of topics the ANOC deals with is lengthy, but some of them are

- seeing to the Olympic program's stability, without precluding changes in order to reflect in due time the development of sports worldwide and in the various regions of the world
- monitoring the conditions of participation for athletes at the Olympic Games and their ceremonies
- monitoring athletes' accommodation in the Olympic Villages

- monitoring the number, working conditions, and accommodation of staff looking after the athletes at the Olympic Games (e.g., officials, coaches, and physicians)
- monitoring the clothing of Olympic delegations (e.g., uniforms, sports clothing, and shirts)
- supporting underprivileged countries through the Olympic Solidarity programs
- coordinating scholarships for athletes and coaches, technical courses, and courses for sport administrators, with the common objective of reducing the gap of unequal development among the NOCs
- contributing to the dissemination of the Olympic ideal through the national Olympic academies and their representatives at the sessions of the International Olympic Academy
- contributing to developing Sport for All by organizing national events and participating in the international Sport for All Congresses (ANOC 2008)

International Sport Federations

These federations are the international nongovernmental organizations that the IOC recognizes as the administrators of one or more sports at the world level. Thus, each IF governs its sport worldwide and is responsible for the international rules and regulations of the sport over which it presides. One of the ways it fulfills its responsibilities is through organizing world or continental championships. Finally, IFs connect sports to the IOC through individual national sport federations, which are organized into four different associations:

- Association of Summer Olympic Federations
- Association of International Olympic Winter Federations
- Association of Recognized IOC International Sports Federations
- General Association of International Sports Federations

Because of their scope and complexity, I will provide a more extended discussion of IFs in a later section of this chapter.

Other Organizations Within the Olympic Movement Network

The IOC contributes Olympic marketing and revenue to the programs of over fifty international organizations that are sport related. Some authors refer to these as Olympic Movement partners. It takes a sizeable document just to list and describe all of them, so I shall identify only several of the most prominent here.

The International Paralympic Committee (IPC) is the international governing body of sports for athletes with disabilities. Its mission is to empower these athletes to achieve sporting excellence, which it does by supervising and co-coordinating the Paralympic Summer and Winter Games and other multidisability competitions, the most important of these being world and regional championships.

Other international sports organizations for athletes with disabilities are limited either to one disability group or to one specific sport, but the IPC is an umbrella organization representing all sports and disabilities.

The World Anti-Doping Agency (WADA) is an international independent organization created to promote, coordinate, and monitor the opposition to doping in sport in all its forms. Created in 1999 through an initiative by the IOC, it led in the development and implementation of the WADA Code, a document integrating antidoping policies in all sports internationally. WADA receives one half of its budgetary requirements from the IOC; the other half is contributed by various governments (Pound 2004; WADA 2009).

The Court of Arbitration for Sport is an international arbitration body established to bring about the resolution of sports-related disputes submitted to it through ordinary arbitration or appeal against the decisions of sports bodies or organizations. Originally conceived by former IOC president Juan Antonio Samaranch to resolve disputes occurring during the Olympic Games, it became a part of the IOC in 1984. It is still closely associated with the IOC, but it became entirely independent in 1993.

The International Committee for Fair Play (ICFP) was established to encourage the universal principles of fair play essential to sport. International Fair Play Prizes are awarded each year by the ICFP based on nominations received by various sport organizations and the public. Athletes, ranging from Olympic champions to beginners and chosen for their particular commitment to fair play, are awarded trophies and diplomas.

The World Olympians Association is an independent global organization representing Olympians. President Samaranch initiated its creation in 1994. It unites Olympians from around the world and involves them in advancing the values and virtues of the Olympic Movement, including the dissemination of Olympic ideals, the promotion of fair play, education against doping, and support for diversity (IOC 2009b).

Global Issues Confronting the Olympic Movement

Any claim to a globalized perspective, for both governments and private organizations, has had to include a principle of inclusion. The proliferation of nations over the past forty years and the increase in UN agencies devoted to resolving environmental and human issues throughout the world illustrate the principle of inclusion. The antidiscriminatory practices and the promotion of multiculturalism adopted by private organizations clearly show that inclusion accompanies globalization.

The IOC has endured a continuing series of off-the-playing-field problems. Three of the most contentious involved issues about inclusion: (1) female eligibility, (2) the amateur requirement for participation, and (3) athletes with special needs.

Females in the Olympics

Pierre de Coubertin had every intention of making the modern Olympic Games a global sporting event, but he was a captive of his own aristocratic social status and nineteenth-century European culture; thus, only male athletes with amateur status were eligible for participation in the Olympic Games.

In his desire to model the modern Olympics after the ancient Greek Olympic Games, Pierre de Coubertin opposed female participation, just as the ancient Greeks had done. Furthermore, a variety of folklore, myths, and slogans supported sport as an exclusively masculine activity. This led de Coubertin to reject female participation in the Olympics because of what he called the "indecency, ugliness and impropriety of women in . . . sports [because] women engaging in strenuous activities were destroying their feminine charm and . . . leading to the downfall and degradation of . . . sport" (quoted in Mitchell 1977, 213).

At another time, de Coubertin drove home the same point: "Would . . . sports practiced by women constitute an edifying sight before crowds assembled for an Olympiad? Such is not [the IOC's] idea of the Olympic Games in which we have tried . . . to achieve the solemn and periodic exaltation of male athleticism with internationalism as a base, loyalty as a means, art for its setting, and female applause as its reward" (quoted in Gerber et al. 1974, 137–138).

Although de Coubertin opposed the participation of women in the Olympics, several female golfers and tennis players participated in the 1900 games. In London at the 1908 games, thirty-six women competed in figure skating and tennis events. In the 1912 games, female swimming and diving were added to the program.[4] By 1924 the IOC had decided to permit greater participation of women in the games, but there was no quick expansion of opportunities for women; even at the 1936 games in Berlin, there were only four sports available to women (IOC 2009a).

Despite de Coubertin's opposition to females participating in the Olympics—one shared by most of the other early members of the IOC— it became increasingly evident that if the Olympic Movement wished to become a truly global entity, it would have to be open and available to females, who make up over one half the population of the world. Consequently, women's Olympic sports and participation have increased significantly during the past three decades, except in Islamic countries, where the level of female participation has remained generally low. Since 1991 all new sports wishing to be added to the Olympic program of approved sports must feature women's events. The Beijing Summer Olympics set a new record for women's participation in Olympic Games. Of more than 11,000 total athletes, 4,746 females—more than 42 percent—participated across the various sports.

The Amateur Issue

Amateur sports require athletes to participate without remuneration. De Coubertin and the IOC intended from the start for all Olympic athletes to be amateurs. De Coubertin was a great admirer of the ethos of amateurism surrounding British sports played in the aristocratic secondary schools called "public schools" and the universities. In this amateur ethos "gentleman" sportsmen competed under a prevailing attitude of fairness and sportsmanship, and serious and extended practicing or training for a sport was considered synonymous with cheating.

Nineteenth-century British amateurism was an upper-class tactic to exclude professional and working-class athletes from competing against socially elite "gentlemen" athletes in sports, such as rowing, tennis, and rugby. Athletes and teams that practiced and played a sport professionally were considered to have an unfair advantage over gentlemen who played it merely as a hobby. De Coubertin viewed this amateur ethos as appropriate for the modern Olympic Games he had created (Allison 2001).

Olympic rules about amateurism became contested terrain almost immediately and caused many controversies about participation eligibility until the late twentieth century, when they were abolished. Questions arose about reimbursement for travel expenses, compensation for time lost from work, payment for commercial endorsements, and whether one could be employed to teach sports and retain one's amateur status. These were difficult questions for the IOC to answer to the satisfaction of all parties concerned, and they often led to confusion about what is and is not professionalism in different sports.

A couple of high-profile incidents that occurred in the first half century of the Olympics illustrate the difficulty of dealing with amateurism. The 1912 Olympic pentathlon and decathlon champion, U.S. athlete Jim Thorpe, was stripped of his medals when it was discovered that he had played semi-professional baseball before competing in the Olympics Games. (In 1983 this action was reversed, his medals were returned, and his championships were restored on compassionate grounds by the IOC.) During the 1936 Winter Olympics, Swiss and Austrian skiers boycotted the events in support of their skiing instructors, who were declared professionals and thus ineligible to compete in the Olympics because they earned money from their sport.

In the three decades following World War II, numerous social, economic, political, and cultural transformations were increasingly making the Olympic amateur athlete rule outdated. It gradually became clear that the amateur rule was exclusionary and discriminatory. While other global government and private organizations were moving toward inclusion and antidiscriminatory practices, the Olympic Movement was not. This raised a significant question: If the Olympic Games were to be the premier global sporting event for the best athletes and teams in the world, as the IOC hoped, how could it exclude working-class athletes who could not afford to make a living and train for Olympic competition at the same time, and how could it exclude professional athletes and teams who demonstrated through their performances in professional competition that they were the best in the world in their sport? Obviously, abolishment of the amateur rule was essential if full globalization was to become a reality for the Olympics.

Other practices related to the amateur rule embarrassed the IOC and placed the entire Olympic Movement in an unfavorable light. Athletes from Western countries were using a variety of subterfuges to maneuver around the amateur rule. They were accepting endorsement contracts from sponsors, with the payments going into trust funds. Some of the athletes' earnings from non-Olympic events were also being placed into trust funds rather than going directly to the athletes themselves. The funds would later be available to them. Western governments were establishing Olympic training centers, where selected athletes trained full time, with all expenses paid. The United States opened the first of three Olympic training centers at the former Ent Air Force Base in Colorado Springs, Colorado, in 1978.

Meanwhile, Communist Bloc countries were entering athletes into the Olympic Games who they said were students, soldiers, or government professionals, but many of them received their incomes from their state government to train and compete in sports as full-time athletes. All of the Communist Bloc countries founded national "sports schools" where boys and girls as young as six or seven years of age were selected and trained, competing year-round until their sports careers ended. They all created a series of Olympic training sites where athletes prepared for Olympic Games.

Because these types of activities were making a mockery of the amateur rule worldwide, amateurism requirements were gradually phased out of the Olympic Charter. By the early 1980s most IOC members recognized that many Olympic athletes were competing professionally in the sense that practicing and playing sports was their main activity and their chief source of income. Eventually decisions on professional participation were left to IFs to determine eligibility in their own sports. Over the next few years, most IFs abolished the distinction between amateurs and professionals, accepting what was called open games. The most immediate consequences of this new IOC policy occurred in 1992, when professional players from the National Basketball Association—the so-called Dream Team—played in the Barcelona Summer Olympics. National Hockey League players became eligible to participate beginning with the 1998 Winter Olympics in Nagano, Japan.

As of 2009, boxing was the only Olympic sport in which professionals could not compete; however, some Olympic boxers collect cash prize money from their NOCs. Men's soccer allows an unlimited number of professionals under the age of twenty-three on a team roster but only three professionals over twenty-three years of age.

Inclusion of Athletes with Special Needs

Paralympics. In an earlier section of this chapter, I identified the International Paralympic Committee as the international governing body of sports for athletes with disabilities. But actions to create the Paralympics also belong with other acts of inclusion taken by the IOC that contributed to positioning the Olympic Movement as global in practice as well as declaration.

People with disabilities, comprising about 20 percent of the population, also make up a group that has historically been subject to systematic prejudice and injustice. Only in the past few decades have laws and enlightened public attitudes worldwide reversed the practices that treated people with disabilities as outcasts. In 1960, in parallel with the Summer Olympic Games in Rome, a games for wheelchair users was organized. Four hundred athletes from twenty-three countries competed, and these games are considered the first Paralympic Games.

Since then, the Paralympics have been held in every Olympic year. Beginning with the 1988 Summer Olympics in Seoul, Korea, and the 1992 Winter Games in Albertville, France, the host city for the Olympics has also played host to the Paralympics, which have also taken place at the same venues as the Olympics. The 2008 Beijing Paralympics had some 4,200 disabled athletes from 148 countries competing for over five hundred gold medals in more than twenty sports. The most recent Winter Paralympics were held in 2010 in Vancouver, Canada, with more than five hundred athletes representing forty-four countries.

Special Olympics. Another world-renowned program for people with special needs is the Special Olympics, an international program of year-round sports training and athletic competition for developmentally disabled children and adults. In 1988, the IOC recognized the Special Olympics, making it the only sport organization authorized by the IOC to use the word "Olympics" in its name. This is another act of inclusion by the IOC that contributes to its reputation as a global organization.

The Special Olympics began in 1968 when Eunice Kennedy Shriver, head of the Joseph P. Kennedy Jr. Foundation, provided funding through the foundation for the First International Special Olympics Games at Soldier Field in Chicago. Since then, millions of developmentally disabled children and adults throughout the world have participated in Special Olympics. Over 2.5 million athletes of all ages participate in accredited Special Olympics sports training and competition in more than 180 countries. There seems little doubt that these programs will continue to grow in the coming years and to provide sporting opportunities to a broad spectrum of individuals with disabilities.

Through the Paralympics and Special Olympics, the Olympic Movement has made it possible for athletes with various kinds of disabilities to have access and opportunities not only to participate in sport but to become elite athletes competing for Olympic gold medals. The future for disabled athletes looks very encouraging because widespread support is now in place for opportunities to increase.

International Sport Federations: GSOs Within the IOC

In an earlier section of this chapter, I identified the IFs collectively as subunits within the Olympic Movement that govern sports at the world level. Each of the IFs can be viewed as a secondary GSO. I return to the IFs now for an expanded discussion of them as GSOs.

Collectively, the IFs are multifaceted organizations that, bewilderingly complex as they are, govern much of global sport. However, while it may seem like the Olympic Movement has every sport organization in the world under its jurisdiction through the IFs, it is important to understand that local communities throughout the world sponsor youth sports and adult sport club programs that are outside the purview of the Olympic Movement. Also, many countries have national-level sports programs that are not linked to the Olympics.

In the United States the National Federation of State High School Associations governs the high school athletic/activity associations of its fifty member states, plus the District of Columbia, reaching 18,500 high schools and over 11 million students involved in sport and activity programs. Two national organizations that govern intercollegiate sports in United States, the National Collegiate Athletic Association and the National Intercollegiate Athletic Association, are not part of the Olympic Movement. Australian Rules Football fits in this same category. It was one of the demonstration sports at the 1956 Melbourne Olympic Games, but it was not endorsed by the IOC. However, it is the most popular spectator sport in Australia.

Individual IFs are the GSOs responsible for managing and monitoring the everyday operations of the world's various sports and supervising the development of athletes participating in these sports at every level. They guarantee the regular organization of competitions, as well as respect for the rules of fair play, and ensure that their statutes, practices, and activities conform to the Olympic Charter. In the hierarchical order, beneath each IF is a national sport federation for each sport.

IFs responsibilities also extend upward. For example, they prepare proposals to the IOC regarding the Olympic Charter and the Olympic Movement in general, including the organizing and holding of the Olympic Games; they advance their opinions about the cities that are candidates for hosting the Olympic Games, especially regarding technical capabilities; they work together in preparing the Olympic congresses; and they participate in the activities of the IOC commissions.

Contributing to the labyrinth of IFs structure are four different associations that connect individual federations to the IOC:

- The Association of Summer Olympic Federations (ASOIF) serves and represents the Summer Olympic IFs at the Summer Olympic Games. At the time this book was written, there were twenty-eight ASOIF members.
- The Association of International Olympic Winter Federations (AIOFW) serves and represents the Winter Olympic IFs at the Winter Olympic Games. At the time this book was written, there were seven AIOFW members.
- The Association of Recognized IOC International Sports Federations (ARISF) includes IFs for those sports that are recognized or provisionally recognized by the IOC but are not included in the Summer or Winter Olympic Games. Sports federations not recognized by the IOC as international federations cannot be members of ARISF, whose main goals are to universalize and promote the Olympic spirit through the sports it represents. At the time this book was written, there were thirty-one ARISF members.
- The General Association of International Sports Federations (AGFIS). All IFs belong to the AGFIS, whose mission is to unite, support, and promote its member international sports federations and organizations for the coordination and protection of their common aims and interests within the Olympic Movement and governmental and nongovernmental bodies. At the time this book was written, there were 102 AGFIS members.

Table 2.1 lists all AGFIS federations. Some IFs belong to one or more of the other three associations as well. One thing needs to be explained about the list: Most readers will be surprised to find that not all of the federations listed represent a specific sport in which athletes compete. Five examples of IFs that are not "sport" federations are listed below with a brief description of how they contribute to the Olympic Movement network:

1. The Commonwealth Games Federation is responsible for direction and control of the Commonwealth Games, a world-class, multisport event held once every four years.

2. The Committee of Mediterranean Games does essentially the same thing for the Mediterranean Games, which is also a multisport event held every four years, mainly for countries bordering the Mediterranean Sea.

3. The World Games are an international multisport event for sports that are not included in the Olympic Games. However, some of the sports that at one time were part of the World Games program eventually became Olympic sports, such as the triathlon. Between twenty-five and thirty-five sports are usually contested at the World Games.

4. The European Broadcasting Union is the largest association of national broadcasters in the world. Much of the world's international sports broadcasts are produced here.

5. The Federation Internationale de Chiropratique du Sport is an organization of national chiropractic sports councils worldwide and individual members that cooperate with international organizations within the chiropractic profession and the world of sports. Its main role is to provide athletes in all sports access, when needed, to the specialized skills of chiropractors as part of overall sports health care.

Table 2.1 General Association of International Sports Federations

Aikido	International Aikido Federation
Air sports	Fédération Aeronautique Internationale
American football	International Federation of American Football
Aquatics	Fédération Internationale de Natation
Archery	International Archery Federation
Athletics	International Association of Athletics Federations
Badminton	Badminton World Federation
Baseball	International Baseball Federation
Basketball	Fédération Internationale de Basketball
Basque pelota	Federacion Internacional de Pelota Vasca
Biathlon	International Biathlon Union
Billiards sports	World Confederation of Billiard Sports
Bobsleigh	Fédération Internationale de Bobsleigh et de Tobogganing
Bodybuilding	International Federation of Bodybuilding and Fitness
Boules sport	Confederation Mondiale des Sports de Boules
Bowling	Federation Internationale des Quilleurs
Boxing	Association Internationale de Boxe
Bridge	World Bridge Federation
Canoeing	International Canoe Federation

table continues

Casting	International Casting Sport Federation
Chess	Fédération Internationale des Echecs
Commonwealth Games	Commonwealth Games Federation
Cricket	International Cricket Council
Curling	World Curling Federation
Cycling	Union Cycliste Internationale
Dancesport	International Dancesport Federation
Darts	World Darts Federation
Deaf sports	International Committee of Sports for the Deaf
Dragon boat	International Dragon Boat Federation
Draughts	Fédération Mondiale du Jeu de Dames
Equestrian sports	Fédération Equestre Internationale
European broadcasting	European Broadcasting Union
Fencing	Fédération Internationale d'Escrime
Fistball	International Fistball Association
Floorball	International Floorball Federation
Flying disc	World Flying Disc Federation
Football	Fédération Internationale de Football Association
Go	International Go Federation
Gymnastics	Fédération Internationale de Gymnastique
Handball	International Handball Federation
Hockey	Fédération Internationale de Hockey
Ice hockey	International Ice Hockey Federation
Jujitsu	Jujitsu International Federation
Karate	World Karate Federation
Kendo	International Kendo Federation
Kickboxing	World Association of Kickboxing Organizations
Korfball	International Korfball Federation
Labor sports	Confederation Sportive Internationale du Travail
Lifesaving	International Lifesaving Federation
Luge	Fédération Internationale de Luge Course
Maccabi	Maccabi World Union
Masters Games	International Masters Games Association
Mediterranean Games	International Committee of Mediterranean Games
Military sport	Conseil International du Sport Militaire
Minigolf	World Minigolf Sport Federation
Modern pentathlon	Union Internationale de Pentathlon Moderne
Motorcycling	Fédération Internationale de Motorcyclisme
Mountineering	Union Internationale des Associations d'Alpinisme
Muaythai	International Federation of Muaythai Amateur
Netball	International Federation of Netball Associations
Orienteering	International Orienteering Federation
Panathlon	Panathlon International
Paralympic	International Paralympic Committee
Polo	Federation of International Polo
Powerboating	Union Internationale Motonautique

table continues

Table 2.1 (continued)

Powerlifting	International Powerlifting Federation
Racquetball	International Racquetball Federation
Roller sports	Fédération Internationale de Roller Sports
Rowing	Fédération Internationale des Sociétés d'Aviron
Rugby Union	International Rugby Board
Sailing	International Sailing Federation
Sambo	Fédération Internationale Amateur de Sambo
School sport	International School Sport Federation
Sepaktakraw	International Sepaktakraw Federation
Shooting sport	International Shooting Sport Federation
Skating	International Skating Union
Skiing	Fédération Internationale de Ski
Sleddog	International Federation of Sleddog Sports
Soft tennis	International Soft Tennis Federation
Softball	International Softball Federation
Special Olympics	Special Olympics, Inc.
Sport climbing	International Federation of Sport Climbing
Sports chiropractic	Fédération Internationale de Chiropratique du Sport
Sports facilities	International Association for Sports and Leisure Facilities
Sports fishing	Confederation Internationale de la Peche Sportive
Sports press	Association Internationale de la Presse Sportive
Squash	World Squash Federation
Subaquatics	Confederation Mondiale des Activities Subaquatiques
Sumo	International Sumo Federation
Surfing	International Surfing Association
Table tennis	International Table Tennis Federation
Taekwondo	World Taekwondo Federation
Tennis	International Tennis Federation
The World Games	International World Games Association
Triathlon	International Triathlon Union
Tug-of-war	Tug-of-War International Federation
University sports	Fédération Internationale du Sport Universitaire
Volleyball	Fédération Internationale de Volleyball
Water skiing	International Water Ski Federation
Weightlifting	International Weightlifting Federation
Wrestling	Fédération Internationale des Luttes Associées
Wushu	International Wushu Federation

The Preeminent International Federation: Fédération Internationale de Football Association

Every IF has its own history, organizational structure, and policies. It is also responsible for the organization and governance of its own competitions; in most cases there is a regular international competitive event to determine the best in the world in that sport. With over one hundred IFs, an extended description of each is not possible, so I have decided to focus on the Fédération Internationale de Football Association (French for "International Federation of Football Association"), known globally by its acronym, FIFA. FIFA is responsible for the organization and governance of its major international tournaments, the best known of which is the World Cup. Although this sport is known in most of the world as association football, or just as "football," or in Latin American countries as "futbol," I shall refer to it as soccer in this book because American football is now well-known throughout the world, so the word "soccer" is increasingly being used globally in speech and print to differentiate the original sport of football from American football (some point to this as an example of Americanization).

I have chosen to elaborate on FIFA for several reasons: First, soccer is the world's most popular sport, and it is played in more countries than any other sport. Second, its most important event, the World Cup, is actually "world," not only in name but in fact, because every country in the world has a chance to participate, unlike with many other sporting events called "world" championships. I realize that other IFs sponsor "world" championship events that meet this criterion, but they do not meet the following two conditions: The World Cup is the most popular single-sport event in the world, and FIFA is one of the largest GSOs in the sports world (Foer 2005).

Figure 2.3 illustrates the governance structure of FIFA. It is established under the laws of Switzerland, with its headquarters in Zurich. FIFA comprises a congress (legislative body), which is an assembly made up of representatives from each affiliated member association. The congress elects the president, the general secretary, and the other members of FIFA's executive committee. The president and general secretary are FIFA's main officeholders and are in charge of its daily administration, carried out by the general secretariat, with its staff of approximately 280 members. The executive committee, chaired by the president, is the main decision-making component of the organization between sessions of the congress.

Figure 2.3 Model outline of FIFA organization chart

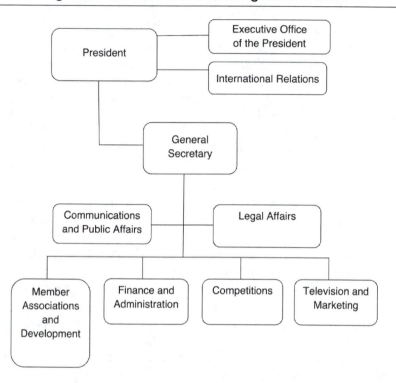

Soccer as an organized sport had acquired some international popularity by the beginning of the twentieth century and was included as a demonstration sport in the 1900 and 1904 Olympic Games; it became an official sport at the 1908 Olympics. In the meantime, FIFA was founded in Paris in 1904 through the initiative of seven European national soccer associations and held its first international competition in 1906. Its membership expanded beyond Europe with the addition of South Africa in 1909, Argentina and Chile in 1912, and Canada in 1913.

In 1914, FIFA began to recognize the Olympics Games as a world football championship for amateurs and agreed to manage the event. Then, in 1928, FIFA decided to organize its own international tournament apart from the Olympics and held the first World Cup in 1930. In front of a crowd of 93,000 people, Uruguay became the first nation to win a World Cup (Lanfanchi et al. 2005).

Except for a couple of exceptions, between 1934 and 1978 sixteen teams competed in each World Cup finals tournament. In 1982 the finals were expanded to twenty-four teams, then to thirty-two in 1998, permitting more teams from Africa, Asia, and North America to take part. European and South American teams have been the strongest. For example, the quarter finalists in 2006 were all from Europe or South America. In 2006, 198 nations challenged to qualify for the FIFA World Cup, and over 200 attempted to qualify for the 2010 World Cup (Crouch 2006; Lisi 2007).

A FIFA Women's World Cup was first held in 1991 in China. Although smaller in scale and profile than the men's World Cup—twelve teams were sent to represent their countries—the women's event has grown in popularity. There were 120 national entrants for the 2007 Women's World Cup, more than double that of 1991. Germany will host the 2011 FIFA Women's World Cup.

FIFA has 208 affiliated associations and their men's national teams as well as 129 women's national teams, leading some commentators to dub this governing body the "United Nations of Soccer." It supports the associations financially and logistically through various programs and grants them a number of attractive rights and privileges (FIFA 2009).

FIFA and the Olympic Games. Except during the first modern Olympic Games in 1896 and again in 1932, men's soccer has been in the program of every Summer Olympic Games. Unlike many other sports, however, the men's Olympics soccer tournament is not considered a top-level soccer tournament; the World Cup is the preeminent men's soccer competition. However, since 1992 professional soccer players under twenty-three years of age and three professionals over age twenty-three have been allowed on each team, raising the level of play and enhancing the popularity of Olympic soccer. Women's Olympic soccer made its debut in 1996 with no age or professional status restrictions on players.

Global Sport Organizations and Solo Sports

My exposition of GSOs has focused on the Olympic Movement network simply because there are dozens of GSOs affiliated with it. No other group of GSOs is affiliated with such a large network. In order to illustrate that there are sports not associated with the Olympic Movement, I now turn the focus onto GSOs with no organizational connection to the Olympic Movement, specifically onto commercial/professional solo sports rather than team sports.

Solo sports are those "for which one-against-one competition is intrinsic to the nature of the game. These sports cannot be re-formulated as team sports without changing their nature" (Forster and Pope 2004, 91). Commercially significant solo-sport competition is typically found within a tournament format, and the athletes must travel the globe following a tournament schedule (or tour) that each year may include dozens of countries on several continents. On the other hand, commercial/professional team sports are typically organized into leagues, and the athletes play in a set of fixed sports venues for their competition.

Several globally popular solo sports played professionally that have well-defined GSOs could serve as exemplars for analysis, but I have chosen to describe the GSOs of men's and women's professional tennis—the Association of Tennis Professionals (ATP) and the Women's Tennis Association (WTA)—because both began in the early 1970s at a time when globalizing developments were materializing in many sectors, especially economic and cultural. Both now have more than thirty years of uninterrupted history with well-defined organizational structures and functions.

Association of Tennis Professionals

The ATP is the GSO for men's professional tennis. It takes as its mission "to serve as the governing body of the men's professional tennis circuit and lead creatively and professionally the worldwide growth of the men's professional game, building on the rich traditions of tennis and innovating to ensure it is always vibrant and relevant" (ATP World Tour 2009). What became the ATP was organized in 1972 to protect the interests of male professional tennis players and to provide a stable source of scheduling and rule making. Until 1990 World Championship Tennis was the tour name for professional male tennis players, but in 1990 the ATP Tour became the major global tennis tour for men; it was renamed the ATP World Tour in 2009.

The ATP's executive offices are in London, England. Its hierarchical governance structure is headed by an executive chairman and president. To accommodate its global reach, there are three CEOs: CEO of Americas, based in the United States; CEO of Europe, headquartered in Monaco; and CEO of the International Division, covering Africa, Asia, and Australasia and based in Australia (CEO locations in 2009).

The ATP's board of directors is composed of the executive chairman and president, three tournament representatives, and three player representatives elected by the ATP Player Council with two-year terms (one is the Americas representative, one is the European representative, and one is the international representative).

Providing representation for ATP players, an eleven-member Player Council consists of four players ranked within the top fifty in singles, two players ranked between fifty-one and one hundred in singles, two top-one-hundred players in doubles, two at-large members, and an alumni representative. The Player Council supplies advisory information to the board of directors, which they can accept or reject.

The 2009 ATP World Tour featured sixty tournaments in thirty-one countries with the following breakdown of tiers: nine ATP World Tour Masters 1000 events, eleven ATP World Tour 500 events, and forty ATP World Tour 250 events, leading to the season-ending Barclays ATP World Tour Finals in London where the ATP World Tour champion Roger Federer was officially crowned (ATP World Tour 2009).

Women's Tennis Association

The WTA, the GSO for women's professional tennis, was organized in 1973, a year after the founding of the ATP. Billie Jean King was the key figure in founding the WTA and uniting all of women's professional tennis in one tour. For many years its worldwide professional tennis tour was called the WTA Tour, but since 2005 it has been called the Sony Ericsson WTA Tour. This tour is the world's leading professional sport for women. In 2009 more than 2,200 players representing more than ninety nations competed for more than $90 million in prize money at the tour's fifty-one events and four grand slams in thirty-one countries (Sony Ericsson WTA Tour, 2009).

The corporate headquarters of the WTA is in the United States, but it also has European headquarters in England and Asia-Pacific headquarters in China. The governance structure of the WTA is less elaborate than that of the ATP. In the hierarchical chain the chair and CEO holds the top position. The board of directors is composed of seven members plus the chair and CEO. A Global Advisory Council of thirteen members makes recommendations and suggestions to the other levels of WTA governance.

Multiple GSOs for a Sport: Professional Boxing

The claim of most current GSOs to legitimate control over their respective sport or sporting event(s) is well established, and they face no challengers.

However, in some sports there is no single controlling GSO. For illustration, I will use professional boxing. Boxing has historically had, and continues to have, a plethora of organizations claiming to be "the" global authority for the sport. The number of those claiming this title fluctuates because boxing organizations often fold, and others emerge. Below is a list of professional boxing organizations claiming to be the supreme governing body for this sport in 2010:

- International Boxing Organization
- International Boxing Association
- World Boxing Organization
- World Boxing Association
- World Boxing Union
- International Boxing Union
- World Boxing Foundation
- World Professional Boxing Federation

Each of these organizations ranks boxers and sanctions bouts in various weight divisions. Thus, it is possible to have more than one "world champion" in a given weight division. Economics-of-sport scholar Rafael Tenorio highlights the ludicrous consequences of the governance situation in boxing: "To make matters worse, none of these organizations uses any kind of objective mathematical formula (based on wins, losses, quality of opposition and so on) to determine their rankings. In fact, rankings are only loosely based on performance.... In addition, business interests, politics, and even bribery have been shown to be important determinants of fighter rankings in many cases" (2006, 366).

The task of unifying, governing, and managing global professional boxing is difficult for several reasons. For at least the past two hundred years, either individual or groups of promoters and "owners" have controlled individual boxers, trainers, and championship bouts. Bouts were agreed to and venues selected by agreement of the boxers' promoters. Several of the current boxing organizations that claim to be the GSO for boxing are merely extensions of this traditional promoter control of boxers and bouts.

Another feature of the boxing culture makes it difficult to establish a single GSO for the sport, namely, that prizefighting has always been a sport of dubious legitimacy. Because boxing was outlawed by many local or national governments until the early twentieth century, prizefights were often held at gambling venues and secret locations so they would not be broken up by law-enforcement agencies. Even today, in most countries of the world, legal professional bouts must be approved by government boxing committees or commissions to guarantee the legitimacy of the proposed bouts and to assure the boxers are in good physical condition. The various laws and conditions required to hold prizefights have thwarted the establishment of a single GSO for boxing.

Global Sporting Organizations and International Games

In the first paragraph of this chapter, I referred to the characteristics of GSOs as transnational authorities that control various sports and sporting events, with each sport or event having a different kind of control or mix of influence (Forster and Pope 2004; Strange 1996). Up to this point, my focus has been on the IOC, which is a hierarchically organized global controlling body of multisports events (the Winter and Summer Olympic Games) and on FIFA and professional tennis associations, all of which are hierarchically organized global controlling bodies of single-sport events, such as the World Cup and tennis tours.

There are also numerous international multisport events that are not under the jurisdiction of any single GSO. Indeed, the organization and management of some of these sporting events is often in the hands of the city in which they are held or handled by an ad hoc committee or commission that changes each time the event is held. Many of these events are global in that organizers and participants are from countries throughout the world, such as the Gay Games and the World Masters Games, so they can accurately be called "global." However, many of these sporting events are international because they involve participants from two or more nations competing in two or more sports in the same location at the same time, but they are geographically regional or specialized in nature, such as the Asian Games or the Firefighters World Games. Therefore, Bell (2003), in his history of these sports events, calls them "international games," and I think that is the appropriate designation for all of them. They also meet Susan Strange's classification of GSOs that have "a different kind of authority, or mix of authorities" (1996, 96).

Most of these international games do not attract global media coverage. Unfortunately, the majority of the events have not kept their own official records; nor is there a central location where data on any particular event is kept. But collectively these international multisports events provide a global spread of sporting events that supplement and broaden the popularity of sport, increase sports participation, and expand sports spectatorship throughout the world.

In his *Encyclopedia of International Games,* Daniel Bell (2003) has documented 1,220 instances of over two hundred types of international sports events held from 1896 until the end of 2000. One of the most remarkable findings of his research is the steady increase in international multisport championship events throughout the twentieth century. These have grown in number every decade for the past one hundred years, and there has been a spectacular growth over the past two decades—at the same time that globalization processes have accelerated. This growth in international multisport competitions is illustrated in Table 2.2 for fifty years.

Table 2.2 Number of International Multisport Competitions per Decade

Decade	Competitions
1950–1959	69
1960–1969	91
1970–1979	144
1980–1989	234
1990–1999	502

Source: Bell 2003.

As an illustration of the rapid proliferation of new international games each year during the decade of the 1990s, in 1993 eight new games were established, in 1996 there were fourteen new games, in 1998 there were nine new games, and in 2000 seven new games were initiated.

Summary

The GSO is the highest level of sport governance body, and each is a private and autonomous entity. GSOs organize the rules under which a sport is played; they develop the competitive events, especially national and international championships; they form leagues and assign teams to them; they assign media and sponsorship rights; and they distribute money from their global revenues.

Although the date, location, and sport involved of the first international sporting event has not been definitively established, there is a record of international sport competitions in the early nineteenth century. By the latter decades of that century, the International Federation of Gymnastics had been founded and had sponsored competitions for gymnasts from different countries. There also were frequent professional boxing matches between boxers from different countries.

The revival of the ancient Olympic Games in 1896 by Pierre de Coubertin became the pinnacle international multisports event. The formation of the IOC as the GSO to organize and manage the modern Olympic Games set the model and standard for subordinate organizations both within and outside the Olympic Movement. With the conclusion of the 2008 Beijing Summer Olympics, there have now been twenty-six Summer Games. The 2010 Vancouver Winter Olympics were the twenty-first Winter Olympics.

The IOC has encountered a continuing series of contentious issues related to its exclusivity. Three of the most significant relate to female eligibility, the amateur requirement, and athletes with special needs. The founder of the modern Olympics opposed female participation, but gradually the percentage of women participating in the Olympics has increased—to the point that in the 2008 Beijing Olympics, they constituted 43 percent of the athletes competing. Pierre de Coubertin insisted that all Olympic athletes be amateurs. But the rule about amateurism became controversial almost immediately. By mid-twentieth century the rule was considered outdated, exclusionary, and discriminatory. Various types of activities made a mockery of the rule, leading to it gradually being phased out. Pleas from various groups for the IOC to become more inclusive persuaded it to endorse the Paralympics and lend its support to the Special Olympics.

FIFA is the most prominent IF because soccer is the world's most popular sport. FIFA is also responsible for the world's second most popular sports event, the World Cup.

Sports in which there is one-against-one competition are called solo sports (e.g., tennis, golf, and boxing). Well-defined GSOs are found in men's and women's professional tennis. On the other hand, professional boxing has no single controlling GSO. Instead, some eight boxing organizations currently claim to be the global governing body of professional boxing.

Many international multisport events are not under the jurisdiction of any single GSO. Over 1,200 instances of over two hundred international sports events have been held over the past one hundred years. There has been a rapid increase in these events during the past two decades.

Notes

1. The committee elected its first Asian member in 1908 and its first African member in 1910. Currently, members from European and North American countries account for much of the IOC membership.

2. When describing the purposes and functions of Olympic Movement organizations (e.g., committees, federations, and associations), I have relied on the accounts by various organizations. They are the most authoritative and up-to-date.

3. The IOC's first president was Demetrius Vikélas of Greece (1894–1896). The other IOC presidents have been Pierre de Coubertin of France (1896–1925), Count Henri de Baillet-Latour of Belgium (1925–1942), J. Sigfrid Edström of Sweden (1946–1952), Avery Brundage of the United States (1952–1972), Michael Morris, Lord Killanin, of Ireland (1972–1980), Juan Antonio Samaranch of Spain (1980–2001), and Jacques Rogge of Belgium (2001–present).

4. Olympic historians differ in their accounts of the sports and number of female participants in the Olympic Games between 1900 and 1928.

References

Allison, Lincoln. 2001. *Amateurism in sport: An analysis and defence.* London: Frank Cass.

Association of the National Olympic Committees (ANOC). 2008. Introduction to ANOC. ANOC. www.en.acnolympic.org/art.php?id=20008.

ATP World Tour. 2009. ATP World Tour. www.atpworldtour.com.

Bell, Daniel. 2003. *Encyclopedia of international games.* Jefferson, NC: McFarland & Company.

Brailsford, Dennis. 1988. *Bareknuckles: A social history of prize-fighting.* Cambridge, UK: Lutterworth Press.

Brundage, Avery. 1968. *The speeches of Avery Brundage.* Lausanne, Switzerland: Comité International Olympique.

Chappelet, Jean-Loup, and Brenda Kübler-Mabbott. 2008. *The International Olympic Committee and the Olympic system: The governance of world sport.* New York: Routledge.

Crouch, Terry. 2006. *The World Cup: The complete history.* Illust. ed. London: Aurum Press.

de Coubertin, Pierre. [1931]1979. *Mémoires Olympiques.* Lausanne, Switzerland: International Olympic Committee.

Fédération Internationale de Football Association (FIFA). 2009. About FIFA. FIFA.com. www.fifa.com/aboutfifa/federation/index.html.

Foer, Franklin. 2005. *How soccer explains the world: An unlikely theory of globalization*. New York: Harper Perennial.

Forster, John, and Osvaldo Croci. 2006. Sport and politics: The question of legitimacy of international sport organizations. Paper presented at the annual meeting of the International Studies Association, Town and Country Resort and Convention Center, March 22, 2006, San Diego, California. www.allacademic.com/meta/p100098_index.html.

Forster, John, and Nigel Pope. 2004. *The political economy of global sporting organizations*. New York: Routledge.

Gerber, Ellen, Jan Felshin, Pearl Berlin, and Waneen Wyrick. 1974. *The American woman in sport*. Reading, MA: Addison-Wesley.

Guttmann, Allen. 2002. *The Olympics: A history of the modern games*. 2nd ed. Urbana: University of Illinois Press.

Hoehn, Thomas. 2006. Governance and governing bodies in sport. In *Handbook on the economics of sport*, ed. Wladimir Andreff and Stefan Szymanski, 227–240. Northampton, MA: Edward Elgar.

International Olympic Committee (IOC). 2007. *Olympic Charter*. IOC, July 7. http://multimedia.olympic.org/pdf/en_report_122.pdf.

———. 2008. Fact sheet: The summer Olympic Games. IOC, January. http://multimedia.olympic.org/pdf/en_report_1138.pdf.

———. 2009a. Fact sheet: Women in the Olympic Movement. IOC, June. http://multimedia.olympic.org/pdf/en_report_846.pdf.

———. 2009b. Official website of the Olympic Movement. www.Olympic.org.

Lanfanchi, Pierre, Christiane Eisenberg, Tony Mason, and Alfred Wahl. 2005. *100 years of football: The FIFA centennial book*. Illust. ed. London: Weidenfeld & Nicolson.

Lisi, Clemente Angelo. 2007. *A history of the World Cup: 1930–2006*. Lanham, MD: Scarecrow Press.

MacAloon, John J. 2008. *This great symbol: Pierre de Coubertin and the origins of the modern Olympic Games*. 25th anniv. ed. New York: Routledge.

Miller, David. 2008. *The official history of the Olympic Games and the IOC: From Athens to Beijing, 1894–2008*. Edinburgh: Mainstream Publishing.

Mitchell, Sheila. 1977. Women's participation in the Olympic Games, 1900–1926. *Journal of Sport History* 4 (summer): 208–228.

Pound, Richard. 2004. *Inside the Olympics: A behind-the-scenes look at the politics, the scandals, and the glory of the games*. Etobicoke, Canada: John Wiley & Sons Canada.

Ronit, Karsten, and Volker Schneider, eds. 2000. *Private organizations in global politics*. New York: Routledge.

Sony Ericsson WTA Tour. 2009. Official website of Women's Professional Tennis. www.sonyericssonwtatour.com.

Strange, Susan. 1996. *The retreat of the state: The diffusion of power in the world economy.* Cambridge: Cambridge University Press.

Tenorio, Rafael. 2006. On the competitive structure in professional boxing, or why the best boxers very seldom fight each other. In *Handbook on the economics of sport,* ed. Wladimir Andreff and Stefan Szymanski, 364–368. Northampton, MA: Edward Elgar.

World Anti-Doping Agency (WADA). 2009. WADA. www.wada-ama.org.

Whannel, Garry. 2008. *Culture, politics and sport: Blowing the whistle, revisited.* New York: Routledge.

Young, David C. 2004. *A brief history of the Olympic Games.* New York: Wiley-Blackwell.

CHAPTER 3
GLOBAL MIGRATION OF SPORTS LABOR

David Beckham has conquered the rest of the world as the most recognized soccer player around. Now, he's ready to take on America.... "I'm coming there to make a difference. I'm coming there to play football," Beckham said.... "I'm not saying me coming to the States is going to make soccer the biggest sport in America. But I think soccer has a huge, huge potential. I wouldn't be doing this if I didn't believe in this project."

—Ken Peters, "Beckham Coming to 'Make a Difference,'" *USA Today,* January 12, 2007

The migration of global soccer icon David Beckham, called by *Time* magazine "the best-known sports star in the world" (Bolt 2003, 1), first from England to Spain, then to the United States, then from the United States to Italy, and then back to the United States, illustrates the globalized sports world. Sports labor includes athletes, as in the case of Beckham, as well as coaches, officials, administrators, sports medicine professionals, and sport scientists; this chapter focuses, however, on athletes. Regardless of their skill or expertise, sports migration is a microcosm of a broader human migration—past and present. Historically situating and culturally locating this broad human migration is a crucial preliminary for understanding migration in globalized sport.

Human Migration: Past and Present

We have always been a "traveling species," declared Kwame Anthony Appiah (2003, 192), professor of philosophy at Princeton University, in a speech for the prestigious Oxford Amnesty Lecture Series. Historians uniformly agree that migration extends back to the beginning of human history. Seeking favorable climate, land, hunting conditions, conquest, or merely slow cultural infiltration and resettlement, human migration has been a continuing feature of human life on earth.

Human migrations in modern times have continued in the form of both voluntary migration within one's country, continent, or beyond and involuntary migration, such as slave trading, racial and ethnic cleansing, and human trafficking. More than in previous generations, migration has become a global phenomenon in the sense that migration flows link all regions of the globe. People migrate for reasons too numerous to list fully, but they include employment, marriage, education, warfare, asylum seeking, and poverty and disaster relief. Currently, though, the most significant general reason is that the global economy, the dominant process of globalization, has unleashed worldwide free market capitalism, stimulating wide-ranging economic development patterns. Figure 3.1 illustrates the growth in world merchandise trading by just one major sector: manufacturing. Since the 1960s manufacturing has grown at an annual rate of 7.5 percent. Growth like this has spawned migrations that stretch across national borders, regularly creating disproportionate flows of people from country to country (Oderth 2002).

Today, more than 140 million people—nearly 3 percent of the world's population—live outside their countries of birth, and migrants account for over 15 percent of the population in over fifty countries. In Canada the foreign-born population is near 18 percent; in Australia it is 22 percent. The pattern of immigration into the United States has been on a sharp upward trajectory for the past twenty-five years. In 2008 there were 38 million foreign-born U.S. residents (about 12.2 percent of the population). In most of the Organization for Economic Cooperation and Development (OECD)[1] countries, immigrants currently account for about 65 percent of the population growth, which is up from 45 percent during the 1990–1995 period. In several oil-producing countries, such as Saudi Arabia, the United Arab Emirates, Oman, and Kuwait, noncitizens outnumber the native population.

These trends are likely to grow through the next decade. Susan F. Martin, an expert on immigration and refugee policy at Georgetown

**Figure 3.1 World merchandise trade volume
for manufacturing, 1960–2009**

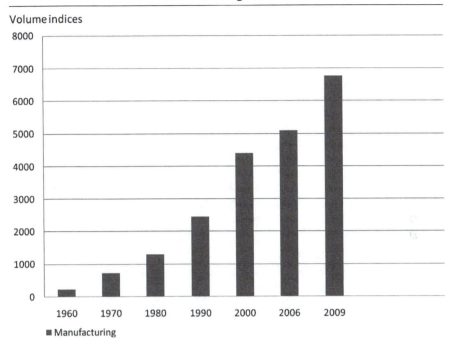

Volume indices

Source: World Trade Organization 2009.

University, asserts, "With poverty, political repression, human rights abuses, and conflict pushing more and more people out of their home countries while economic opportunities, political freedom, physical safety, and security pull both highly skilled and unskilled workers into new lands, the pace of international migration is unlikely to slow any time soon" (2009, 31).

The production of goods and services for the global economy relies on a prolific force of entrepreneurs, intelligent creators, professionals, and skilled and unskilled workers. Persons with these competencies are not equally distributed throughout the world; nor is the demand for them. Therefore, a great deal of cross-border migration takes place as the dynamics of supply and demand for the global workforce change. Business investors, owners, managers, executives, professionals—such as physicians, attorneys, nurses, teachers, professors, technicians (e.g., CAT, computer)—and various kinds of skilled and unskilled workers now globally migrate in search of jobs and financial security. For example, over two-thirds of IBM employees, both foreigners and U.S. citizens, work outside the United States. Much global migration is a consequence of global employment inequalities and arises as millions of individuals seek better lives.

The Migration of Sports Labor: Sports Workers Throughout the World

With the current omnipresence of organized sports—leisure oriented, youth, club, high school, intercollegiate, professional—it is easy to understand why we tend to believe that the wide array of formalized participant and spectator sports that we enjoy has always existed. But, unimaginable as it seems, there were no formally organized participant or spectator sports in the world before the nineteenth century. Even then, it was not until the latter half of that century that sports became more than casual pastimes in the emerging industrializing countries.

There were reasons for that state of affairs. In the first place, people had very little leisure time or opportunity to engage in games and sports. The harsh circumstances of wresting a living from the environment necessitated arduous daily work, so most people had to devote most of their efforts to basic survival tasks. Second, religion was a powerful institution that dominated social life, and playful physical activities were frowned upon. Third, sociocultural conditions—urbanization, motorized transportation, telegraphic and wireless communication—necessary for the development of organized sports did not exist until the emergence of a more technologically and economically advanced industrialization.

Currently, the commercial sports industry, which is a component of the contemporary global entertainment industry, has, like other parts of the global economy, a migratory labor force of highly skilled sports workers. As organized sports gained commercial appeal, sport organizations began to seek talented sports workers from distant locations, and sports workers began to find employment beyond their local residences in what was increasingly becoming an interdependent and shrinking world (Maguire 2009). The current system of sports-worker migration that has evolved takes place at three levels:

- within nations
- between nations on the same continent

- between nations located on different continents and in different hemispheres

Sports-Labor Migration Within Nations

The first form of sport migration began with the professionalization of sport, as sport organizations were organized as private business enterprises. Some professionalization of sport took place in the industrialized countries during the latter nineteenth and early twentieth century, but it was in the latter three decades of the twentieth century that professional sports became a global industry and sports workers joined the global labor force of migrating workers.

The newly formed sport businesses, similar to other business enterprises, sought employees with skills at affordable wages wherever they could find them. In the case of sport labor, athletes and coaches with these competencies were most often found by the team-sport owners within the country where the sports organizations were headquartered. In the United States, Major League Baseball (MLB) is a good example. I shall use MLB as a within-country migration model for what also occurred in many other countries in several sports.

From an informal children's game played throughout the eighteenth century, baseball developed codified rules in the 1840s, and groups of upper-class men organized clubs, taking care to keep out lower-class persons. The Civil War wiped out this upper-class patronage of the game, and a broad base of popularity existed in 1869 when the first professional baseball team, the Cincinnati Red Stockings, was formed. The team was a touring team made up of itinerant players who played games from coast to coast in the United States—winning sixty-five games without a defeat in its first year. This was followed in 1871 by the organization of the first baseball sports league—the National Association of Professional Baseball Players. In 1876 the National League of Professional Baseball Clubs—or simply National League—was founded to replace the National Association. It is presently the world's oldest extant professional team-sport league.

Each team in what became known as Major League Baseball was an independent private business. Team owners recruited players and coaches from throughout the United States, and the recruited players on these early teams became the first professional team-sport migrants. The team owners organized a league primarily for scheduling purposes, but also to control the migration of players. Indeed, MLB owners created a plan known as the reserve clause to severely limit player migration (Koppett 2004).

The reserve clause was a provision in every player's contract that enabled owners to control players' mobility. Once a player signed a contract with a team (aka club), that team had exclusive rights over him; he was no longer free to negotiate with other teams because his contract had a clause that "reserved" his services to his original team for the succeeding year. The reserve clause specified that the owner had the exclusive right to renew the player's contract annually, thereby binding the player perpetually to negotiate with only one club. He became a team owner's property and could even be sold to another club without his own consent. In all succeeding years, then, the player had to sell his services solely to the club that owned his contract, unless the club released, sold, or traded him or he chose to retire (Koppett 2004).

MLB owners imposed another limitation on baseball player migration. Emancipation of African Americans after the Civil War gave them hopes of participating in professional sports along with whites, but the postwar years saw a mass social disenfranchisement of African Americans. Although a few African Americans played on professional baseball teams in the latter nineteenth century, MLB team owners adopted an unwritten "gentleman's agreement" pledging they would not recruit or employ African American players (Koppett 2004; see also Peterson 1992).

Between the latter nineteenth and mid-twentieth centuries, many other team sports, such as soccer (originally called football), ice hockey, American football, and basketball, became professionalized and established a commercial market for their sporting events. Like MLB, athletes and coaches for these sport organizations migrated within the country of the sports teams on which they played, moving to sports teams based on salaries, coaching, level of competition, facilities, and so forth. Although most professional sports leagues did not impose a reserve clause like MLB, many did formulate provisions to limit player migration within their league.

Sports-Labor Migration: Intra- and Intercontinental Migration

Intra- and intercontinental sport migrations have been a significant feature of global sports. As described above, when most team sports were organized as private commercial enterprises in the late nineteenth and early twentieth centuries, the operations—games, matches, contests, leagues, conferences—all took place within a single country. During the past fifty years, especially the past twenty-five, the globalization occurring in the economic, political, technological, and cultural sectors has also impacted sports. Among the most prominent trends of sport-labor migration is movement beyond national boundaries into, first, neighboring countries, then into continents across the globe. Movement of baseball players from Canada, the Caribbean islands, and then South America into MLB teams provides a good example of a pattern of intra- and intercontinental sport migration. After the fall of the Soviet Union, the movement between western and eastern Europe among soccer, basketball, and ice hockey sports workers illustrates intracontinental sport-labor migration. While the massive recruitment and influx of African soccer players to European soccer clubs illustrates the intercontinental migration pattern.

Most nations have various laws and policies with regard to immigration, which sports workers crossing national borders must confront. In order to permit workers with special skills or knowledge needed by the government or private business to enter a country quickly—and thus bypass quota or other laws that limit immigration—many countries have enacted legislation to facilitate what is called guest-worker immigration.

Guest-Worker Programs. One of the by-products of globalization is the great increase in cross-border migration. That trend is especially prominent in the labor force of the global economy. As I noted above, to facilitate cross-border migrations of workers, many countries created guest-worker programs. The titles for these programs differ from country to country, but they all provide a means by which employers in a country can sponsor foreign laborers for a specific period—such as three years. These immigrants can be deported when their employment contract expires if they are no longer needed or have not obtained a permanent work permit (called a green card in the United States). At the same time, in order to prevent unwanted immigrants from entering a country illegally, most countries have established laws and an agency to enforce them. In the United States that agency is U.S. Immigration and Customs Enforcement.

Early guest-worker laws applied mostly to unskilled agricultural and manufacturing workers. However, in order to be competitive in the global economy in cutting-edge information technology (e.g., computer science) and other high-status professions (e.g., physician) that require high-level skills, all of the developed countries have created "special" immigration programs that allow foreigners with specific competencies to enter. For example, in the United States the H-1B visa (Immigration and Nationality Act, section 101[a][15][H]) enables professionals in "specialty occupations" to immigrate to work in their specialties. Specialty occupations include engineers, architects, computer analysts, programmers, database administrators, web designers, social scientists, physical scientists, doctors, nurses, business specialists, educators, lawyers, accounts, and artists. Petitions are submitted by employers based on their need for the non-U.S.-resident employees. The H-1B visa is issued for up to three years but may be extended.

Sports Workers As Guest Workers. With the expanding professionalization of sports in the early twentieth century, sport-labor migration was common, but migration beyond national borders was infrequent before mid-century. However, rapid development of the global economy during the latter twentieth century featured a more cohesive global integration supported by technical change and international economic policies, all of which motivated multilateral cooperation. These combined to reduce barriers to international flows and accelerate the growth rate of world output; thus, people, money, images, and ideas were able to travel the globe quickly.

The interweaving of economic, political, social, and cultural patterns of globalization greatly expanded the intra- and intercontinental migration potential for elite-level sports workers. Indeed, a global labor market for sports workers became another component of the global economy. During the past twenty years, with the expanding global spread of sport, most nations have passed laws to facilitate the migration of sports workers. In the United States, since the H-1B legislation did not include the importation of athletes and coaches, two U.S. immigration laws, H-2B and P-1, were passed to include athlete, artist, and entertainer as specialty occupations.

Under this legislation any internationally recognized professional or amateur elite-level athlete or coach, individually or as part of a group, is eligible for admission into the United States to participate in his or her sport. Sport organizations wishing to employ foreign athletes or coaches are required to submit a petition of support and promise of employment. Similar laws applying to sports workers have been enacted in many other countries to facilitate the importation of athletes and coaches.

There is currently a globally active sports-worker recruitment and migration in over a dozen sports. This "free trade" in sports workers occurs most often between developed countries; it also migrates from developed to developing countries, but rarely from developing to developed countries. The reasons for this is rather obvious: Developed countries have the largest reservoir of sports workers, and the sport-organization owners in developed countries have the most capital to spend on foreign athletes and coaches.

Global Patterns of Migration Among Sports Labor in Selected Sports

It would be an encyclopedic undertaking to attempt to identify and describe sports-worker migration patterns for all commercially played sports. Instead, I have selected four of the most globally popular team sports: soccer, basketball, ice hockey, and baseball. I describe the globalizing pattern of sports-worker migration in these sports, for the latter three focusing on the highest level of play: the National Basketball Association (NBA) in basketball; the National Hockey League (NHL) in ice hockey; and Major League Baseball in baseball. (At least, these are the leagues most acclaimed by those who play and coach in each sport.) In the case of soccer, because it is played at the highest level in so many countries, it is problematic to claim that any one league is the "best." I also include the Olympic Movement because the Olympic Games are the most widely acclaimed global multisports event, and sports workers in every sport worldwide aspire to membership on their country's Olympic team.

Sports-Labor Migration and Soccer

There may be no cultural practice more global than soccer. Rites of birth and marriage are infinitely diverse, but the rules of soccer are universal. No world religion can match its geographical scope. The single greatest simultaneous collective human experience is the World Cup final (Review of *The Ball Is Round* 2008).

I have chosen to examine sport-labor migration in soccer first among the major professional team sports because it has several unique features: First, worldwide, it is the world's most popular sport, and it is played in more countries than any other sport. Second, of the sports I identified above, only its most prestigious professional league is not located in North America; indeed, no single country can claim the "best" league because many countries have elite professional leagues. Third, the World Cup is the most popular single-sport championship worldwide (Foer 2005).

Soccer evolved in different parts of the world where play has involved the kicking of a ball. Every early culture seems to have had its own version of the game, but the concept was the same: kicking the ball with the feet. So every group has its "footprint" in soccer history, and this may be the reason why soccer is so popular around the globe.

The modern rules of soccer were formulated in England in the mid-nineteenth century in an effort to standardize the widely varying forms of that sport. In 1885 professional soccer players were first recognized by the Football Association, which was, and is, the governing body of soccer in England. By 1888, the first professional soccer league was formed by twelve English soccer clubs.

Soccer spread from England and, by the first decade of the twentieth century, had become so popular that a worldwide association, the Fédération Internationale de Football Association (FIFA), was formed in 1904. By 1930 many countries throughout the world had professional soccer leagues, and the first World Cup was held in that year. Soccer has continued to grow and become even more popular over the last eight decades (Goldblatt 2008). According to a FIFA survey, at the beginning of the twenty-first century more than 250 million people from more than two hundred countries regularly played football (FIFA 2001). Its simple rules and minimal equipment needs have aided its spread and growth in popularity.

In analyzing sports-worker migration patterns in the premier professional leagues of the NBA, NHL, and MLB, it is possible to show clearly the increase in foreign-born athletes in each sport. In soccer this is impossible, first because there are so many elite professional soccer leagues throughout the world; second, there has been a global free-flowing migration of professional soccer athletes over the last twenty years because limits on the number of foreign players in the European leagues were lifted in 1995 by the Bosman ruling, which allows soccer players to move freely from club to club, league to league, and country to country. It also removed restrictions on the number of foreign players a team could have from other European Union countries (Fordyce 2005).

The nation-state has been virtually abolished for league soccer, better enabling it to participate in the growing global economy and expanding global sports industry. Branko Milanovic, a scholar at the Carnegie Endowment for International Peace, declares that "soccer is not only the world's most popular sport, but also probably its most globalized profession. It is inconceivable that Brazilian, Cameroonian or Japanese doctors, computer scientists, blue-collar workers, or bank tellers could move from one country to another as easily as Brazilian, Cameroonian or Japanese soccer players do" (2006, 1; see also Goldblatt 2008).

The numbers and percentages of foreign players in the premier professional soccer leagues of Europe and Asia change on a daily basis, and there are so many of those leagues that accurate figures cannot be cited. Based on the figures provided by various sources that follow soccer leagues throughout the world, however, in the 2007 season the following percentages of foreign players in Europe and England were reported (The Offside 2007):

England: 55.4 percent
Germany: 44.8 percent
Spain: 34.3 percent
France: 32.2 percent
Italy: 28.9 percent

Additional data about the globalization of soccer was reported in the second edition of the *Annual Review of the European Football Players' Labour Market*. According to the review, in 2007 homegrown players represented only 24.3 percent of the 2,744 soccer players employed by the ninety-eight clubs of the five top European leagues in the countries listed above (Poli and Ravenel 2007; see also Lanfranchi and Taylor 2001). Box 3.1 illustrates how thoroughly globalized European professional soccer has become.

Americans like to consider their country an exception in a variety of matters. While their belief may be problematic in several of these, in one area there is no doubt that the United States is exceptional, and that is in the popularity (or unpopularity) of soccer. "Americans have never taken to soccer" is an often-heard comment about Americans' relationship with soccer. However, that has been changing during the past two decades. Youth soccer programs are thriving. In fact, youth soccer has been growing faster than any other youth team sport over the past decade and now has some 10,000 teams and 4.8 million young boys and girls playing (U.S. Youth Soccer 2008).

Major League Soccer (MLS) is the premier professional soccer league in the United States. It was founded in 1993, and its first playing season took place in 1996 with ten teams in the league. Presently, there are fifteen MLS teams, fourteen in the United States and one in Canada, divided into two conferences. Each club (or team) is allowed twenty players on its senior roster, in addition to four developmental players.

From its beginnings, MLS has had foreign players, but since 2006 its league leadership has made a concerted effort to globalize the league to

Box 3.1 Foreign-Born Players Rise to the Top: Importing Goals at Euro 2008

The 2008 Union of European Football Associations (UEFA) championship (Euro 2008), a quadrennial soccer tournament contested by European nations, was the thirteenth. The tournament was hosted by Austria and Switzerland; it began on June 7, 2008, and concluded with the final in Vienna on June 29, 2008.

The following is an edited account of Euro 2008 by Spiegel Online:

Europe is a continent shaped by migration. Nowhere can that be seen more clearly than on the football pitch. So far in this year's tournament, almost 30 percent of the goals have been netted by foreign-born players. For the German team, the total is much higher.

Three times in the first 20 minutes of Thursday night's game between Austria and Poland, the Austrians were virtually alone in front of Polish keeper Artur Boruc. Three times they failed to put the ball in the net. . . . But then, in the 93rd minute, an Austrian player went down in the Polish box and the referee gave a penalty. Ivica Vastic, long a fixture on the Austrian national team, calmly fired the ball past Boruc. Finally, after two games and over 180 minutes of football, Austria had its first goal of the tournament.

Vastic's goal, though, was significant for another reason as well: Of the 28 goals scored so far in this year's European Championship tournament, it was the eighth goal by a player not born in the country he is playing for. Indeed, so far almost 30 percent of Euro 2008 goals have been by foreign-born players. On Tuesday night, three of the five goals scored were netted by foreign-born players. Brazilian-born Roger Guerreiro scored Poland's lone goal on Thursday night.

A glance at the squads shows that this is hardly a statistical anomaly. The Turkish team boasts five foreign-born players, including Colin Kazim-Richards, originally of England. Portugal also has five. Croatia and France have seven each. And four of the five strikers on the German national team were not born in Germany. (The fifth, Mario Gómez, has a Spanish father.) Only four teams—Romania, Czech Republic, Netherlands and Russia—don't have a single foreign-born player in their squads. Even FIFA President Sepp Blatter has turned his attention to the issue of foreign players—albeit on the club level. In early June, he pushed through a new rule requiring clubs to start games with at least six non-foreign players on the field. . . . Otherwise, he worries, club teams will simply recruit players from abroad instead of investing in youth sports closer to home.

He even went so far as to say that England's failure to qualify for this year's Euro 2008 was partly as a result of the fact that top Premiership teams employ so many foreign play-ers. "So where are the best English players coming from? They are coming from the less strong teams, which is weakening the English national team," Blatter said in an interview last week. . . . "What is happening in England is that the best teams are preparing the national team players for England's opponents."

Another way of looking at it, however, is that England isn't taking enough advantage of European cosmopolitanism. Most of the foreign-born players on Euro 2008 rosters are simply a reflection of a Europe that has grown closer together in recent years. . . .

Indeed, a reliance on foreign-born players is an absolute must for many teams. Like Germany, for example. In the 2002 World Cup, seven of Germany's 14 goals were scored by foreign-born players. In the 2006 tournament in Germany, if one eliminates the pen-alty shootout with Argentina and the goals scored in the match for third place, nine of Germany's 11 goals were fired in by Germans not born in the country—with Miroslav Klose and Lukas Podolski, both born in Poland, leading the charge.

And in this year's European Championship? So far, the ratio for Germany is 100 percent.

Source: Spiegel Online International 2008.

raise the quality of play. The most significant action was the implementation of the Designated Player Rule, which allows teams to pay, at their own expense, up to two players a salary beyond that covered in the salary cap. As a result, several veteran foreign players joined MLS, improving the league's level of play and overall profile in the United States and abroad (Davis 2007).

The Designated Player Rule has helped build on the foreign-born supply of MLS players, despite the relatively meager MLS salary cap compared to European soccer leagues. Consequently, of the roughly 375 MLS players, American-born players make up almost two-thirds of the League's fifteen rosters, with the remaining one-third being foreign-born players from forty-seven countries (MLSnet 2009). Based on the number of nations in which its sports workers were born, MLS is more globalized than the other North American professional sports leagues and is about average compared with the premier professional leagues in Europe in the percentage its foreign players.

Women's organized soccer clubs were present in the United Kingdom and most European countries in the early twentieth century, but national tournaments were rare, and recognized international tournaments did not exist. In 1969 and 1979, women's international tournaments for national teams were held in Europe as unofficial European championships, but there was no formal international tournament until 1982, when the first Union of European Football Associations (UEFA) international tournament, the European Competition for Representative Women's Teams, began. This competition was subsequently named the UEFA Women's Championship and is currently referred to as the Women's Euro.

Following these and other unofficial international tournaments in the 1970s and 1980s, FIFA sponsored the Women's FIFA Invitational Tournament in 1988. This was followed in 1991 by FIFA's establishing the Women's World Cup, played in China, with twelve teams representing their countries, and named the Women's World Championship. This was sixty-one years after the first men's FIFA World Cup held in 1930. Even with these breakthroughs, women's professional soccer still awaits the globalizing features of men's professional soccer.

This is illustrated by the events in U.S. women's soccer over the past two decades. The success of a U.S. women's national soccer team that has won two Women's World Cups and three Olympic women's tournaments since 1991 has not translated into a stable women's professional soccer league in the United States. In 2000 the Women's United Soccer Association (WUSA) was founded as the world's first women's soccer league in which the athletes were paid professionals. It began play in 2001 with eight teams, all of which were located in U.S. cities.

Most of the WUSA rosters comprised primarily American players but were allowed up to four international players. International players from the following countries played in the WUSA: Australia, Brazil, Canada, China, England, France, Germany, Japan, Norway, Mexico, Scotland, and Sweden. In brief, the WUSA showed the same globalizing features of sport-labor migration that we see in other professional team sports. Unfortunately, the WUSA ceased operation at the end of 2003, shortly after completing its third season.

A new U.S. women's soccer league was formed in 2007 and took the name Women's Professional Soccer (WPS). It began play in March 2009 with seven teams spread across the country. Franchises are individually owned and operated by a group of investors in each market. Of the 159 players on the WPS rosters for its first season, 37, or 23 percent, were from outside the United States, and virtually the entire world was represented. There were players from Australia, Brazil, Canada, China, England, France, Japan, and Sweden, among others—certainly a global representation. The average salary was reported to be about $32,000 for the season. It was reported that Marta Vieira da Silva, the Brazilian superstar who plays for the Los Angeles Sol, was being paid $1.5 million over three years, or $500,000 per year, not counting incentive bonuses (Whiteside 2009).

The WPS discontinued operations of the Los Angeles Sol for the 2010 season, but it expanded to include the Philadelphia Independence and the Atlanta Beat (Marta da Silva is signed to a multiyear, guaranteed contract and is expected to play in the WPS with another team for the remainder of her contract). The WPS plans to continue to explore additional potential franchises beyond 2010. It has taken as its mission to become the premier women's soccer league in the world and the global standard by which women's professional sports are measured (WPS 2010).

Sports-Labor Migration and Basketball

From its humble beginnings in 1891 at Springfield College as a physical education activity designed by the instructor James Naismith, in less than 120 years basketball has become a global sport rivaling soccer as the most popular worldwide. Today, professional basketball leagues are found in dozens of countries, but male players and athletes consider the

National Basketball Association the best in the world and aspire to play and coach in the NBA.

As professional sports leagues go, the NBA is one of the youngest. It began operations in 1949 after previous attempts at forming a professional basketball league had failed. Like many other commercial businesses, by the mid-1980s the NBA was flowing in the stream of the expanding global economy and exploring prospects for attracting basketball players from foreign countries. After several failed attempts, the arrival of political refugees from Cold War nations began in the late 1980s, right after the international governing organization for basketball made it legal for professionals to play in the Olympics. That permitted foreign-born players to play in the NBA and remain eligible to play for their home country—if they wished—during the Olympic Games. Like businesses in all kinds of industries, NBA owners actively began to recruit international-level basketball players. Figure 3.2 illustrates how rapidly basketball players from around the world have migrated to the United States and helped to make the NBA a global sport.

The migration of basketball players from throughout the world to play in the NBA is only the tip of the iceberg in the globalization of basketball.

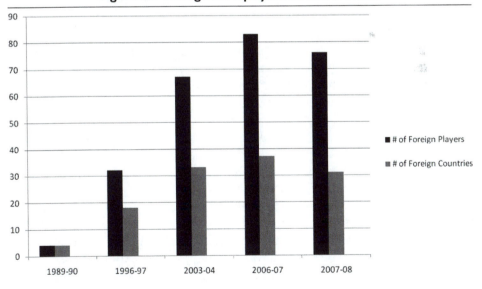

Figure 3.2 Foreign-born players on NBA rosters

Source: NBA.com 2008.

There are dozens of professional basketball leagues worldwide. The Union of European Leagues of Basketball (ULEB), headquartered in Spain, was founded in 1991 to assist in the development of European basketball leagues, and by 2005 fourteen countries had joined. ULEB sponsors the EuroLeague, one of the professional basketball competitions for elite European clubs. Several hundred Americans have been playing in Europe's professional men's basketball leagues every year for over a decade.

Throughout the world, women's professional basketball has struggled to establish permanent leagues. The Women's Professional Basketball League, considered the first American professional women's basketball league, played three seasons, from 1978 to the spring of 1981, before folding. Then, in 1996 the American Basketball League was founded, but it folded two years later, when it became evident that it could not compete successfully against the women's counterpart to the NBA, the Women's National Basketball Association (WNBA), which had begun play in 1997. From the beginning, the WNBA attracted a substantial percentage of players from foreign countries. By 2010, 22 percent of WNBA players were foreign-born from nineteen countries and territories. The international players have proven to be key contributors on many WNBA teams.

Even though the WNBA quickly became the destination for the best players from every country, professional women's basketball has been played in some countries for over thirty years, and women's professional basketball leagues now exist in Australia, Asia, Europe (including Russia), and South America. EuroLeague Women—officially called FIBA EuroLeague Women—is the highest-level professional basketball league in Europe for women's clubs. In 2009 twenty-four teams from twelve countries were members of EuroLeague Women.

With the WNBA and other countries having nonoverlapping seasons, many WNBA players temporarily emigrate to play in Europe or Australia during the WNBA off-season. Of the 256 players on WNBA rosters in 2008, 133 migrated in the off-season to play for professional basketball teams abroad (Poms 2009; Wolff 2008).

Eurobasket.com, with related websites in Africa, Asia, Australia, and Latin America, illustrates the global scope of elite basketball. It claims to be the most popular website about global basketball—both men's and women's—with Internet traffic comparable to NBA.com. It advertises itself as providing basketball news coverage for over 191 countries and worldwide coverage of 463 leagues, garnering over 160 million hits per month. Some three hundred people from different countries provide information about all pro and semi-pro basketball around the world.

The site covers basketball—including professional, semi-professional, and many amateur leagues—on all continents. The database has profiles of over 182,000 players and coaches.

Sports-Labor Migration and Ice Hockey

Ice hockey is another team sport that first became popular in the late 1800s, especially in Canada. The first Canadian professional hockey league was formed in 1904. In 1917 the National Hockey League was organized with five teams all located in Canadian cities. In 1924 the Boston Bruins were granted the first American franchise to join the NHL, making the it the first international professional team-sport league. With over ninety plus years of expansions, contractions, and relocations, the NHL now comprises thirty teams. At the same time, a huge migration of franchises has occurred because twenty-four of the NHL franchises are now based in the United States, leaving only six in Canada (Hughes, Fischler, and Fischler 2007).

During its first fifty years the NHL consisted overwhelmingly of Canadian players. Players migrated from one Canadian province to another, with only Canadian players on the teams. There is some dispute about the identity of the first foreigner to play in the NHL. According to Canadian hockey history expert Liam McGuire, George "Gerry" Geran, born in Massachusetts, was the first player from the United States to play in the NHL, starting with the Montreal Wanders in the NHL's inaugural 1917–1918 season. Other accounts claim that Clarence "Taffy" Abel was the first American to play in the NHL. He signed with the New York Rangers as a free agent in 1926 and played for eight years in the NHL. During most of his career, he was the only American in the league.

Even though Canadians dominated the NHL for half a century, in the past thirty years American- and European-born players have become abundant in the league because of its continued expansion into the United States and the availability of highly skilled European players. Swedish-born Ulf Sterner is considered the first European to play in the NHL. He accepted a New York Rangers training-camp invitation in 1963, but it was 1965 before the Rangers called him up. He played in four NHL contests before returning to the minors.

Stocking NHL teams with Europeans became common practice during the 1980s. Table 3.1 shows the migration pattern of European-born players over the past twenty years.

Table 3.1 Migration of European-Born Players in the NHL

Year	Percentage of Europeans
1989–1990	12
1995–1996	20.8
2000–2001	31.8
2004–2004	29.1
2008–2009	25.8

Source: Figures from Podnieks 2008.

In 2008 players from eighteen different countries were on NHL rosters. As the migration pattern in Table 3.1 shows, European-born players increased dramatically over the past two decades. Even so, in recent years there has been a decline in European players from every significant European nation, apparently for two main reasons: First, as just noted, more American players have entered the league; second, professional European ice hockey players are choosing to remain in Europe because many can make more money playing in European leagues, so the NHL is not as attractive to them as it once was (Podnieks 2008; see also Allen 2009). (Figure 3.3 shows the nationality of NHL players from three major nationalistic categories during 2008.)

Despite significant immigration of foreign-born ice hockey players into the NHL, Canadian representation in the league has remained steady at about 52 percent for several years. American representation has experienced

Figure 3.3 NHL by nationality

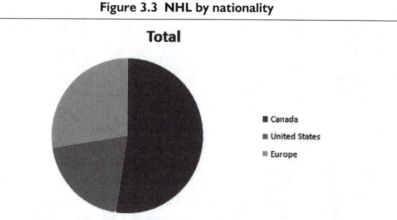

Total

- Canada
- United States
- Europe

Source: Mirtle 2008.

a significant surge. For example, there were 183 (19 percent) Americans in the NHL in the 2006–2007 season, but that number rose to 204 (22 percent) in the 2007–2008 season (Podnieks 2008).

Professional ice hockey leagues are widespread throughout Europe, including the Scandinavian countries and Russia, as well as in Asia. There are far too many of these leagues, most of which permit foreign-born players on the teams, to describe sport-labor migration patterns. The clubs within these leagues are structured slightly differently than those in their North American counterpart, the NHL.

Most of those hockey leagues are governed by their league rules, and this includes rules about foreign-born players. Sports-worker migration has impacted all of these leagues, just as globalization has influenced the various nations' economies, societies, and cultures. A similar pattern of increased sport-labor migration has occurred with professional ice hockey. With respect to immigrant players, one common rule found in many leagues is a limitation on the number of foreign-born players a team may employ. This rule is primarily a response to the desire to maintain national identity through the professional hockey teams.

Sports-Labor Migration and Baseball

As I noted earlier, the National Association of Professional Base Ball Players was established in 1871, making it the first professional team-sport league in the world. Five years later, in 1876, the National League of Professional Baseball Clubs was founded to replace the National Association. A companion league, the American League of Professional Baseball Clubs, was founded in 1901. Since then, the two leagues have made up Major League Baseball.

It is true, as Yale University anthropologist William W. Kelly argues, "that baseball has never developed the global character of soccer" (2007, 80); of course, neither has any other sport. Kelly does grant that "baseball is a significant international sport with rich and well-documented autonomous histories in several countries. It is also a transnational sport because, among these national spheres, organizational templates, players, techniques, strategies and spectatorship have continuously circulated" (2007, 82). There is general agreement among sport-studies scholars that baseball is an international sport (Bjarkman 2005; Gmelch 2006), and in his book *Growing the Game: The Globalization of Major League Baseball*, sport anthropologist Alan Klein declares that his seven-year study of "the political, economic, and structural arrangements of contemporary baseball on a global scale" has convinced him that baseball is making significant globalizing strides (2008, 1).

For my purposes in this chapter, it is not important whether baseball can be assigned "global" sport status. More important here is that MLB has been a model for supporting and sustaining international sport-labor migration in baseball for several decades. That is the reason I devote a place for baseball in this chapter, which focuses on sport-labor migration.

Table 3.2 illustrates the association between the increasing percentages of foreign-born MLB players and its expanding globalization over the past fifty years. The increase in foreign players resulted not from one or two factors related to globalization but instead from a variety of factors in the total processes of globalization. Taking it one step further, the percentage of minor-league baseball players who are foreign-born is even higher than for MLB. In 2009, of the 6,973 minor leaguers, 48 percent were foreign-born (MLB.com 2009).

MLB player immigration from the Dominican Republic best exemplifies the increase in foreign-born major leaguers. Dominicans' passion for baseball is unsurpassed. Professional baseball in the Dominican Republic began in 1890 with the founding of the country's first professional league. The Dominican Republic was the first North American country to adopt baseball enthusiastically as "its national sport."

Historically, the Dominican Republic has been linked to MLB since 1956, when Ozzie Virgil Sr. became the first Dominican to make an MLB team; he remained in the league until 1969. Since Virgil debuted in MLB over fifty years ago, some 450 Dominicans have played in the league. Opening Day rosters in 2009 included eighty-one players from the Dominican Republic; of all foreign players, 35 percent came from the Dominican Republic. After the United States, the Dominican Republic

**Table 3.2 Percentage of Foreign-Born Players
on Major League Baseball Rosters**

Year	Percentage
1958	4
1968	7
1978	9
1988	12
1998	20
2010	28

Source: Figures from MLB 2010.

has the second-highest number of players in MLB, and its contribution goes beyond just players. Between 1992 and 2008 four MLB managers were born in the Dominican Republic (Klein 1991a, 2008; Ruck 1999).

The Dominican Republic is not the only Caribbean country with a passion for baseball. Other countries in that region have contributed to what has become an increasing number of MLB players. Puerto Rico has produced more than 250 MLB players. In 2009 there were thirty-five MLB players combined from Puerto Rico and Cuba. In the case of Cuban baseball players, the situation is unique. Restrictions on emigration by the Cuban government have meant that Cuban MLB players have had to defect to become major-league players.

Because the United States has historically had fairly open borders with Canada and Mexico, these two other North American countries have contributed numerous players to MLB over the past thirty years, a fact only minimally impacted by the globalizing economy. Over eighty Canadians have played in the major leagues since 1970, and in 2009 there were thirteen Canadians on MLB rosters. There were fourteen Mexican nationals on 2009 MLB rosters, and there are approximately one hundred currently in the MLB minor-league system.

As for intercontinental migration from Latin American countries (here I include both Central and South America), Venezuela, Colombia, and Panama were the largest contributors to MLB in 2009: Venezuela gave fifty-two, Panama four, and Colombia two.

Outside the American continents, Asia has been the most prolific contributor to MLB, especially Japan. Baseball has a long history in Japan. Organized baseball was played there during the latter nineteenth century in athletic clubs and universities. A professional baseball league called the Japanese Baseball League was established in 1936. Currently there are two professional baseball leagues in Japan: the Central League and the Pacific League, each consisting of six teams. Baseball has long been considered the most popular sport in Japan. Table 3.3 illustrates the increased numbers of Japanese baseball players in MLB over the past forty-five years.

The migration of baseball players is not all toward MLB in the United States. Japanese professional baseball leagues attract migrating foreign players from various countries. A steady influx of foreign-born players has taken place. In 2008, sixty-two foreign-born players were contracted to play professional baseball in Japan, including players from Australia, Canada, the Dominican Republic, Puerto Rico, South Korea, Taiwan, the United States, and Venezuela (Dannheisser 2008).

Table 3.3 Number of Japanese Baseball Players
on Major League Baseball Rosters

Year	Number of Japanese
1964	1
1965	1
1966–1994	0
1995	1
1998	6
2000	8
2003	11
2005	15
2007	14
2009	18

Source: Figures from JapaneseBallPlayers.com 2009.

Sports-Labor Migration and Intercollegiate Sports

The system of intercollegiate sports in the United States is unique. Although many universities in other countries have intercollegiate sporting events, none has the elaborate structural organization, financial investment, media coverage, and public popularity of American intercollegiate sports. Sport competition between colleges in the United States began in the mid-nineteenth century and was well established in American higher education by the beginning of the twentieth century. By the end of that century, college sports had become a central cultural institution because their events were enormously popular among fans and spectators, despite persistent controversy, scandals, and criticism over excesses.

Intercollegiate sports are organized into two national associations: the National Collegiate Athletic Association (NCAA) and the National Association for Intercollegiate Athletics (NAIA). The former is by far the larger and more prominent of the two, with about 1,285 member institutions; the latter has about 300 members.[2] Both organize the intercollegiate sports programs for their member colleges and universities.

There seems to be no agreement as to who the first foreign-born immigrant to play on an intercollegiate sport team was, but there was certainly no large migration of foreign student-athletes until the late 1950s and early 1960s. About that time objections began to surface about the recruitment of foreign student-athletes, some in their late twenties and even early thirties, with physical maturity and sporting experience far beyond that of the typical American college athlete. To counter this criticism, in 1961 the NCAA adopted an alien-student rule aimed at slowing recruitment of older foreign athletes. The rule was challenged by Howard University, and in 1973 the court ruled that the alien-student rule violated the equal-protection clause of the Fourteenth Amendment of the U.S. Constitution. The NCAA complied with the decision and dropped the alien-student rule, thus allowing coaches to recruit foreign athletes without regard to age.

As the global economy and entertainment industry gained momentum during the 1960s and 1970s, intercollegiate athletes entered the flow of migrant workers that accompanied these movements. In 1977 sports writer Neil Amdur claimed, "As many as 1,000 foreign athletes, from as far away as Australia, Sweden, Kenya and Japan, are competing on scholarships in the United States, including 400 in track and field" (1977, 46).

A decade later sports geographer John Bale (1988) estimated that approximately 16 percent of NCAA Division I players were foreign. Three years later, in a comprehensive book-length analysis of foreign student-athletes in American universities, titled *The Brawn Drain: Foreign Student-Athletes in American Universities,* Bale declared that in the late 1980s, "a figure of around 6,000 foreign student-athletes [including NAIA, junior colleges, and women's sports] in the United States does not seem unreasonable.... The numbers have grown over time and ... in some sports ... the foreign involvement extends beyond 10 percent of the total number of athletes in the most sport-oriented universities" (1991, 64–65).

In 1991 and 1992 and in 1995 and 1996, the NCAA (1996) carried out studies of the number of foreign student-athletes in NCAA member institutions. The total number of international student-athletes rose by approximately 2,000 in that four-year period, from 6,833 to 8,851. Commenting on the 1996 NCAA report, Bale said, "If non-NCAA colleges and universities were taken into account the overall figure would certainly be in excess of 10,000" (2003, 104). During the same period the average number of foreign student-athletes at NCAA schools rose from 8.55 per institution to 10.52. Ten years later, a 2006–2007 NCAA study revealed the increase in foreign student-athletes: More than 16,000 foreign athletes dotted NCAA rosters, nearly two-thirds of them in Division I. They accounted for 6.2 percent of all Division I athletes, up from 2.4 percent eight years earlier. Table 3.4 lists the percentages of foreign athletes in the NCAA's top-tier Division I. According to *Sports Illustrated* writer Luke Winn (2010), foreign basketball players are currently being called "luxury imports" because they are proving to be as valuable as top

American basketball recruits. Some 1,500 Canadian athletes were playing for U.S. colleges and universities in 2009, although not all of them were playing in Division I.

Table 3.4 Percentages of Foreign Athletes in the NCAA's Top-Tier Division I

Sport	Percentage (2006–2007)
Women's ice hockey	50
Women's tennis	50
Men's tennis	38
Men's ice hockey	31
Women's golf	20
Men's soccer	13
Men's skiing	19

Source: Figures from Wieberg 2008.

Sports-Labor Migration and the Olympic Games

In 1894 Baron Pierre de Coubertin founded the first global sport organization, the International Olympic Committee (IOC), which two years later organized the first modern Olympic Games—the first global multisport event. This was before the word "globalization" had entered the popular lexicon. Although a number of international sporting events preceded the first modern Olympic Games in Athens, Greece, none had the structure and scope of the modern Olympics (Guttmann 2002; MacAloon 2008).

De Coubertin's ambition was to foster sports competition between athletes from different countries—a sporting celebration of the world's best athletes. For him, the Olympic Games were designed as a competition not between nations but rather between athletes. However, since all the athletes had to be certified by their respective nations, much of the attention garnered by the Olympic Games quickly centered on the country the athletes were "representing," and their achievements became attached to their respective countries' medal count. National medal counts inherently pitted nation against nation, turning the Olympic Games into a global sports competition between countries. As a *Time* magazine reporter said, "National pride always takes center stage at the Olympics, where the medals table measures a country's worth and the victors beam as they hear their national anthems" (Larmer 2008).

As a global undertaking, the Olympic Movement has encountered many issues, controversies, and challenges over the past one hundred plus years, but perhaps the most persistent and contentious has been the eligibility of athletes. Eligibility issues are relevant in this chapter because they bear on the migration of sports workers. Any form of restriction on participation eligibility will adversely impact sports laborers' migration options. As you will see below, this has indeed happened in the case of Olympic athletes' migration. However, a variety of globalizing forces have weakened the restrictions, so much so that some Olympic scholars contend that today there exists a "global free agency" for elite athletes.

Male amateur athletes of every race, religion, and nationality were eligible to participate in the Olympic Games from their beginning. Women's participation was gradually adopted under the same conditions. But, as I explained in Chapter 2, the "amateur issue" (involving, for instance, how to define an "amateur," reimbursement for travel expenses, and compensation for time lost at work) dogged the IOC for decades. Finally, under political pressure and after complaints from corporate sponsors, by the early 1990s the IOC had abolished the distinction between amateurs and professionals with what was called open participation; that is, professional athletes could compete in the Olympic Games.

A second incessant eligibility problem has centered on the IOC requirement that all participants be national citizens of the country they are representing. National Olympic committees (NOCs) are the national constituents of the worldwide Olympic Movement (as of 2010, there were 205 NOCs). They are responsible for organizing participation in the Olympic Games by selecting and sending teams and certifying competitors to the games. National citizenship and the changing of competitors' sporting nationality are governed by the Olympic Charter, particularly by Rule 42 and its bylaws. NOCs are required to apply this rule when certifying athletes in their country. The basic Olympic Charter rule is quite clear (IOC 2007):

Rule 42: Nationality of Competitors
1. Any competitor in the Olympic Games must be a national of the country of the National Olympic Committee (NOC) which is entering such competitor.

Bylaw to Rule 42
1. A competitor who is a national of two or more countries at the same time may represent either one of them, as he may elect.

There are additional bylaws about the nationality of competitors, but they need not concern us.

While Rule 42: Nationality of Competitors seems simple enough, many issues and questions have arisen about "nationality." In the history of the modern Olympic Movement, one of the most common issues has concerned individuals born in one country who then become citizens of another. In one way, Rule 42 and its bylaws cover this, but often at issue are the *conditions* under which the changes in citizenship occurred: was the migration voluntary? was it done merely to participate in the Olympics? was it forced or coerced? and so forth. A 2008 *Christian Science Monitor* article titled "Now More Than Ever, Olympic Teams Go Multinational," stated, "Increasingly, athletes are switching national alliances—sometimes for money, but also for better training opportunities or a chance to compete in a sport that's too saturated with talent back home" (Bryant and Harman 2008). Olympic historian Bill Mallon argues, "These are people who are basically being [global] athletic mercenaries" (quoted in Bryant and Harman 2008).

Another common concern is that the presence of foreign-born athletes on Olympic teams generates resentment and criticism from native-born athletes who lose a place on their country's Olympic team to a non-native-born athlete who has become a naturalized citizen. Despite such criticism, foreign-born athletes are competing on Olympic teams throughout the world. They represent another example of the effects of globalization on the migration of sports workers. As Abby Hoffman, a four-time Olympic runner for Canada in the eight hundred meters and a council member of the International Association of Athletics Federations, said, "If you think on a global scale, people are moving around for business reasons, because they're refugees, because they're dislocated by wars. We can't have a system in sport that fails to recognize that global migration is a reality" (quoted in Bryant and Harman 2008).

The migration of sport labor for opportunities to participate on Olympic teams is global, and it exists in all directions and involves all nations—rich and poor, developed and developing, large and small. Moreover, the phenomenon is not recent; it has been a feature of the Olympic Movement for decades. Over the past decade the International Association of Athletics Federation has approved approximately three hundred changes in citizenship for just one sport—track and field.[3]

Because countless countries have used foreign-born athletes on their Olympic teams, I cannot possibly list all of them, or even estimate their number, since neither the IOC nor any of the various NOCs collects that information. However, to illustrate this pattern of migration, I cite some examples: The first Olympic medal awarded to the small, oil-rich kingdom of Qatar was won in 1992 by Somali-born runner Mohammed Suleiman. In 2008 Bahrain's top Olympic woman track hopeful was Maryam Yusuf Jamal, an Ethiopian-born athlete who lives in Switzerland. All of Germany's Olympic boxers at the 2008 Beijing Olympics were foreign-born: Rustam Rahimov, born in Tajikistan; Wilhelm Gratschow, born in Uzbekistan; Jack Culcay-Keth, born in Ecuador; and Konstantin Buga, born in Kazakhstan. Over fifty foreign-born athletes were on Canada's Beijing Olympic team.

During the 2008 Summer Olympics in Beijing, thirty-three members of the 596-person U.S. Olympic team were foreign-born; they came from twenty-five different foreign countries. The United States had eight foreign-born Olympians at the 2006 Winter Games in Turin, Italy. Included in the 2008 U.S. foreign-born group in Beijing were "four Chinese-born table tennis players, a kayaker from Britain, Russian-born world champion gymnast Nastia Liukin ... [on the] men's 1,500 meter [track] squad—Kenya native Bernard Lagat; Lopez Lomong, one of the 'lost boys' of Sudan's civil war who spent a decade in a refugee camp; and Leo Manzano, a Mexican laborer's son who moved to the U.S. when he was 4 but didn't gain citizenship until 2004" (Crary 2008; see also Liwag 2008).

Related Features of Sports Migration

In addition to the migration patterns of sports workers, several related topics have been identified by sport-studies scholars. Their research has revealed interesting information about sports migrants' motivations, employers' recruitment of sports labor, and consequences of sport-labor migration (Elliott and Maguire 2008a).

Sports Migrants' Motivations

It is typically assumed that sports workers migrate throughout the world to gain employment, make money, and become financially secure, but studies have revealed that their motivations are much more complex. Recently, Joseph Maguire, a scholar at Loughborough University in England and perhaps the most prominent scholar in the area of sports migration, and his colleague Richard Elliott from Southampton Solent University synthesized their research findings about global sport-labor migration. They then compared and contrasted sports-worker migration with global migration of highly skilled workers employed in information technology, medical sciences, law, accounting, and banking, all of which are part of the globalization of intellectual capital, or "brain drain," as it is often called (Elliott and Maguire 2008a). They argue that "the migration experience is contoured by a series of complex interdependent processes. Politics, history, economics, geography, and culture can all be seen to be influential in determining the motivations of athletic migrants and in affecting the ways in which they experience the migration process" (2008a, 485). To be sure, some sports migrants do seek financial gain, but a single causal factor, such as "following the money," does not capture the complexities of sport migration.

A range of factors—ethnicity, politics, culture, challenge seeking—in addition to economics contour migratory decisions by athletes and coaches. A study of Nordic/Scandinavian soccer migrants into English league soccer found that the immigrant players were seeking a challenge to test their abilities at the highest level of soccer competition. The researchers say, "Although our sample of Nordic/Scandinavian players were clearly aware of the immediate benefits of their move and were qualified in their attachment to English club and area, they did not fit the mercenary mold. There is a high level of instrumentality involved but not in any narrow economic sense" (Stead and Maguire 2000, 54). A study of Hungarian professional soccer players who emigrated after the collapse of Soviet-style communism revealed they were seeking new opportunities, new challenges, and better working conditions, not merely financial gain (Molnar 2006).

The opportunity structure in global professional sports accounts for a great deal of sports migration. By opportunity structure I mean the exogenous factors that limit or expand sports workers access to employment. Related terms are *supply and demand* and *surplus and scarcity*. Highly skilled elite-level athletes have a rare talent, and like workers in every profession and occupation, most elite athletes want to take advantage of their "human capital," their skills and talents. There is great variability throughout the world in the supply of and demand for professional athletes. Likewise, there is large variability in the surplus and scarcity of elite athletes.

This worldwide opportunity structure creates motivations for athletes in one country to seek out, and be sought by, sport organizations in other countries. One general example is the immigration of athletes from throughout the African continent over the past twenty-five years to

English and European soccer leagues, to American universities' track and field teams, and to the Olympic teams of Arab countries as runners. Why would African athletes join Arab Olympic teams? As Olympic historian Bill Mallon has said, "Kenya has so many good distance runners, but only three spots on their national team" (quoted in Weeks 2009). The surplus of talented basketball players in the United States, where the only elite professional league is the NBA, has supplied European leagues with basketball players for years. Likewise, with only one MLB in baseball, surplus excellent baseball athletes have migrated to Japan and a few other countries that have professional baseball.

One controversial issue during the 2008 Beijing Olympics involved three American basketball players, two who played on Russian Olympic basketball teams and one who played on Germany's national basketball team. Each illustrates how the opportunity structure of global basketball, with an oversupply of elite-level American players, works. Becky Hammon, a member of San Antonio's WNBA team, did not make the U.S. Olympic women's basketball team, so although she has no family links to Russia, she gained Russian citizenship and won a spot on the Russian national team. She contends that this was her chance to fulfill her Olympic dream, after being overlooked by the U.S. team. She argued, "I don't expect everybody to understand" (quoted in Larmer 2008). J. R. Holden never made it to the NBA, but he became a naturalized Russian citizen and was a member of Russia's national basketball team. Chris Kaman, a center for the NBA's Los Angeles Clippers, is an American citizen with great-grandparents who were German. This helped him acquire German citizenship, making him eligible to join the German national team for the Beijing Olympics.

These are examples of the migratory flows of hundreds of sports workers each year. These flows move in all directions and are driven by the opportunity structure much more than merely financial considerations.

Recruitment of Sports Labor

Previous sections in this chapter have demonstrated that there is a global marketplace for elite athletes, and most barriers and restrictions that once existed to limit sport-labor migration no longer exist. Some claim there is a global free market for sports labor. Elite athletes rely on a variety of sources as they seek employment opportunities for themselves in the global labor market. Expanding global sports occupational opportunities during the past three decades has increased the demand for elite athletes. Thus, athlete talent pools are constantly drawn upon to meet the demands.

Bale's research identified several methods used to recruit foreign student-athletes to American universities. He noted that "recruiting systems range from the well-planned network of contacts … to almost random events … which cost the university nothing. … Most foreign recipients of athletic scholarships are initially approached by the head coach, an athlete, an alumnus or someone somehow associated with the institution. … The nature of these contacts varies from the carefully planned to almost chance events" (1991, 100, 104–105).

Anthropologist Alan Klein's (1991a, 1991b, 2008) extensive study of Dominican Republic baseball provides an in-depth description of the recruitment mechanisms that MLB clubs use to train and recruit young Dominican boys. The system of baseball academies established by MLB clubs is arguably the most systematic instrument of sport-labor recruitment in the world. All thirty MLB teams have established player-development academies, often called baseball factories, that select promising young Dominican baseball players—as young as twelve years old—house the prospects in year-round training facilities, and then recruit the best players, when they are sixteen or seventeen years old, to their major-league organization. An average of 450 young Dominicans sign baseball contracts annually with the thirty MLB teams in the United States and Canada. During the 2008 season, about 100 Dominicans were playing in the major leagues, while another 2,000 were members of the seventy-eight U.S. minor-league teams affiliated with MLB (Green 2008).

In a study of global athletic-labor migration examining the mechanisms through which Canadian athletes are recruited into Britain's Elite Ice Hockey League, researchers found that recruitment was not necessarily "facilitated by a formal mediator such as an agent. Instead, informal communicative 'friends-of-friends' networks and 'bridgehead' contacts [migrants who have already experienced the sports-migration process] more commonly facilitate flows of information to the potential employer and potential migrant employee"; they conclude that "mutually beneficial recruitments can be seen to be occurring as the result of human mediation facilitated by a series of informal interdependent networks of social relationships" (Elliott and Maguire 2008b, 158).

One of the most widespread and significant mechanisms of sport-labor recruitment is the informal system that Michael Smith (1999) calls "translocal," which involves both local nationals and international migrants who participate in regular cross-border transnational social and cultural networks. Elliott and Maguire describe the relevance of this system for athletes and coaches: "Coaches not only develop local connections via face-to-face contact with other coaches and players, they can also strengthen a series of transnational bonds via regular telephone or e-mail contact with coaching colleagues and players around the globe" (2008a, 492).

Consequences of Sports-Labor Migration

The system of global sport-labor migration may have consequences or effects for several constituents: sports workers, donor nations, host nations, sports organizations, and the sport itself. For many sports workers this system provides employment, a means to pursue a career in a sport for which they have talent but, for one reason or another, cannot find work in within their native country. In addition to the contributions that sports migrants make to elevating the level of performance of their host team, they sometimes contribute to the development of their teammates in the host nation.

There are drawbacks to emigrating, but there are also rewards and satisfactions. Most sports migrants report positive feelings about the personally, socially, and culturally enriching experiences they have while playing in a foreign country. For talented athletes from developing countries especially, not only does joining professional sports leagues throughout the developed countries allow them to showcase their sport talent on a global level, but a career in professional sports allows them to escape the economic realities they face in their native countries (Kapur and McHale 2005).

It must be acknowledged that a persistent pattern of criticism has issued from various sources in most donor and host countries where migrant sport labor is a prominent feature of the professional sports programs. Some coaches, athletes, journalists, and radio and TV commentators in donor countries complain of a "brawn drain," meaning that the emigration of the country's best athletes is "deskilling" the nation and weakening its sport status, especially for international sports competition.

A similar group of critics disparages global sport-labor migration in host countries, but their complaints fall into the tradition of nativism, that is, an opposition to immigration and an advocacy for policies favoring native-born inhabitants over immigrants. The common objection here is that foreign athletes are "taking over our sports," and "our" athletes are being deprived of opportunities to play at the highest level on "our" teams.

Despite these criticisms, in both donor and host countries elite sports migration continues to proliferate worldwide. Indeed, new sport leagues and their teams must rely on the global sports-migrant pool of labor to be successful enterprises, and these new sport organizations go global in their recruitment of athletes.

Few would argue that the now mature global sports system has not improved the skill of the athletes playing every sport, the global popularity of every sport, and the expansion of media coverage of most sports, as well as enlarged the fan base in every sport. In short, every sport has benefited in a variety of ways as the sports industry has globalized along with other industries in the global economy.

Summary

Human migrations extend back into the earliest human history, but the frequency of human migration has accelerated in conjunction with globalization. Rapid changes in global economies force workers in every profession and occupation to become mobile, and this has included professional sports workers as well. Global sports-worker migration has dramatically increased in the past two decades, and this labor flow has occurred within national boundaries, between nations on the same continent, and across continents.

To accommodate cross-border migrations, many countries have established guest-worker programs. While the rules and policies of these programs vary from country to country, sports workers usually have to enter a foreign country under its guest-worker policies.

Several of the most popular team sports, such as soccer, basketball, ice hockey, and baseball, have a high rate of athlete migration, and that migration has been increasing rapidly in recent years. Some observers declare there is now an unrestricted free flow of sports workers in those sports. For example, in 2009 players from forty-seven different countries played on Major League Soccer teams.

A persistent issue for the Olympic Movement throughout its history has revolved around the eligibility of athletes. The IOC requires that all participants be citizens of the countries they represent. However, many issues and questions have arisen concerning the meaning of "nationality." Nevertheless, many countries have used foreign-born athletes on their Olympic teams.

Analyses of migrant sports workers' motivations reveal that they are much more complex than just a desire to find higher-paying employment to become financially secure. The opportunity structure in global sports is a motivational mechanism that accounts for considerable sports migration. Recruitment of foreign sports workers involves coaches, team owners, and personal and social connections, along with a variety of spontaneous forms and practices.

The system of global sport-labor migration has consequences not only for the sports workers themselves but also for the host and donor nations, sport leagues and teams, and the sport itself. For each there are positive effects and benefits, but there are also disappointments and drawbacks as well.

Notes

1. The OECD is an international organization of thirty nations that accept the principles of representative democracy and free market economy. Most OECD members are high-income economies with a high Human Development Index (HDI) and are regarded as developed countries.

2. The NAIA has five member institutions in Canada. In 2009, the Canadian Simon Fraser University became the first non-U.S. college admitted to the NCAA. Its sports teams will compete at the Division II level.

3. The IOC now requires a three-year waiting period between an athlete's getting citizenship in a country and competing on its Olympic team.

References

Allen, Kevin. 2009. More Russians say "nyet" to NHL grind. *USA Today,* December 17, 1C.

Amdur, Neil. 1977. Is college recruiting of foreigners excessive? *New York Times,* March 15, 46.

Appiah, Kwame Anthony. 2003. Citizens of the world. In *Globalizing rights,* ed. Matthew J. Gibney, 189–232. New York: Oxford University Press.

Bale, John. 1988. Foreign student-athletes in NCAA Division I universities: An empirical study of six men's sports. *Journal of Comparative Physical Education and Sport* 10, no. 1: 21–31.

———. 1991. *The brawn drain: Foreign student-athletes in American universities.* Urbana: University of Illinois Press.

———. 2003. *Sports geography.* 2nd ed. New York: Routledge.

Bjarkman, Peter. C. 2005. *Diamonds around the globe: The encyclopedia of international baseball.* Westport, CT: Greenwood Press.

Bolt, Kristen. 2003. Brand it like Beckham. *Time,* June 23. www.time.com/time/columnist/elliott/article/0,9565,460400,00.html.

Bryant, Christa Case, and Danna Harman. 2008. Now more than ever, Olympic teams go multinational. *Christian Science Monitor,* August 4. http://features.csmonitor.com/olympics08/2008/08/04/now-more-than-ever-olympic-teams-go-multinational.

Crary, David. 2008. Foreign-born athletes take Olympic stage for US. *USA Today,* July 18. www.usatoday.com/sports/olympics/beijing/2008-07-18-immigrants_N.htm.

Dannheisser, Ralph. 2008. Baseball, once just an American game, extends reach worldwide. America.gov, July 24. www.america.gov/st/sports-english/2008/July/20080331164120zjsredna0.6307947.html.

Davis, Steve. 2007. Desire to maintain quality drives foreign player rule. *ESPNsoccernet,* December 26. http://soccernet.espn.go.com/news/story?id=493683&cc=5901.

Elliott, Richard, and Joseph Maguire. 2008a. Thinking outside of the box: Exploring a conceptual synthesis for research in the area of athletic labor migration. *Sociology of Sport Journal* 25: 482–497.

———. 2008b. "Getting caught in the net": Examining the recruitment of Canadian players in British professional ice hockey. *Journal of Sport and Social Issues* 32: 158–176.

Fédération Internationale de Football Association (FIFA). 2001. FIFA survey: Approximately 250 million footballers worldwide. FIFA. http://web.archive.org/web/20060915133001/http://access.fifa.com/infoplus/IP-199_01E_big-count.pdf.

Foer, Franklin. 2005. *How soccer explains the world: An unlikely theory of globalization.* New York: HarperCollins.

Fordyce, Tom. 2005. 10 years since Bosman. *BBC Sport,* December 14. http://news.bbc.co.uk/sport2/hi/football/4528732.stm.

Gmelch, George, ed. 2006. *Baseball without borders: The international pastime.* Lincoln: University of Nebraska Press.

Goldblatt, David. 2008. *The ball is round: A global history of soccer.* New York: Riverhead Trade.

Green, Eric. 2008. Passion for baseball used in Dominican Republic development plan. America.gov, December 22. www.america.gov/st/sportsenglish/2008/December/20081222132726maduobba0.218609.html.

Guttmann, Allen. 2002. *The Olympics: A history of the modern games.* 2nd ed. Urbana: University of Illinois Press.

Hughes, Morgan, Stan Fischler, and Shirley Fischler. 2007. *Hockey chronicle:*

Year-by-year history of the National Hockey League. Lincolnwood, IL: Publications International.

International Olympic Committee (IOC). 2007. *Olympic Charter.* Lausanne, Switzerland: IOC.

JapaneseBallPlayers. 2009. Japanese players who were active in year 2009. JapaneseBallPlayers. www.japaneseballplayers.com/en/year. php?year=2009.

Kapur, Devesh, and John McHale. 2005. African soccer goes global. *The Globalist,* November 21. www.theglobalist.com/StoryId.aspx?StoryId=4915.

Kelly, William W. 2007. Is baseball a global sport? America's "national pastime" as global field and international sport. In *Globalization and sport,* ed. Richard Giulianotti and Roland Robertson, 79–93. Malden, MA: Blackwell Publishers.

Klein, Alan M. 1991a. *Sugarball: The American game, the Dominican dream.* New Haven, CT: Yale University Press.

———. 1991b. Sport and culture as contested terrain: Americanization in the Caribbean. *Sociology of Sport Journal* 8: 79–85.

———. 2008. *Growing the game: The globalization of Major League Baseball.* New Haven, CT: Yale University Press.

Koppett, Leonard. 2004. *Koppett's concise history of Major League Baseball.* Rev. ed. New York: Carroll & Graf Publishers.

Lanfranchi, Pierre, and Matthew Taylor. 2001. *Moving with the ball: The migration of professional footballers.* Oxford, UK: Berg Publishers.

Larmer, Brook. 2008. The year of the mercenary athlete. *Time,* August 19. www .time.com/time/world/article/0,8599,1833856,00.html.

Liwag, Roland. 2008. Graphic of the day: Foreign-born athletes playing for the U.S. Olympic team. CBSSports.com, August, 7. www.cbssports.com/ olympics/story/10922554.

MacAloon, John J. 2008. *This great symbol: Pierre de Coubertin and the origins of the modern Olympic Games.* 25th anniv. ed. New York: Routledge.

Maguire, Joseph. 2009. "Real politic" or "ethically based": Sport, globalization, migration and nation-state politics. In *Sport and foreign policy in a globalizing world,* ed. Steven J. Jackson, 95–110. New York: Routledge.

Martin, Susan F. 2009. Heavy traffic: International migration in an era of globalization. In *Globalization: The transformation of social worlds,* ed. D. Stanley Eitzen and Maxine Baca Zinn, 31–36. 2nd ed. Belmont, CA: Wadsworth Cengage Learning.

Milanovic, Branko. 2006. Learning about globalization by watching a soccer game. *Taipei Times,* February 12. www.carnegieendowment.org/

publications/index.cfm?fa=view&id=18064&prog=zgp&proj=zted&
zoom_highlight=branko.

Mirtle, James. 2008. The NHL by nationality. From the Rink, November 26.
www.fromtherink.com/2008/11/26/673622/the-nhl-by-nationality-52.

MLB. 2010. Rosters showcase foreign-born players. MLB.com, April 6.
http://mlb.mlb.com/news/article.jsp?ymd=20100406&content_
id=9103912&vkey=news_mlb&fext=.jsp&c_id=mlb.

MLSnet. 2009. MLS players. MLSnet.com. http://web.mlsnet.com/players.

Molnar, Gyozo. 2006. Mapping migrations: Hungary-related migrations of
professional footballers after the collapse of communism. *Soccer and Society*
7 (December): 463–485.

National Collegiate Athletic Association (NCAA). 1996. *1996 NCAA study of
international student-athletes.* Kansas City, MO: NCAA.

NBA.com. 2008. NBA players from around the world: 2007–08 Season. NBA
.com, August 7. www.nba.com/players/int_players_0708.html.

Oderth, Reidar. 2002. *An introduction to the study of human migration: An
interdisciplinary perspective.* Bloomington, IN: Author House.

Offside, The. 2007. How MLS stacks up in the foreign players department,
TheOffside.com, September 19. www.theoffside.com/leagues/mls/how-
mls-stacks-up-in-the-foreign-players-department.html.

Peters, Ken. 2007. "Beckham Coming to 'Make a Difference,'" *USA Today,*
January 12.

Peterson, Robert. 1992. *Only the ball was white: A history of legendary black players
and all-black professional teams.* New York: Oxford University Press.

Podnieks, Andrew. 2008. NHL landscape changes. International Ice Hockey
Federation, October 5. www.iihf.com/en/home-of-hockey/news/news-
singleview/browse/33/article/nhl-landscape-changes.html?tx_ttnews%
5BbackPid%5D=187&cHash=862d9bf602.

Poli, R., and L. Ravenel. 2007. *Annual review of the European football players'
labour market [Etude annuelle du marché du travail européen des footballeurs].*
Neuchâtel, Switzerland: International Centre for Sports Studies.

Poms, Matt. 2009. Foreign affairs spur WNBA to later start. *USA Today,* June
4, 6C.

Review of *The ball is round: A global history of soccer.* 2008. Barnes &
Noble. http://search.barnesandnoble.com/Ball-Is-Round/David-
Goldblatt/e/9781594482960.

Ruck, Rob. 1999. *The tropic of baseball: Baseball in the Dominican Republic.*
Lincoln, NE: Bison Books.

Smith, Michael, P. 1999. Transnationalism and the city. In *The urban movement:*

Cosmopolitan essays on the late-20th-century city, ed. Robert A. Beauregard and Sophie Body-Gendrot, 119–139. Thousand Oaks, CA: Sage.

Spiegel Online International. 2008. Foreign-born players rise to the top: Importing goals at Euro 2008. Spiegel Online International, June 13. www.spiegel.de/international/europe/0,1518,559493,00.html.

Stead, David, and Joseph Maguire. 2000. "Rite de passage" or passage to riches? The motivation and objectives of Nordic/Scandinavian players in English league soccer. *Journal of Sport and Social Issues* 24: 36–60.

U.S. Youth Soccer. 2008. U.S. Soccer Youth website. www.usyouthsoccer.org.

Weeks, Linton. 2009. Changing home teams: Olympians shift allegiances. NPR, January 30. www.npr.org/templates/story/story.php?storyId=93741707.

Whiteside, Kelly. 2009. Superstar Marta's magical feat. *USA Today,* July 8, 1C–2C.

Wieberg, Steve. 2008. Division I sees unprecedented foreign influx. *USA Today,* October 1. www.usatoday.com/sports/college/2008-10-01-foreign-influx_N.htm.

Winn, Luke. 2010. The luxury imports are here. *Sports Illustrated,* March 1, 59–61.

Wolff, Alexander. 2008. To Russia with love. *Sports Illustrated,* December 15, 58–67.

Women's Professional Soccer (WPS). 2010. WPS discontinues operations of Los Angeles Sol. WPS, January 28. www.womensprosoccer.com/news/press_releases/100128-sol-discontinues

World Trade Organization (WTO). 2009. International trade statistics 2009—Charts. Chart 3, World merchandise trade volume by major product group, 1950–2008. WTO. www.wto.org/english/res_e/statis_e/its2009_e/its09_charts_e.htm.

CHAPTER 4

THE GLOBAL SPORT INDUSTRY

PRODUCTION AND PROMOTION

Despite more than 15 years of codes of conduct adopted
by major sportswear brands ... workers making their
products still face ... excessive, undocumented and unpaid
overtime, verbal abuse, threats to health and safety and ...
exposure to toxic chemicals.
—Play Fair Alliance, *Clearing the Hurdles: Steps to
Improving Wages and Working Conditions in
the Global Sportswear Industry,* 2008, 6.

The previous two chapters focused on the sport-performance segment of
Brenda Pitts and David Stotlar's (2007) sport-industry segment model
(see Figure 1.1), with global sport organizations being the specific topic
of Chapter 2 and the migration of sport labor being that of Chapter 3. In
this chapter I turn attention to the sport-production and sport-promotion
segments. The first part of this chapter examines the global sporting goods
and equipment component of the global sport industry; in the second part
I examine the promotion segment of the Pitts and Stotlar model.

Even though the sporting goods and equipment market is dominated
by a handful of transnational corporations (TNCs), there are over 4,000
sporting goods and equipment manufacturers competing in the global
market. One reason for this is that such an enormous number of sporting

goods and equipment items is necessary to fulfill the needs of more than a hundred activities classified as sports. The result is an industry so fragmented that the ten largest sporting goods and equipment companies account for only about 35 percent of industry revenue (in the automobile industry, for example, just the top five auto makers have about 72 percent of market share) (Andreff 2006).

The largest TNCs in sporting goods and equipment include Wilson Sporting Goods (a subsidiary of Finland-based Amer Sports Corporation), Adidas AG, Reebok International, Mizuno Corporation, and Nike, Inc. Free trade in the global economy makes it possible for the majority of sporting goods and equipment manufacturers to have some international presence; however, I shall focus only on these five sporting goods and equipment manufacturing corporations and describe their positioning and operations in this industry.

When the topic is sport, attention is almost always on the athletes, teams, coaches, schedules, and fans; attention to sporting goods and equipment usually concerns what is in and what is out. When I make a presentation to a college class, professional conference, or community-service group about the global sporting goods and equipment industry, I begin by holding up several items, such as a basketball jersey, soccer cleats, or a baseball glove, and ask if anyone in the audience has seen any of them growing on trees, like apples, or on the ground, like watermelons, or underground, like potatoes. The response is always the same: the shaking of heads back and forth, meaning no.

I then explain that sporting goods and equipment are not gifts of nature; they are all made by people working in manufacturing plants throughout the world. It is their labor that produces all sporting goods and equipment, products that are essential to the world of sport because they are universally used in sports of all kinds. I conclude by suggesting that workers making those products are as much a part of the sports world as coaches, athletic trainers, fans, and even athletes.

The Sporting Goods Manufacturers Association (SGMA) defines the sporting goods manufacturing industry as "a composition of manufacturers of athletic footwear, sports apparel, and sporting goods equipment, as well as manufacturers of accessory items to the sports and recreation market" (SGMA 2009a). More specifically, sporting goods and equipment are the uniforms, footwear, balls, bats, gloves, footwear, protective equipment, uniforms, and so forth that are necessary to playing organized sports. In many cases, these are required and regulated by the rules. They make playing sports more comfortable, efficient, and safe.

Sporting goods and equipment manufacturing currently makes up a $285 billion global industry; the United States' share of this market is 36 percent. In the past five years, Asia-Pacific has been the second-largest market, maintaining a 34 percent share; Europe is ranked third, with a 29 percent share (NPD Group 2009). Nike, the world's leading manufacturer of athletic shoes and apparel and a major manufacturer of sports equipment, generated revenue in excess of $19.2 billion in its 2009 fiscal year. Thus, the manufacturing of sporting goods and equipment is a key component in global sport.

Understanding the manufacture of contemporary sporting goods requires that this segment of the sport industry be historically situated within the rise of factory manufacturing, the evolution of modern sport forms, the increase of manufacturing in the global economy, and the growth of the sporting goods manufacturing industry. Combined, these are the foundational pillars upon which the global sporting goods manufacturing industry rests.

The Rise of Factory Manufacturing

The system of sporting goods production has evolved over the past two hundred years in connection with many other transforming forces of modernity. Today, sporting goods and equipment are produced in large mechanized factories throughout the world, where hundreds, even thousands, of workers are employed. But these manufacturing plants are only the latest stage in a two-century evolution of industrial manufacturing.

In the latter eighteenth century, technological innovations and economic changes launched what became known as the Industrial Revolution, which involved a change from handwork to machine production and from industry in the home to manufacturing in factories.

Great Britain, where the Industrial Revolution originated, maintained its dominance in the first half of the nineteenth century. However, technological innovations and capitalist industrial development spread to Europe and America, and a factory system of manufacturing evolved wherever industrialization took place.

As this system evolved during the first half of the nineteenth century, factories in Britain and the United States were located mostly in the textile industry. By the mid-nineteenth century, most British, American, and European industrial enterprises were still predominantly small-scale businesses (Nelson 1995). By the beginning of the twentieth century, the

United States had passed Britain in the quantity and value of its manufactured products and had become the world's foremost industrial nation. As a factory system grew and manufacturing flourished, production on a large scale for a national market expanded rapidly (Perrow 2005; Roy 1999).

The tendency toward profit maximization among manufacturers in the industrializing countries during the latter nineteenth century led to massive exploitation of workers. Owners of the early factories quickly established a pattern of hiring workers as cheaply as possible. They often employed women and children, who could be hired for lower wages than men. These low-paid employees worked as many as sixteen hours per day, and many were subjected to various pressures, even physical punishment, in an effort to make them speed up production. Thus, the early years of factory manufacturing were characterized by appalling and dangerous conditions for large numbers of workers (Le Blanc 1999).

In time, labor organizations were formed to force owners to correct some of the worst abuses. Workers agitated for and obtained the right to organize, and they established political parties and labor unions. The unions, after a considerable struggle and frequent setbacks, won important concessions from management and government, including the right to organize workers in factories and to represent them in negotiations (Skurzynski 2008; Zieger and Gall 2002).

Patterns of industrial expansion varied among the Western industrializing nations, and each experienced the inevitable business cycles, but industrial growth continued unabated in the three decades between the beginning of the twentieth century and the Great Depression of the 1930s. The number of manufacturing workers continued to increase in industrialized countries in the two decades following World War II, as did the value added to their economies by manufacture. However, during the mid-1970s, many manufacturers in the industrialized countries began an accelerated pattern of foreign direct investment in developing countries. Relocation of manufacturing plants to offshore sites increasingly led to factory closings in developed countries, with accompanying job loss and even economic devastation in some regions. These TNC practices became a major feature of the global economy and the early phase of globalization from above (Blackford 1998).

I delay analysis of TNC practices in the global economy because it is important to show first how the growth of commercial sports accompanied the evolution of the manufacturing industry. Both were foundations for the creation and development of the sporting goods and equipment manufacturing industry.

The Growth of Commercial Sports

Over the past two centuries, the rise of commercial sport forms evolved hand in hand with the growth of industrialization and large-scale manufacturing. This is not the place to provide a detailed chronicle of the rise of commercial sport; however, an overview of modern sport's evolution is important to understanding the linkages between this social practice, industrialization, and sporting goods manufacturing (Birley 1995; Gems, Borish, and Pfister 2008; McDevitt 2004; Morrow and Wamsley 2005).

It seems unimaginable today, but there was little by way of what could be called organized participant or spectator sports prior to the mid-nineteenth century. A commercial sport industry requires technologies that support rapid transportation, communication, and mass production modes. It also requires an infrastructure of large numbers of people living in close proximity—an urban population—with substantial amounts of discretionary time and money. These conditions did not exist at the beginning of the nineteenth century.

Urban influences on the world of the newly emerging commercialized sport industry made their appearance in the mid-nineteenth century and became more significant with each ensuing decade of the 1800s. The growing towns and cities were natural centers for organizing sports. The increasing concentration of city populations and the wearisome monotony of the industrial workplace created a demand for more recreational outlets. Urbanization created favorable conditions for commercialized spectator sports, while industrialization gradually provided the leisure time and standard of living so crucial to the growth and development of all forms of commercial sport and recreation.

Other significant forces for transforming sport from informal village festivals into highly organized commercial events include the technological advances that made possible the steam engine, railroads, riverboats, and large-scale manufacturing. All contributed to creating, promoting, and expanding interest in sports in the latter nineteenth century. By this time regular sports events, such as horse racing, prizefighting, rowing, foot racing (the runners were called pedestrians), and similar activities were held in towns and villages throughout the Western countries.

The final three decades of the nineteenth century saw the rising tide of organized sports take on an increasing role in people's lives. Expanding industrialization and urbanization, enhanced by the revolutionary transformations in communication, transportation, and other technological advances, provided the framework for the rise of commercial sport.

In Britain, the lure of commercialization gradually undermined amateurism in a number of sports. By the mid-1880s professional soccer had been accepted, and while the Rugby Union fought more fiercely to preserve amateurism, by the end of the nineteenth century this sport, too, had a professional organization. Thus, the framework of modern commercial sport was established during the last half of the nineteenth century, setting the stage for the remarkable developments in mass popular and professional sport that followed during the twentieth century. Sport historian Wray Vamplew, asserts that "commercialized spectator sport for the mass market became one of the economic success stories of late Victorian England" and claims that "by 1910 there were over 200 first-class professional cricketers plus several hundred country ground staff and league professionals; [there were] some 400 jockeys and ... in soccer there were 6,800 registered professionals ... earning money from playing sport" (1988, 13).

During the first half of the twentieth century, organized sport grew and prospered, becoming a massive commodified industry. Growing urban areas, better transportation facilities, a growing affluent class, a higher standard of living, and more discretionary funds for purchasing sporting equipment fostered sport and facilitated the formation of numerous leagues and teams. Commercialized sport penetrated into many levels of the business world: fashion, mass media, transportation, communication, advertising, and a variety of marginal enterprises that profit from commercial sport. The sporting spirit became a prominent part of the social life of large numbers of people.

One of the major trends in commercial sport in countries throughout the world over the past thirty years has been the colossal expansion of professional spectator sports and the increased active participation by the general public in sports activities. Professional sports are a form of corporate organization that functions very similarly in many respects to corporations of any other kind, albeit with certain tax and monopolistic advantages not given to other businesses. The professional team-sport industry has been one of the most successful growth industries in recent decades. The number of teams in all of the professional leagues has grown at an unbelievable rate, more than doubling their numbers in the past three decades. At the same time, the number of sports in which there are now professional leagues and tours—for example, the Professional Golfers' Association (PGA) tour—has expanded rapidly.

The evolution of mass manufacturing and the growth of commercialized sport have had major impacts on the sporting goods manufacturing industry. Professional athletes as well as the average sports participant require appropriate apparel, footwear, and equipment for their activities. As professional sports and general-public participation have expanded, the demand for sporting goods and equipment has been incredible; thus the sporting goods industry has become a major growth industry during the past thirty years.

All sports apparel, footwear, and equipment must be manufactured, and an understanding of contemporary sporting goods manufacturing requires that the industry be contextualized within manufacturing in the global economy. The connection between the manufacturing industry and the global economy is the topic of the next section.

Manufacturing in the Global Economy

Although most people regard international commerce as a recent phenomenon, in fact trade across borders has taken place for centuries. It has only been in the past forty years, however, that production, distribution, and consumption of products and services has become global. According to the Organization for Economic Cooperation and Development (OECD), the global economy has its origins in the changing patterns of "transborder operations of firms undertaken to organize their development, production, sourcing, marketing, and financing activities" (1996, 15).

The expansion of what is now called the global economy can be seen by the increase in global foreign direct investment, which grew from $629 billion in 1960 to $15 trillion in 2008. TNCs have increased in number from 7,000 in the 1960s to 79,000 worldwide today, and they own about 790,000 foreign affiliates globally (UN Conference on Trade and Development 2008; see also Thun 2008). These TNCs are huge and powerful enterprises. Economically, they exceed the size of most governments; indeed, of the world's one hundred largest economies, more than half are TNCs. Here we see an exemplary illustration of the globalization from above that I described in Chapter 1. All of its features are discernible.

Product manufacturing is a major driving force of the global economy, as advanced capitalist and developing countries seek to increase their shares of the wealth of nations. In this system, product research, design, development, and marketing take place in industrial developed countries, while the labor-intensive, assembly line phases of product manufacture are relegated to developing (aka Third World) nations. A key component of global manufacturing utilized by TNCs is export-processing zones

(EPZs), which "are areas within developing countries that offer incentives and a barrier-free environment to promote economic growth by attracting foreign investment for export-oriented production" (Papadopoulos and Malhotra 2007, 148).

The finished products are then exported for distribution in the developed countries of the world. EPZs are intended to increase foreign-currency earnings for impoverished developing nations through these exports, while providing cheap labor and tax breaks to foreign corporations, thus achieving their economic objectives of export-led growth. Because manufactured goods from developing countries have increased sharply in the past twenty-five years, over one-third of the earnings of the two hundred largest U.S. TNCs are now from their export-processing operations.

EPZs are typically established in developing countries with authoritarian governments, where production costs are cheap, labor protections are not enforced, workers are most repressed, the workforce is not unionized, and weak or nonexistent safety and environmental laws prevail. This process is widely known throughout the world as the "race to the bottom," which refers to shifting production to the lowest-wage countries. The most dramatic shift of this kind in the past decade has been to China, where average wages are less than 5 percent of those in the United States.

One of the consequences of the export-processing system for workers in developed countries is that manufacturing employment has plummeted. TNCs have closed factories in those countries and moved the jobs to developing countries throughout the world. The percentage of U.S. workers employed in manufacturing dropped from 20 percent in 1980 to 11 percent in 2009. Most of those jobs have gone to Mexico and East Asia. Manufacturing employment over the past ten years has declined 4.7 percent in England, 6.1 percent in Germany, and 5.2 percent in Japan. Meanwhile, manufacturing accounts for 33 percent of gross domestic product in China, a country with arguably the lowest manufacturing wages in the world (Schwartz 2009).

For workers and their communities in developed countries, the consequences of export-processing industrialization have been grim: closed plants, replacement jobs paying minimal wages, community disintegration, and various physical and mental worker afflictions linked to the global economy.

The consequences of export-processing industrialization for workers in developing countries have been horrible. Although this system has provided employment for many workers, there have been adverse outcomes as well. This form of manufacturing leads to environmental devastation and is built on the backs of an exploited labor force largely made up of young women and children; 70 to 90 percent of workers in EPZs are women who frequently suffer mistreatment, especially sexual harassment, long working hours, wages so low that they cannot provide for their basic needs, unjust and inhumane working conditions, prohibition of union organization, and the near absence of social welfare facilities (such as child care) (Silverstein 2010). Even worse, according to the International Labour Organization, 218 million children aged five to fourteen are engaged in some form of child labor, with Asia-Pacific having the largest number of child workers (International Labour Organization 2009; see also Flanagan 2006). These are the existing conditions that globalization from below aims to combat.

Today, transnational companies in dozens of industries outsource production to contractors in the most corrupt and repressive countries in the world in search of cheap labor, generous tax benefits, and weak safety, health, and environmental regulations. These are the conditions in developing countries where direct investment in export processing favors transnational corporate profit—that is, globalization from above (Human Rights Watch 2009).

Global Sporting Goods Manufacturing: From Humble Beginnings to Transnational Corporations

As the number of popular individual and team sports grew during the latter nineteenth century, recreational participation in sports expanded, commercialized sports proliferated, and sports participants began using special apparel for competition, mostly for comfort but also to distinguish members of different teams. They also began to use specialized equipment for safety and to perform the required tasks for each sport efficiently. To meet the demands for these sporting goods and equipment, an industry took root in parallel with the growth of mass manufacturing in other industries. Indeed, mass-produced goods developed in sporting and equipment just as they did in other industries, and a national market expanded rapidly.

Like in other industries, sporting goods production and distribution were rudimentary and poorly organized until the last three decades of the nineteenth century. Athletes and sportsmen either fashioned their own uniforms and equipment or acquired apparel and equipment supplied by home-crafting, merchant importers, or local craftsmen who produced sporting goods and equipment as a sideline (Hardy 1990).

Conditions changed rapidly as favorable economic, social, and cultural conditions created a market for standardized manufactured sporting goods and equipment. Although the popularity of sport and outdoor recreation was still in the early stages of development, entrepreneurs saw the potential for profits in supplying and fueling the demand for these products. This fostered the manufacture of bicycles, billiard tables, baseball and football equipment, sporting rifles, fishing rods, and numerous other items. By 1880 the U.S. Census Bureau listed eighty-six firms in the category of "sporting goods" manufacture. Between 1879 and 1899 the growth in the value of products manufactured by the sporting and athletics goods industry increased by 133 percent (Thomas and Day 1976). In 1899 Henry Chadwick, the acclaimed father of baseball, wrote, "Our Yankee manufacturers now control the supply of sport goods the world over" (quoted in Hardy 1990, 72).

An indication of the growing significance of sporting goods manufacturing is that in 1906 a group of sporting goods manufacturers assembled to form an organization to meet the industry needs that individual companies could not handle. They took the name Sporting Goods Manufacturers Association (SGMA 2009b). Several of the sporting goods firms that were to dominate the industry in the twentieth century were thriving businesses by the 1920s. In addition, dozens of other sporting goods firms were actively in the market.

As I said in a previous section, there are over 4,000 sporting goods and equipment manufacturing firms worldwide, so I must limit the number that I highlight in this chapter. The firms that I have chosen for attention are Wilson Sporting Goods, Adidas AG, Reebok International, Mizuno Corporation, and Nike, Inc. (see Table 4.1). This book is about global sport, so I have chosen sporting goods and equipment companies that originated in different geographical regions of the world, and they are all currently TNCs representing global ownership, production, distribution, and sales.

All of these corporations have a lengthy history in a dynamic and rapidly changing industry. I briefly describe each company's transformation from an individual entrepreneurial firm to a TNC. These corporate biographies are important to understanding global sport because sporting goods and equipment corporations supply essential components for the conduct of all global sports.[1]

Table 4.1 Leading Global Sporting Goods and Equipment Manufacturers

Wilson Sporting Goods Subsidiary of Amer Sports Corporation
Incorporated: Finland
Number of employees: 6,338
Financial highlights (2008):

Total revenue	$1.576 billion
Total assets	$1,662 billion
Principal offices	Helsinki, Finland
	Chicago, Illinois, USA

Adidas AG Sporting Goods
Incorporated: Germany
Number of employees: 39,982
Financial highlights (2008):

Total revenue	$10,799 billion
Total assets	$9,533 billion
Principal offices	Herzogenaurach, Germany

Reebok International Subsidiary of Adidas AG
Incorporated: Massachusetts, USA
Number of employees: 9,102
Financial highlights (2008):

Total revenue	$3,785 billion
Total assets	$2,441 billion
Principal offices	Canton, Massachusetts

Mizuno Corporation
Incorporated: Japan
Number of employees: 5,731
Financial highlights (2008):

Total revenue	$174,019 billion
Total assets	$144,169 billion
Principal offices	Osaka, Japan

Nike, Inc.
Incorporated: Oregon, USA
Number of employees: 32,500
Financial highlights (2008):

Total revenue	$18,627 billion
Total assets	$12,443 billion
Principal offices	Beaverton, Oregon

Wilson Sporting Goods

Wilson Sporting Goods, currently a subsidiary of Amer Sports Corporation, designs, manufactures, and distributes ball-sports equipment. It is
the world's leading such manufacturer, offering products for baseball,
football, basketball, softball, volleyball, soccer, and golf, as well as for
racquet sports, such as tennis, racquetball, squash, badminton, and platform tennis. It reported $670.5 million net sales for 2008 (Amer Sports
2008). Wilson also produces uniforms and apparel, footwear for men and
women, and accessories like bags, strings, and grips. As the originator of
breakthrough technologies, Wilson has earned worldwide legitimacy in
each sport for which it has produced goods and equipment.

What became Wilson Sporting Goods was founded in 1913 in Chicago
as Ashland Manufacturing and was originally established to find unique
ways of using slaughterhouse by-products from a nearby meat-packing
firm. Within its first two years, the company was producing items like
tennis-racket and violin strings and surgical sutures, and it had expanded
into baseball shoes and tennis racquets. The president, Thomas E. Wilson, saw the potential of the firm's becoming exclusively a sporting goods
company, so he began to concentrate on the manufacture of sporting and
athletic equipment. In 1916, the company was renamed the Thomas E.
Wilson Company, a name it retained until 1931, when it was changed to
Wilson Sporting Goods Company. By the mid-twentieth century, Wilson
Sporting Goods had become the leading sporting goods manufacturer
in the United States.

Beginning in 1967, Wilson Sporting Goods went through a series of
ownership changes. It was first purchased by the aerospace conglomerate Ling-Temco-Vought Corporation. In 1970 Wilson was acquired by
Pepsico, the New York soft drink giant, which gave Wilson the financial
base it needed to expand into the international market. By 1976, Wilson
had opened a manufacturing plant in Galway, Ireland. In 1985 the company reemerged as an independent entity, Wilson Sporting Goods Inc.,
with its headquarters in River Grove, Illinois. But four years later Wilson
Sporting Goods became a wholly owned subsidiary of the Amer Sports
Corporation based in Helsinki, Finland.

The Amer Sports Corporation is a leading company for technically
advanced products that improve the performance of sports participants.
Its major brands include Arc'teryx, Atomic, Mavic, Precor, Salomon, Su-
unto, and Wilson. Thus, the company's business is balanced by its broad

portfolio of sports and its presence in all major markets. Under Amer's direction, Wilson opened subsidiaries in Canada, France, Germany, Japan, and the United Kingdom. Through a comprehensive marketing and global distribution network, Wilson is able to sell its sporting equipment and uniforms in over one hundred countries worldwide (Wilson 2010).

Adidas AG

Currently, Adidas (legal name Adidas AG) is one of the global leaders within the sporting goods industry and the largest sportswear manufacturer in Europe. It offers a broad range of products around three core segments: Adidas, Reebok, and TaylorMade-adidas Golf. With its headquarters located in Herzogenaurach, Germany, it has 190 subsidiaries worldwide delivering state-of-the-art sports footwear, apparel, and accessories. It has also assembled an unparalleled portfolio of promotion partnerships around the world, including sports associations, events, teams, and individual athletes (Adidas Group 2009).

Also located in Herzogenaurach are the strategic business units for running, soccer, and tennis as well as a research and development center. Additional key corporate units are based in Portland, Oregon, home to the strategic business units for basketball, adventure, and alternative sports.

Adolph ("Adi") Dassler, a German craftsman and avid track athlete, began making shoes by hand for running and training in 1920. Four years later he and his brother Rudolf ("Rudi") became partners and registered their shoe company under the name Dassler OHG; they leased their first production facility in 1927, calling it Dassler Brothers Sports Shoe Factory. In 1936 Dassler shoes begin its long domination of Olympic sports when Jesse Owens won four gold medals for track and field events at the Berlin Olympics while wearing Dassler shoes.

Shortly after World War II, a bitter dispute between the Dassler brothers resulted in Rudi's leaving the company and opening his own shoe manufacturing business and naming his shoes Puma. At this point, Adi registered the famous three stripes as his company's trademark and Adidas became the official company name after its founder: "Adi" for Adolph and "Das" from Dassler (Smit 2008).

Between the 1952 Olympic Games in Helsinki, Finland, and the 1984 Olympic Games in Los Angeles—spanning seven Summer Olympics—Adidas was overwhelmingly the sport-shoe brand most widely worn by the athletes. At the Los Angeles Summer Olympics, 124 out of 140 nations competed in Adidas products. Adi was also a devoted soccer fan, and when the 1954 German Nation Team won the Football (Soccer) World Cup in 1954 for the first time, all the players were wearing Adidas shoes. Again, in 1974 Germany became the World Cup champion, and 80 percent of all players at the competition were wearing Adidas shoes and apparel.

Unfortunately, the death of Horst Dassler in 1987 marked the beginning of a period of serious instability and financial trouble for Adidas. After a period spanning almost seventy years, the Dassler family withdrew from the company in 1989. In an effort to save money, those managing Adidas manufacturing moved operations to Asia. In 1997 Adidas acquired the French Salomon Worldwide Group, which broadened the Adidas product range to include TaylorMade for golf products and Mavic for cycle components. The newly formed group took the name adidas-Salomon AG.

Early in 2006, Adidas-Salomon AG acquired Reebok International, Ltd. The closing of the Reebok transaction marked a new chapter in the history of the Adidas Group. Taking over Reebok doubled its share of the U.S. athletic shoe market and intensified competition with rival Nike, which has nearly 40 percent of the worldwide market. The marriage of number two Adidas and number three Reebok also gave the combined firm increased clout among merchants to command shelf space and deeper pockets to bid on endorsement contracts.

By combining two of the most respected and well-known brands in the worldwide sporting goods industry, the new group has benefitted from a more competitive global platform, well-defined and complementary brand identities, a wider range of products, and a stronger presence across teams, athletes, events, and leagues. In June 2006, the company's name was changed to Adidas AG (Adidas Group, n.d.).

Reebok International

Reebok International is a Fortune 500 corporation and one of the world's leading manufacturers of sports footwear, apparel, and accessories. The name is the South African spelling of the word "rhebok," a species of antelope endemic to South Africa. But this was not the company's original name; I will explain below. As I mentioned above, Reebok is currently a subsidiary of the Adidas Group.

Reebok has been recognized for its innovations and breakthrough concepts and technologies for numerous sports and fitness activities. Under the leadership of Paul Fireman, who had acquired the North American license for the company's products from its British owner in 1979, Reebok gained its original international prominence by creating a new market for aerobic training shoes for women interested in fashion. That initial success allowed the company to expand into other sports and products and to market its products throughout the world. In the past decade, Reebok has become the world's leading producer of hockey apparel and equipment with its acquisition of The Hockey Company.

Widely considered the oldest manufacturer of athletic shoes in the world, J. W. Foster and Sons was founded in England in 1895 (some accounts say 1898) by Joseph William Foster. Foster made some of the first-known running shoes by hand for runners of that period, and before long his fledgling company developed an international clientele of distinguished athletes. A big breakthrough for the family-owned business came when its running shoes were worn by the British athletes competing in the 1924 Paris Summer Olympic Games—the runners featured in the movie *Chariots of Fire.*

It was not until 1958, when Foster's two grandsons took over the company, that the name was changed to Reebok. Reebok maintained a presence in sporting goods in the United Kingdom and Europe in the three decades following World War II, but its transformation into an international corporation was given a boost when Paul Fireman, an American and a partner in an outdoor sporting goods distributorship, noticed some Reebok shoes at an international trade show. He was impressed and acquired a North American distribution license. In 1979 Firman introduced three Reebok running shoes in the United States, at $60 a pair, the most expensive running shoes on the market.

Under Fireman's leadership, Reebok quickly became the top athletic footwear maker in United States, riding the aerobics craze with revolutionary sneakers like the Pump. By 1981, Reebok's sales exceeded $1.5 million. Fireman took the company public in 1985, and shortly thereafter Reebok began an aggressive expansion into overseas markets. Explosive growth followed, which Reebok fueled with new product categories, making it an industry leader. International sales contributed 10 percent of revenues, showing that Reebok had become a global corporation.

In 1992, Reebok began a transition from a company identified principally with fitness and exercise to one equally involved in sports by creating several new footwear and apparel products for baseball, football, soccer, track and field, and other sports. That same year, Reebok began its partnership with golfer Greg Norman, resulting in the creation of the Greg Norman Collection. In the late 1990s, Reebok made a strategic commitment to align its brand with a select few of the world's most talented, exciting, and cutting-edge athletes. Since then, the company has focused on those athletes who represent the top echelon of sports and fitness (I'll discuss this further in the following section).

As mentioned above, in 2006 Adidas AG acquired Reebok, making it a subsidiary and thus merging two of the largest global sporting goods and equipment manufacturers.

Mizuno Corporation

Mizuno Corporation, founded and still headquartered in Japan, is a world leader in the manufacture and sale of baseball, golf, mountaineering, skiing, and other sports equipment, footwear, and sportswear. Its operations are carried out through two divisions namely: sporting goods and other. The sporting goods division deals in golf goods, various sporting goods, sportswear, and shoes. The other division's operations include sports facilities, such as management of track fields, tennis courts, gyms, golf driving ranges, and golf courses. Mizuno is considered one of the top three brands for baseball equipment, and its golf irons are among the leading clubs used on the PGA Tour. The company maintains offices and operating facilities across the globe.

A devoted fan of baseball, Rihachi Mizuno opened a baseball equipment store in 1906 in Osaka, Japan, offering custom uniforms as well as sports clothing. Eventually, Mizuno expanded into manufacturing sports equipment. His baseballs became the standard of excellence for the product in Japan, and the store gradually grew into a successful TNC. During the 1920s and 1930s, Mizuno expanded the operations of his company into skiing and golf equipment manufacturing. In 1934 he opened a factory based near Osaka for making baseball bats, balls, and uniforms, as well as for manufacturing golf clubs and skis. The company continued to expand into other areas of sports until the onset of World War II. After the war, the company returned to producing baseball equipment, in particular sailcloth for gloves and wooden bats with resin added for longevity.

By the 1970s Mizuno was at the forefront of an emerging global sporting goods industry. The company gained recognition as an innovator in its field, creating, among other items, customized gloves for Major League Baseball (MLB) players. Its growing reputation stimulated a desire for a global presence, so in 1982 Mizuno launched an American division under the direction of Jack Curran, a sports equipment veteran. Curran started Mizuno Corporation of America. Within a relatively short time, Mizuno entered the American sporting goods and equipment market with several technologically advanced products and nationally known endorsers.

Masato Mizuno, a grandson of the firm's founder, gained control of all the company's operations in 1987, acquiring the presidency from his father. Masato helped the company prosper. Within two years, Mizuno controlled 30 percent of the Japanese golf club and baseball markets. But Masato's goal became global dominance. "We want to be able to meet every sports need," he explained to *Sports Illustrated*, "and we want true internationalization. Those are our goals" (quoted in Smith 1989, 63). And it did seem like Mizuno was on a path to accomplishing them. During the 1989 MLB season 240 MLB players in the United States used Mizuno equipment, notably gloves and shoes. Roger Craig, then San Francisco Giants manager, could see it. He told *Sports Illustrated*, "You see the name so much you hardly think it's Japanese" (Smith 1989, 62).

Over the past twenty years, Mizuno has launched new items with products built around technology and innovation, such as the Reactor tennis racquet, which claimed a 200 percent increase in accuracy owing to its symmetrical head and patented string system. During this time, Mizuno liquidated the Mizuno Corporation of America and closed the golf equipment and apparel distribution company located in Georgia, owing to unprecedented losses. Instead, the company established Mizuno USA Corporation as its presence in the United States, consolidating its golf brands into T-ZOID and cutting its shoe line by 40 percent (Mizuno 2009).

Nike, Inc.

Nike is the world's leading manufacturer of sporting goods and equipment (Amer Sports Corporation also claims this distinction). It sells its products to retail stores and a variety of independent distributors and licensees in over 180 countries around the world. The company has consistently relied on innovation in the design of its products and aggressive promotion and marketing to fuel its growth in both U.S. and foreign markets. Through its suppliers, shippers, retailers, and other service providers, it directly or indirectly employs nearly 1 million people, which includes some 32,000 Nike employees across six continents. In addition to manufacturing sportswear and equipment, the corporation operates Niketown retail stores and factory outlets (Nike 2009).

Like the other sporting goods and equipment firms described in this chapter, what became Nike, Inc., was founded by a single individual, Philip H. Knight, a Stanford University business graduate. On a trip to Japan in 1963, Knight arranged with a Japanese firm that made sport footwear to import some of its products to the United States. Knight felt that Japanese running shoes could compete significantly with the German products, Adidas and Puma, which were dominating the American market. To convince the Japanese owners that he represented an actual company, Knight claimed he represented a firm named Blue Ribbon Sports (BRS), a firm that did not actually exist at that time. A year later, Knight and Bill Bowerman, Knight's college track coach, established a partnership in a company they named Blue Ribbon Sports.

By the early 1970s, BRS began manufacturing its own products, and the company introduced its swoosh trademark and the brand name Nike (for the Greek goddess of victory). Over the next decade the official name of the corporation became Nike, Inc. During that decade, the first line of clothing was launched, the Nike Air shoe-cushioning device debuted, and Nike International, Ltd., was created to spearhead worldwide investment and sales, targeting Africa, Asia, Europe, and Latin America.

Entering the 1980s, Nike's line of products included more than two hundred different kinds of sports footwear, and its combination of innovative design and aggressive marketing allowed it to overtake Adidas AG, previously the leader in U.S. sales. It signed Michael Jordan to an extended endorsement contract in the mid-1980s, and aggressive marketing featuring Michael Jordan ads proved key to the company's successes for several years (Jordan 2006).

The fickle tastes of teenagers and young adults, the core consumer groups for sporting goods and equipment, created great swings from stagnation to waves of buying in annual Nike sales, but by the mid-1990s, Nike was the dominant force in sports footwear, with about 30 percent of the U.S. market, far outdistancing its nearest competitor, Reebok. It also had its next superstar endorser, Tiger Woods, just as Michael Jordan's career was drawing to a close. At age twenty, Woods agreed to a twenty-year, $40 million endorsement contract, thought to be the highest in sports endorsement history at that time. Two years later, in 2000, Woods renegotiated his Nike contract to $100 million (Sirak 2005).

Nike rang in the new millennium in the traditional Nike manner that had proven successful in the past, with a new footwear cushioning system called Nike Shox, which proved worthy of joining Nike Air as the industry's gold standard. Nike continued to seek new and innovative ways to develop sporting goods; Nike Free, Nike+, and Nike Sphere are just three examples of this approach. Just as Nike's products have evolved, so has Nike's approach to global marketing.

Nike focuses on lifestyle marketing, which combines sporting goods and everyday life to make its products useful both on and off the field. At the same time the firm has continued signing new superstars to endorsement contracts and sponsoring some of the best teams and sporting events in the world.

Sporting Goods Manufacturing in the Global Economy: The Case of Nike

Sporting goods manufacturing is one of the most flourishing export-processing industries. Indeed, sporting goods manufacturers that produce all of their products domestically are now a minority because many of them have "run away" to various low-wage export-processing countries across the world. Over 90 percent of the sneakers and other sporting goods sold in the United State are imports made in foreign countries. China alone, arguably the country with the most abhorrent working conditions in the world, accounts for approximately 65 percent of global sporting goods production (Harley 2007; Harney 2008; Lee 2007; Sage 2004).

This section focuses on a single sporting goods manufacturing firm—Nike—but it is important for readers to understand that there are several thousand sporting goods product manufacturers whose products are made in developing countries, much like Nike's. I have chosen Nike to illustrate how sporting goods firms have transferred their productive operations from the country in which they are incorporated to foreign export-processing operations in developing countries because Nike is the exemplar of, the "poster boy" for, this practice. Two writers for the *Washington Post* agree: "No company symbolizes the mobilization of American companies overseas more than Nike. Its 30-year history in Asia is as close as any one company's story can be to the history of globalization, to the spread of dollars ... into the poor corners of the earth.... It is a story of restless and ruthless capital, continually moving from country to country in search of new markets and untapped low-wage labor" (Swardson and Bugawara 1996).

As I said in an earlier section, the corporation that is now Nike was founded in 1964, with Blue Ribbon Sports as the company's original name. Nike was adopted as the name for a new style of running shoes in the early 1970s; the corporate name was changed to Nike, Inc., in 1977.

At first, the sneakers sold by Blue Ribbon Sports were made in Japan, at that time a low-wage country. But by the time the corporate name Nike, Inc. was adopted, a factory in South Korea had been opened. By the early 1980s, nearly 90 percent of Nike's sports footwear was produced by South Korean and Taiwanese shoe manufacturers because both were low-wage countries with cooperative governments for export-processing plants. Nike's operations in Asia were carried out through subcontracting with local manufacturers, mostly located in cheap labor countries, thus eliminating the need for Nike to build plants, hire workers, and carry out the day-to-day tasks of production.

In the late 1980s, democratic reforms came to South Korea and Taiwan; wages increased dramatically, and the labor movement won the right to form independent unions and strike. Nike began shifting much of its footwear operations out of these two countries into politically autocratic, military-dominated countries like Indonesia and Thailand, then later to China and Vietnam, in a relentless drive for a favorable political climate and the lowest-cost labor to make its shoes and apparel. Nike CEO Philip Knight knew that political leaders in these countries were attracting foreign corporations with promises of weak or poorly enforced labor and environmental standards, and unions were outlawed or state controlled (Korzeniewicz 2008; Senser 2009).

By 1998 about 40 percent of all Nike shoes were produced in Indonesia, with China and Vietnam being the other major Asian Nike footwear manufacturing nations. Currently, Nike has around 800,000 workers making Nike products in its global supply chain; about 65 percent of Nike-brand footwear is made in China and Vietnam. None of Nike's footwear is manufactured within the United States.

Nike's Asian Factories: Not a Pretty Sight

During the 1990s, sixteen major investigations were made of factories producing Nike footwear in China, Indonesia, and Vietnam. Investigations were carried out by a variety of organizations—academic, religious, labor, human rights, and development—from various countries. The length of time spent collecting data, the expertise of the investigators, and the methodology used for data collection varied considerably, but the investigations revealed similar patterns and conditions in Nike's Asian shoe factories.

The factory investigations can be summarized as follows: 75 to 80 percent of Nike workers were women, mostly under the age of twenty-four, who regularly put in ten- to thirteen-hour days, worked six days a week, and were forced to work overtime two to three times per week; worker abuse by supervisors was widespread. The typical worker earned around 50 percent of the wage the governments considered as meeting "minimum physical needs"—meaning subsistence for a single adult worker in a given country. Several of the reports found that Nike's record on workers rights in these countries was deplorable. Independent unions were not permitted in the factories. Working conditions were horrendous (Sage 1999).

The abysmally low wages and poor factory conditions quickly led to strikes and protests in the Indonesian sport-shoe factories and later in Nike factories in Vietnam and China. These actions resulted in increased scrutiny of Nike's factories, at first by the Indonesian press, then by the foreign media and nongovernmental organizations (NGOs), which focused on wages and working conditions. Throughout the 1990s labor problems arose in every Asian country where Nike contractors were located. A Stanford University professor who studied Nike's Indonesian factories said, "Nike's got business in Indonesia because the workers are docile by virtue of government repression and they can't protest. The world that Nike and Philip Knight represent is the opposite of human rights and civilized values" (quoted in Mohtashemi 1997).

At the same time as investigations of Nike factories were being reported and the appalling workers' wages and working conditions revealed, the Nike corporation was expanding rapidly and recording record-breaking revenue almost annually. Moreover, Nike was spending lavishly on promoting its products, paying out $1.13 billion on advertising alone in 1998.

Between 1992 and 1996, as global understanding and consciousness grew about Nike's labor practices, they struck a collective chord of horror and outrage, spurring collective actions by workers in Nike's Asian factories and launching what ultimately became the Nike Social Movement. This movement comprised a coalition of organizations, each with its own maze of affiliates, members, friends, and allies. As it grew, it became so dense and diverse, with so many interlocking links, that the organizational matrix became difficult to identify clearly.

Figure 4.1 illustrates the types of organizations that became part of the Nike Social Movement. Many NGOs throughout the world took up the workers' cause, thereby forming the broad structure for the Nike Social Movement, which then organized a variety of campaigns against Nike. Those campaigns took the form of demonstrations, protests, op-ed columns, TV spots, sit-ins, and marches and were devoted to increasing public awareness of Nike's labor practices. All of these campaigns portrayed Nike as a repressive, abusive, unjust, and inhuman corporation. Between 1993 and 1998 the Nike Social Movement reached its peak of action and influence. The ultimate goal was to create enough public outrage against Nike that governments, business organizations, unions, religious organizations, and human rights groups would pressure the corporation to change its labor practices and move forcefully to improve conditions in the factories.

Figure 4.1 Types of organizations composing the Nike Social Movement

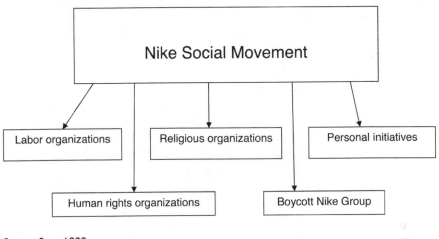

Source: Sage 1999.

Nike's Responses to Factory Reports and the Social Movement

From its beginnings, Nike had carefully crafted its image as a company with an "attitude." Nike CEO Philip Knight himself admitted, "What we are all about is being against the establishment" (Egan 1998, 69). At the same time, Nike scrupulously honed a rhetoric of social responsibility, suggesting it was a socially conscious global corporate citizen with a sensitivity to racial, gender, and disability discrimination, as well as a concern for the environment. The company also engaged in a variety of promotional ventures designed to illustrate its support for empowering minority and disadvantaged groups (Knight and Greenberg 2002).

With such a corporate perspective, it is perhaps not surprising that Nike's initial response to the reports about its Asian factories was overwhelmingly denial and anger. At first, Nike management denied responsibility for conditions in the Asian factories, arguing that Nike merely contracted with suppliers, who actually manufactured the shoes, and therefore Nike could not control what went on inside. This was, of course, absurd; Nike always had overall control of its productive operations through the power it wielded over its contractors. In all its contracts with suppliers, Nike specified very precisely the quality standards that must be met in the manufacture of its products. There is no reason at all that

Nike management could not also specify labor standards with regard to the workers in the factories.

Nike also responded to reports about conditions in its factories by undertaking its own investigations of them. In 1994 Nike hired the accounting firm Ernst & Young to conduct audits of labor and environmental conditions inside it factories, and in 1997 it commissioned former American UN ambassador Andrew Young and his company GoodWorks International to investigate Nike factory operations in China, Indonesia, and Vietnam. In the same year Nike released a summary of an investigation of its Asian factories by a group of MBA students at the Amos Tuck School of Business at Dartmouth College—an investigation it had funded. All three reports were prepared and paid for by Nike; none was an independent inspection of Nike factories.

Not surprisingly, all three reports found little to criticize about wages and working conditions in Nike's factories. Also not surprisingly, those investigations received scathing condemnation from international human rights groups, labor organizations, and religious organizations, as well as a number of investigative journalists.

Perhaps the most consistent and persistent response Nike management made during the 1990s to the reports about its Asian factories was, "Why is Nike being singled out when the Asia factories of other sports footwear and apparel manufacturers are very similar to Nike's?" Nike Social Movement leaders gave several types of replies: They argued that because Nike was the industry pioneer in moving its productive operations overseas, complaints about its labor practices were the first to surface in the Asian sports footwear industry. They was also pointed out that a basic principle of labor and human rights organizations seeking social justice is to go after the market leader, and Nike was far and away the market leader in the sports footwear industry, with approximately 40 percent of the market. Moreover, according to Nike's own research, its corporate icon, the swoosh, was recognized worldwide. Lastly, they argued that as Nike was the "marquee corporation" in the global sports footwear and apparel industry, other corporations in the industry looked to it for leadership. Even Nike CEO Philip Knight acknowledged, "Our competitors just follow our lead."

Therefore, there was reason to believe that when Nike agreed to resolve its problems with wages, working conditions, and worker treatment and to permit collective bargaining in its factories, other companies in the sports manufacturing industry would follow. As the founder of a Nike campaign called "Justice! Do It Nike" put it, "Nike is ... the largest company [in the sport-shoe industry] and has set the precedent for ... [the] race to the bottom. If Nike reforms, they will trumpet the change and other manufacturers will have to follow."

The reports about conditions in Asian Nike factories and the campaign of the Nike Social Movement damaged the Nike brand name and reputation severely for millions of people throughout the world. For many, the Nike swoosh became associated with sweatshops[2] and the oppression of workers. Even Nike CEO Philip Knight admitted this. Speaking at a National Press Club luncheon in Washington, D.C., in May 1998, he said, "The Nike product has become synonymous with slave wages, forced overtime and arbitrary abuse." He also said, "I truly believe that ... [consumers do] not want to buy products made in abusive conditions" (Cushman 1998).

Knight's admission of the Nike brand's reputation clearly illustrated that the campaigns against Nike's manufacturing practices had won sympathy and support. As a matter of fact, they helped to change governmental policies in several foreign countries, including increases in minimum wages, reforms in working-condition standards, and limitations on hours of work per day and week. Several governments adopted new public policies to permit independent union organization.

Nike Social Movement campaigns also brought their message about Nike's Asian factories to American university campuses. Many students were moved to organize and campaign in a variety of ways to show their support for the movement. This led to the founding of United Students Against Sweatshops (USAS) in the summer of 1998, and USAS is still active. In 2009 more than 250 college and university campuses in the United States had member chapters, and another two hundred similar campus organizations worldwide were not formally linked to USAS. At many colleges and universities, USAS has successfully had antisweatshop codes and institutional policies adopted against sweatshops.

Nike's New Initiatives: A Commitment to Reform or a Public Relations Ploy?

During Philip Knight's National Press Club speech in May 1998, he announced plans for a substantially new course for the company. This course, which he called "New Labor Initiatives," was Nike's plan for significant reforms in the company's labor practices. As this was followed up by a number of actions appearing to show that those initiatives were underway, many of the individuals and organizations in the Nike Social

Movement felt they had accomplished most of their objectives and turned to other issues. But within a year after the "New Labor Initiatives" announcement, reports about Nike's factories began coming in. I briefly summarize them:

1999: The Urban Community Mission (Jakarta) conducted a survey of Nike's Indonesian workers. Their report summarized the findings: "Contradicting claims by Nike to have reformed [its Asian factories], this survey indicated that excessive and compulsory overtime, abusive management practices and inadequate wages are still features of Nike contracted factories in Indonesia" (Urban Community Mission 1999).

2000: A group of international labor-rights organizations reported on a series of investigations made at various Nike factories in Cambodia, Indonesia, Vietnam, and Thailand. Their report concluded, "This leads us to believe that labour abuses are the norm in ... suppliers' factories and not isolated incidents as Nike has frequently suggested to the media" (quoted in UNITE! Report 2000, 1).

2001: The Global Alliance for Workers and Communities released a 106-page report on the labor conditions at nine Nike factories in Indonesia. The report was titled *Workers' Voices: An Interim Report on Workers' Needs and Aspirations in Nine Nike Contract Factories in Indonesia,* and many of the findings confirmed what investigations of Nike's Asian factories had been reporting for over ten years (Global Alliance 2001). Even Nike management found the report findings "disturbing."

2001: Global Exchange, an international human rights organization, published a 115-page report titled *Still Waiting for Nike to Do It.* The report concluded, "Nike has misled consumers and let down the workers who make its products and who continue to suffer extreme injustice while Nike touts itself as an 'industry leader' in corporate responsibility"; it also charged Nike with treating the "sweatshop issue as an issue of public relations rather than human rights" (Global Exchange 2001, 92, 94; Richman 2001).

2002: A report titled *We Are Not Machines* was published by a coalition of labor-rights organizations based on interviews with Indonesian workers from four sport-shoe factories producing Nike and Adidas products. The report detailed continued abuse of workers' human rights, including verbal abuse, humiliation in front of other workers, excessively long workweeks, below-subsistence wages, and denial of rights to freedom of association and collective bargaining (Conner 2002).

2006: The findings of a study by the Massachusetts Institute of Technology Sloan School of Management "suggest[ed] that notwithstanding Nike's very real interests in improving its image vis-à-vis these issues and the company's significant efforts and investments over the last decade to improve working conditions among its suppliers … analyses of Nike's own data suggest that conditions in some of its suppliers have improved somewhat but that in many of them, things have either remained stable or deteriorated" (Locke, Qin, and Brause 2006, 36).

These reports add to what has become a long list of Nike factories where serious labor problems have been found. Between 2006 and 2009, there were at least twelve strikes in over thirty-five Nike-producing factories. The findings of the various studies of Nike's Asian factories during the ten years after Knight's "New Labor Initiatives" announcement convincingly show a huge gap between Nike's claims about improvements in its factory workplaces and persisting reports of the same conditions over ten years later (Danish Consumer Council 2009; Knorr 2007). As one Nike Social Movement organizer remarked, "Persuading Nike to reform its factories is like pulling a reluctant tomcat across a carpet."

To be sure, Nike is not the only company that has followed this global "race-to-the-bottom" economic model. For example, the Reebok website reports the following: Reebok "uses footwear factories in 14 countries. Most factories making Reebok footwear are based in Asia—primarily China (accounting for 51% of total footwear production), Indonesia (21%), Vietnam (17%) and Thailand (7%). Production is consolidated, with 88% of Reebok footwear manufactured in 11 factories, employing over 75,000 workers.... Our apparel supply chain is larger, with factories in 45 countries.... Most (52%) of our apparel sold in the US is produced in Asia" (Reebok Human Rights Programs 2009). The Adidas AG website reports that "on December 31, 2007, we worked with more than 1,070 independent factories (excluding factories of our licensees) who manufacture our products in 67 countries. 67% of our factories are located in Asia, 17% in the Americas and 16% in Europe and Africa. 24% of all these factories are in China" (Adidas Group 2007).

The contradiction between what Nike has claimed about its factories and what study after study has reported about them has continued because Nike persistently projects a corporate image of concern for the working conditions in its factories and a commitment to reform them, but the company's basic strategy has largely relied on damage control and public relations. This strategy has preserved Nike's core company policies, which have allowed it to profit from sweatshop labor.

Beyond Sport Production to Sport Promotion

Individual Athlete Endorsements

Figure 1.1 in Chapter 1 illustrates the three segments of the sport industry: sport performance, sport promotion, and sport production. In that figure, the three segments are separated by spaces, but in the real world they are closely integrated. Thus, the double arrows in the figure represent this integration.

Sporting goods and equipment manufacturers are part of the sport-production segment. In order to be profitable businesses, however, they must promote the sale of their products through various marketing strategies, such as employing athletes to endorse their products. Endorsements are part of the sport-promotion segment, and the use of athletes and coaches as endorsers has become a universal practice in sports marketing.

The global relevance of this integration of sport-industry segments is apparent in the employment of globally popular athletes to endorse the products of transnational sporting goods and equipment manufacturers. In their widely used text on sport marketing, Pitts and Stotlar assert that "sport marketers have used individual athletes through sport product endorsements with the hope that their endorsements will result in increased sales" (2007, 293). The principle behind this practice is that global celebrity athletes are seen as opinion leaders, and their endorsements can enhance consumer recognition of a brand and increase the relative perceived value of the products being endorsed (Pride and Ferrell 2006).

The most famous early example of a sporting goods and equipment manufacturer using individual athletes to endorse its products is Adidas founder Adi Dassler's providing free running shoes to Jesse Owens at the 1936 Berlin Olympics. Owens won four gold medals in track and field events while wearing Dassler (now Adidas AG) shoes. Owens became world-famous for his achievements, and Dassler shoes gained global recognition as well. However, Owens was not a paid endorser and did not receive any direct remuneration for wearing Dassler shoes because, at that time, Olympic athletes were required to be amateurs. Nevertheless, the worldwide attention he received for his Olympic gold medal performances while wearing Dassler footwear was a global commercial windfall for the Dassler sporting goods business.

Golf equipment manufacturers were pioneers in realizing the benefits of having the top athletes endorse their products. Walter Hagen and Gene Sarazen, two of the most influential figures in the popularization of professional golf in the early twentieth century, were the pioneers of golf product endorsement. Walter Hagen's golf apparel is still sold in golf shops, and Sarazen had what is still the longest-running endorsement contract in professional sports—with Wilson Sporting Goods—from 1923 until his death in 1999, a total of seventy-six years.

The U.S. "national pastime," baseball, was played at the highest level in MLB beginning in the latter nineteenth century, and manufacturers of baseball equipment were quick to see the benefits of securing the endorsement of baseball equipment by MLB players. Over the past one hundred years, the two items most often carrying the names of major-league players have been gloves and bats. Through most of the twentieth century, Rawlings Company baseball gloves were the favorites of MLB players. These gloves were endorsed by the best major leaguers, and their names were burned into the leather of the glove. As for bats, throughout the twentieth century Hillerich & Bradsby's Louisville Slugger was the number one bat in the United States, and legends like Honus Wagner, Babe Ruth, Ty Cobb, and Lou Gehrig all endorsed and swung them. "This trend has continued throughout the history of the company, giving rise to more than 7,000 contracts between players and Louisville Slugger" (Mondore 2007, 1).

Leading the list of the "best" soccer players in the world during the twentieth century is the Brazilian virtuoso Pelé. During his soccer-playing career, and for years after he retired, Pelé was a sought-after endorser of many sport products, and for good reason. David Carter of Sports Business Group, a sports marketing firm, said, "Pelé is known by more people than Muhammad Ali. He's the global face of a global sport" (quoted in Horovitz 2002).

The sea change that created a global boon for athlete endorsements occurred with the confluence of several trends during the late 1980s: rapid expansion of the global economy; global migration of athletes, teams, and leagues; abolition of the amateur requirement by the International Olympic Committee, allowing professional athletes to participate in the Olympics; and the maturation of Michael Jordan into a full-blown superstar.

Michael Jordan lifted athlete endorsements to a whole new level. *Time* magazine called Jordan "the hottest player in America's hottest sport" (Donnelly 1989, 50). Just the title of Walter La Feber's *Michael Jordan and the New Global Capitalism* (1999) powerfully illustrates the extent to which Michael Jordan played a leading role in the globalization of sport.

Michael Jordan is best known for his Nike endorsement, which earned him $16 million annually in his peak years. Sonny Vaccaro, the man who was instrumental in establishing the Jordan-Nike relationship, declared that "the marriage of Michael and Nike is the biggest story in the history of sports marketing" (quoted in Wetzel and Yaeger 2000, 2; see also Jordan 2006). But Jordan was a multiproduct endorser during the years he was endorsing Nike, and he was also being paid millions of dollars for endorsing a variety of other products: "$5 million from Gatorade, $5 million from Bijan Cologne, $4 million from MCI, $2 million from Ray-O-Vac, $2 million from Hanes, $2 million from Ball Park Franks, $2 million from Wheaties, $2 million from Wilson Sporting Goods, $2 million from Oakley, $1 million from AMF Bowling, $1 million from CBS Sportsline, and $1 million from Chicagoland Chevrolet" (Wetzel and Yaeger 2000, 5–6). In 1997, Jordan earned an estimated $45 million a year in endorsements.

All five of the sporting goods and equipment manufacturers described in previous sections of this chapter have had aggressive campaigns to secure global celebrity athlete endorsers during the past two decades. I shall not attempt to identify all of the athletes who have endorsement contracts with these manufacturers because these types of contracts have proliferated to the point that each of the firms listed in Table 4.1 have some form of endorsement arrangement with dozens of athletes. A few examples will suffice to illustrate.

Wilson Sporting Goods. Few other sporting goods companies in the world have garnered the high-powered endorsements Wilson Sporting Goods has—from Gene Sarazen to Babe Didrikson Zaharias, arguably the greatest woman athlete of the modern era, to Arnold Palmer, to Irishman Padraig Harrington. Wilson Golf has had an enviable string of globally renowned endorsers. Michael Jordan had his own line of Wilson signature basketballs, selling over 1 million annually for nearly fourteen consecutive years.

Adidas AG. Ian Thorpe, a swimmer from Australia, won five Olympic gold medals to become the star of the Sydney Olympics while wearing the Adidas AG Full Body Suit (it resembles a wetsuit). In 2001 he became the first person to win six gold medals in one world championship. His reputation in swimming circles helped raise sales of Adidas swimming suits globally. A new generation of athletes, including basketball superstar Kobe Bryant and soccer legend David Beckham, are recent endorsers for Adidas AG. Spanish golfer Sergio Garcia has an endorsement contract with TaylorMade-adidas Golf. Endorsement contracts are overwhelmingly made with male athletes, but three Women's Tennis Association players—Sania Mirza from India, Ana Ivanovic from Serbia, and Anna Chakvetadze from Russia—all have endorsement deals with Adidas AG.

Reebok International. When the National Basketball Association's prolific scorer Allen Iverson first signed with the Philadelphia 76ers in 1996, he negotiated a ten-year, $50 million endorsement contract with Reebok. In 2001, he got a lifetime extension on that deal. His signature shoe, The Answer, was among the top-selling basketball shoes. Reebok rebuilt its basketball and clothing lines around him.

Among female athletes, the pro-tennis-playing Williams sisters have made endorsement breakthroughs for women. In 2000 Venus Williams signed a five-year, $40 million contract extension with Reebok. At the time, it was considered the richest endorsement deal for a female athlete. In 2005 Reebok signed Canadian hockey phenomenon Sidney Crosby, who has lived up to his billing as the National Hockey League's (NHL) next great player by winning the league's MVP award, the Hart Trophy, in 2007.

Mizuno Corporation. Endorsers for Mizuno are called Mizuno brand ambassadors, and since Mizuno is a TNC manufacturing products for a variety of sports, its brand ambassadors are drawn worldwide from several sports. Luke Donald, a native of England, is one of the brightest young stars on both the PGA and European tours. In 2006 he signed a multiyear contract with the Mizuno Corporation. Two female Ethiopian long-distance runners, Tirunesh Dibaba and Meseret Defar, are Mizuno brand ambassadors. Both have won Olympic and World championships at distances between 3,000 and 10,000 meters. At the 2008 Major League All-Star Game, ten Mizuno brand ambassadors were on the American and National League rosters. Mizuno brand ambassadors with international reputations in professional baseball include Ichiro Suzuki from Japan, Miguel Tejada from the Dominican Republic, Carlos Guillen from Venezuela, and Chipper Jones from the United States.

Nike, Inc. Nike certainly did not create individual athlete endorsements as a sporting goods marketing tool, but it was Nike that raised endorsements to the forefront of sports marketing. With its highly recognized trademarks of "Just do it" and the swoosh logo, Nike sponsors many high-profile athletes and sports teams around the world. The company had the good fortune to sign Michael Jordan just as Nike was on its way up in the sports manufacturing industry and just as Jordan was beginning his professional basketball career. Michael Jordan went on to become one of the most marketed sports figures in history, actually becoming a brand name within the Nike brand (Jordan 2006; La Feber 1999).

Nike's roster of endorsers goes well beyond Michael Jordan. It is a who's who of global sports over the past twenty-five years. The company's first professional athlete endorser was Romanian tennis player Ilie Năstase, and its first track endorser was distance-running legend Steve Prefontaine. Following Michael Jordan, a few of the most renowned Nike endorsers have been soccer players Ronaldinho (Brazilian) and Mia Hamm (American); American basketball players LeBron James and Kobe Bryant; tennis players Roger Federer (Swiss), Rafael Nadal (Spanish), and Maria Sharapova (Russian); Formula One racer Michael Schumacher (German); American cyclist Lance Armstrong; and American golfer Tiger Woods. In 2003 Serena Williams signed a $60 million endorsement deal with Nike, eclipsing the $40 million her sister was receiving from Reebok. Nike signed Serena as not just a tennis player but as a global icon, a trademarked Nike goddess.

After turning pro, Tiger Woods was on his way to affluence by signing a five-year, $40 million endorsement contract with Nike. Over the past fourteen years, he has appeared in many of the sneaker company's advertisements and established his own brand of clothing and shoes. Woods also helped Nike make a big splash in the golf equipment business. In 2009, he was the highest-paid professional athlete, having earned an estimated $100 million from winnings and endorsements. More impressive, that year Woods became sport's first billion-dollar athlete in career earnings, the majority of them coming from endorsements of a variety of products in addition to Nike. Unfortunately for him, near the end of that same year it was publically revealed that Woods had been engaged in a series of martial infidelities. Several corporations withdrew their endorsement deals with, but at the time this book was written, Nike had not dropped him.

Event and Team Sponsorships

Sponsorship involves a company's making a commitment to support a business or an event. Sponsorship marketing by corporations as a component of their brand-management strategy is prevalent in the sporting goods and equipment industry. It has a number of advantages over conventional advertising techniques. One of them is that advertising delivers forthright commercial messages, while sponsorship connects with people in a less direct but more generous way.

Globally, sponsorship spending increased to $43.5 billion in 2008. North American sponsorship spending alone rose to $16.78 billion, with sports sponsorship spending accounting for 69 percent, or $11.6 billion, of the total (Klayman 2008; see also Klayman 2009). The sponsorship of sports activities ranges from local Little League tournaments, to the Union of European Football Associations (UEFA) European Football Championship, to the Olympic Games. The massive scope of sport sponsorship is difficult to convey, but one way is to note that the *Sports Sponsor Fact Book,* which lists sport sponsor profiles, is 550 pages long (Gluskin and Danney 2007).

Global sport sponsorship is "an investment in an individual, event, team or organization with the expectation of achieving certain corporate objectives in multiple countries" (Amis and Cornwell 2005, 2). All of the five sporting goods and equipment manufacturers that this chapter has focused on actively participate in global sports event and team sponsorships. They are TNCs whose marketing strategies target sporting events and teams worldwide; indeed, many of the events and teams they sponsor are international sporting events. As with individual athlete endorsements, each sports manufacturer sponsors dozens of events and teams, so I am only going to identify a couple of the sponsorships in which each of these five sporting goods and equipment firms is involved. Even these few examples clearly illustrate the global scope of sponsorships.

Wilson Sporting Goods. Wilson Golf, a division of Chicago-based Wilson Sporting Goods, sponsors the First Tee of Chicago and the Illinois Junior Golf Association, locally based organizations that have championed the youth golf movement in the Chicago area and throughout the state of Illinois. The mission of the First Tee of Chicago is to introduce the game of golf to inner-city youth and provide ongoing golf instruction to interested juniors free of charge.

Wilson is the Official Sporting Goods Equipment Sponsor of the Breast Cancer Research Foundation (BCRF), a nonprofit organization whose mission is to achieve prevention of and a cure for breast cancer. To date, Wilson has donated nearly $1.5 million to the foundation and has developed a line of Hope racket and golf sports equipment and accessories, from which a portion of the proceeds is directed to the BCRF.

In January 2009 Wilson Sporting Goods announced that the National Collegiate Athletic Association (NCAA) had given Wilson sponsorship rights, making the company Official Soccer Ball Supplier to the NCAA starting immediately. This further enhances the Wilson soccer brand as one of the fastest growing in North and South America.

Adidas AG. In 2008 Adidas and the International Association of Athletics (track and field) Federations (IAAF) announced an eleven-year partnership agreement granting Adidas AG the worldwide sponsorship rights for all IAAF World Athletic Series events from 2009 until 2019. Under the agreement, Adidas will be the official IAAF athletic sponsor and licensed product supplier.

Adidas is the official sponsor and ball supplier for the most important Fédération Internationale de Football Association (FIFA) and UEFA football tournaments, including the 2010 FIFA World Cup in South Africa and the UEFA Champions League.

Reebok International. In 2007 the Bolton Wanderers Football (Soccer) Club, an English professional team that plays in the British Premier League, one of the strongest leagues in Europe, announced that they had signed a new sponsorship agreement with Reebok, which will also continue as naming rights sponsor of Reebok Stadium until 2016.

Reebok sponsors four teams in the Australian Football League: the Fremantle Football Club, the North Melbourne Football Club, the Port Adelaide Football Club, and the Richmond Football Club.

Mizuno Corporation. The Mizuno Corporation is the official sponsor of the Russian men's and women's national and junior volleyball teams. This means the global Mizuno sports brand will be providing the official team kit and footwear for the coming four years, including at the 2012 London Olympics.

In 1998 at the Nagano Olympics, because Mizuno was a Gold Sponsor, 850 athletes from sixteen countries used Mizuno products. Sponsorships usually involve only a single team. In 2005 Mizuno signed a sponsorship contract with China's Liaoning table tennis team.

Nike, Inc. In 1996 Nike signed a ten-year, $100 million sponsorship deal with the Brazilian Football Confederation, the governing body of the Brazilian national soccer team. This agreement was extended through 2018 for an estimated $144 million.

A $506 million sponsorship deal between Nike and the French Football Federation (FFF) in 2008 made Nike the official equipment supplier of the FFF, including France's national soccer team, beginning in 2011 and continuing through the end of the 2017–2018 season.

A 2010 report by Covalent Marketing on celebrity endorsements and brand image illustrate the full extent of Nike's endorsement and sponsorship commitments. That report lists Nike obligations at $3.5 billion in 2009 (Ahuja 2010).

Summary

The sporting goods and equipment manufacturing industry is dominated by a few TNCs, but there are over 4,000 companies in this industry. Thus, the industry is fragmented, largely because there are over a hundred activities classified as sports for which sporting goods and equipment are needed. It is, however, a $285 billion global industry.

Sporting goods and equipment firms have evolved in conjunction with the growth of organized sports. All of the organized sports require the use of apparel, equipment, and accessory items. Factory manufacturing has also been a key component in meeting the needs of both sporting goods companies and sport participants.

The largest sporting goods and equipment TNCs, such as Wilson, Adidas AG, Reebok, Mizuno, and Nike, were all founded by individual entrepreneurs. Through hard work, perseverance, business acumen, and in some cases luck, they were able to grow their companies to the point at which they were selling their productions globally. As the original founders were displaced by death or corporate acquisition, the businesses achieved TNC status.

As the global economy became the driving force in business in the later two decades of the twentieth century, the labor-intensive assembly line phases of product manufacturing shifted to developing—mostly Asian and Central and South American—countries and to a manufacturing system called export-processing manufacturing. Export-processing production costs were cheap, labor protections for workers were absent or not enforced, collective bargaining was not required, and worker safety laws did not prevail. This is widely called the "race to the bottom." For the labor forces in these export-processing counties, this was an example of the other side of globalization—globalization from below.

Sporting goods manufacturers, especially those that had evolved into TNCs, became among the most flourishing export-processing supporters. Those that produced sport products domestically had become a minority by the mid-1990s because most had outsourced their manufacturing to various low-wage developing countries. To make the public aware of the low wages and horrendous working conditions in Nike's Asian footwear factories, the Nike Social Movement was launched in the 1990s. As of 2010 some 800,000 workers were making Nike products in the company's offshore global supply chain.

Sporting goods and equipment manufacturers use individual athletes— mostly global celebrity athletes—to endorse their products. This is a marketing strategy; because the athletes are viewed as opinion leaders, their endorsements may enhance consumer connection with the brand and influence purchase of its products. Sponsorship of sporting events and sports teams by sporting goods manufacturers forms another component of their corporate marketing strategy.

Notes

1. Each of these companies' websites were the primary source of information about them.

2. After Denis G. Arnold and Norman E. Bowie (2003), I define a "sweatshop" as any workplace in which workers are subject to more than one of the following conditions: forced overtime, health and safety risks resulting from employer disregard of employee welfare, coercion, underpayment of earnings, and wages for full-time work that keep workers below the poverty level in that country.

References

Adidas Group. n.d. At a glance: The story of the Adidas Group. Adidas Group. www.adidas-group.com/en/ourgroup/assets/History/pdfs/History-e .pdf.

———. 2007. Supplier. Adidas Group, December 31. www.adidas-group.com/ en/sustainability/performance_data/2007/supplier_a_2007.aspx.

———. 2009. Adidas Group. www.adidasgroup.com/en/home/Welcome. aspx.

Ahuja, Tripti. 2010. Celebrity endorsements and brand image. Covalent Marketing, January 18. www.covalentmarketing.com/blog/read.aspx?blogId=2226.

Amer Sports. 2008. *Amer Sports Annual Report*. Helsinki, Finland: Amer Sports.

Amis, John, and T. Bettina Cornwell. 2005. Sport sponsorship in a global age. In *Global sport sponsorship*, ed. John Amis and T. Bettina Cornwell, 1–17. New York: Berg.

Andreff, Wladimir. 2006. The sporting goods industry. In *Handbook of the economics of sport*, ed. Wladimir Andreff and Stefan Szymanski, 27–39. Northampton, MA: Edward Elgar.

Arnold, Denis G., and Norman E. Bowie. 2003. Sweatshops and respect for persons. *Business Ethics Quarterly* 13 (April): 221–242.

Birley, Derek. 1995. *Land of sport and glory: Sport and British society, 1887–1910*. Manchester, UK: Manchester University Press.

Blackford, Mansel G. 1998. *The rise of modern business in Great Britain, the United States, and Japan*. 2nd ed. Chapel Hill, NC: University of North Carolina Press.

Connor, Timothy. 2002. *We are not machines*. Oxfam Australia. www.caa.org .au/campaigns/nike/reports/machines/index.html.

Cushman, John H. 1998. International business; Nike pledges to end child labor and apply U.S. rules abroad. *New York Times,* May 13. www.nytimes. com/1998/05/13/business/international-business-nike-pledges-to-end-child-labor-and-apply-us-rules-abroad.html.

Danish Consumer Council. 2009. Nike turns a blind eye to factory worker abuses. *Consumer's International,* July 2. www.consumersinternational.org/ Templates/Internal.asp?NodeID=99649.

Donnelly, S. B. 1989. Great leapin' lizards. *Time,* January 9, 50–52.

Egan, Timothy. 1998. The swoon of Swoosh. *New York Times Magazine,* September 13, 69.

Flanagan, Robert J. 2006. *Globalization and labor conditions: Working conditions and worker rights in a global economy*. New York: Oxford University Press.

Gems, Gerald R., Linda J. Borish, and Gertrud Pfister. 2008. *Sports in American history: From colonization to globalization*. Champaign, IL: Human Kinetics.

Global Alliance. 2001. Workers' voices: An interim report on workers' needs and aspirations in nine Nike contract factories in Indonesia. A three-part report of the Global Alliance for workers and communities. California Baptist University, February 22. www.calbaptist.edu/dskubik/nike_rpt.pdf.

Global Exchange. 2001. Still waiting for Nike to do it. Global Exchange, May. www.globalexchange.org/campaigns/sweatshops/nike/NikeReport.pdf.

Gluskin, Jonathan, and Jeremy Danney, eds. 2007. *Sports sponsor fact book 2007*. Chicago: Team Marketing Report.

Hardy, Stephen. 1990. "Adopted by all the leading clubs": Sporting goods and the shaping of leisure, 1800–1900. In *For fun and profit: The transformation of leisure into consumption,* ed. Richard Butsch, 71–101, Philadelphia: Temple University Press.

Harley, Sharon, ed. 2007. *Women's labor in the global economy: Speaking in multiple voices.* New Brunswick, NJ: Rutgers University Press.

Harney, Alexandra. 2008. *The China price: The true cost of Chinese competitive advantage.* New York: Penguin Press.

Horovitz, Bruce. 2002. Pelé scores with endorsement deals. *USA Today,* May 6. www.usatoday.com/money/advertising/2002-05-07-pele.htm.

Human Rights Watch. 2009. *Not yet a workers' paradise: Vietnam's suppression of the independent workers' movement.* Human Rights Watch, May. http://hrw .org/sites/default/files/reports/vietnam0509webwcover.pdf.

International Labour Organization (ILO). 2009. Child labour by sector. ILO. www.ilo.org/ipec/areas/lang-en/index.htm.

Jordan, Michael. 2006. *Driven from within.* New York: Atria.

Klayman, Ben. 2008. North American sponsorship spending seen up in '08. IEG Sponsorship.com, January 22. www.sponsorship.com/About-IEG/IEG-In-The-News/North-American-Sponsorship-Spending-Seen-Up-in-08.aspx.

———. 2009. U.S. sports sponsorship spending likely off in '09. Reuters, February 11. www.reuters.com/article/reutersEdge/idUSTRE51A84T20090211.

Knight, Graham, and Josh Greenberg. 2002. Promotionalism and subpolitics: Nike and its critics. *Management Communication Quarterly* 15 (May): 541–570.

Knorr, Zack. 2007. Nike is leading the race ... to the bottom. AlterNet, March 9. www.alternet.org/workplace/48982.

Korzeniewicz, Miguel. 2008. Commodity chains and marketing strategies: Nike and the global athletic footwear industry. In *The globalization reader,* ed. Frank J. Lechner and John Boli, 163–172. 3rd ed. Malden, MA: Blackwell.

La Feber, Walter. 1999. *Michael Jordan and the new global capitalism.* New York: W. W. Norton.

Le Blanc, Paul. 1999. *A short history of the U.S. working class: From Colonial times to the twenty-first century.* Amherst, NY: Humanity Books.

Lee, Ching Kwan. 2007. *Against the law: Labor protests in China's rustbelt and sunbelt.* Berkeley: University of California Press.

Locke, Richard, Fei Qin, and Alberto Brause. 2006. *Does monitoring improve labor standards? Lessons from Nike.* Cambridge, MA: MIT Sloan School of Management. July.

McDevitt, Patrick F. 2004. *May the best man win: Sport, masculinity, and nationalism in Great Britain and the empire, 1880–1935.* New York: Palgrave Macmillan.

Mizuno. 2009. Mizuno history. Mizuno. www.mizuno.com/aboutus/history
.html.

Mohtashemi, Marjie. 1997. Knight defends firm's Asian wages. Global Exchange
Campaigns, April 30. www.globalexchange.org/campaigns/sweatshops/
nike/protests.html#defends.

Mondore, Scot. 2007. One hundred years of player endorsements: Honus Wagner and Louisville slugger. National Baseball Hall of Fame,
February 19. www.baseballhalloffame.org/news/article.jsp?ymd=
20070219&content_id=859&vkey=hof_news.

Morrow, Don, and Kevin B. Wamsley. 2005. *Sport in Canada: A History.* New
York: Oxford University Press.

Nelson, Daniel. 1995. *Managers and workers: Origins of the twentieth-century
factory system in the United States, 1880–1920.* 2nd ed. Madison: University
of Wisconsin Press, 1995.

Nike. 2009. Company overview. Nike. www.nikebiz.com/company_overview.

NPD Group. 2009. NPD releases global sports market estimate 2009. NPD Group,
July 1. www.wfsgi.org/taggon_cmd.php?_taggon_cmd=popup&aid=458.

Organization for Economic Cooperation and Development (OECD). 1996. *Globalization of industry: Overview and sector reports.* Paris, France: OECD.

Papadopoulos, Nicolas, and Shavin Malhotra. 2007. Export processing zones in
development and international marketing: An integrative review and research
agenda. *Journal of Macromarketing* 27, no. 2: 148–161.

Perrow, Charles. 2005. *Organizing America: Wealth, power, and the origins of
corporate capitalism.* Princeton, NJ: Princeton University Press.

Pitts, Brenda G., and David K. Stotlar. 2007. *Fundamentals of sport marketing.*
3rd ed. Morgantown, WV: Fitness Information Technology.

Pride, William M., and O. C. Ferrell. 2006. *Marketing concepts and strategies.*
Cincinnati, OH: South Western College Pub.

Reebok Human Rights Programs. 2009. Where are our suppliers? Reebok.com.
www.reebok.com/Static/global/initiatives/rights/business/suppliers.
html.

Richman, Josh. 2001. Is Nike still doing it? *Mother Jones,* May 16, 1. www
.motherjones.com/politics/2001/05/nike-still-doing-it.

Roy, William G. 1999. *Socializing capital: The rise of the large industrial corporation in America.* Princeton, NJ: Princeton University Press.

Sage, George H. 1999. Justice do it! The Nike transactional advocacy network:
Organization, collective actions, and outcomes. *Sociology of Sport Journal*
16, no. 3: 206–235.

———. 2004. The sporting goods industry: From struggling entrepreneurs to national businesses to transnational corporations. In *The Commercialisation of sport,* ed. Trevor Slack, 29–51. New York: Routledge.

Schwartz, Nelson D. 2009. Rapid declines in manufacturing spread global anxiety. *New York Times,* March 20, B1.

Senser, Robert. 2009. *Justice at work: Globalization and the human rights of workers.* Bloomington, IN: Xlibris Corporation.

Silverstein, Ken. 2010. Shopping for sweat: The human cost of a two-dollar T-shirt. *Harper's Magazine,* January. http://harpers.org/archive/2010/01/0082784.

————. 2009b. About SGMA. SGMA. www.sgma.com/about.

Sirak, Ron. 2005. The *Golf Digest* 50—on and off the course. *Golf Digest* 56, no. 2: 99–101.

Skurzynski, Gloria. 2008. *Sweat and blood: A history of U.S. labor unions.* Breckenridge, CO: Twenty-First Century Books.

Smit, Barbara. 2008. *Sneaker wars: The enemy brothers who founded Adidas and Puma and the family feud that forever changed the business of sport.* New York: Ecco.

Smith, Shelley. 1989. Grandpa would be pleased. *Sports Illustrated,* August 21, 62–63.

Sporting Goods Manufacturers Association (SGMA). 2009a. *SGMA state of the industry report 2009.* SGMA. www.sgma.com/reports/248_SGMA-State-of-the-Industry-Report-2009.

Swardson, Anne, and Sandra Bugawara. 1996. Asian workers become customers. *Washington Post,* December 30, A1, A16.

Thomas, Woodlief, and Edmund E. Day. 1976. *The growth of manufacturers, 1899 to 1923.* New York: Arno Press.

Thun, Eric. 2008. Globalization and production. In *Global political economy,* ed. John Ravenhill, 346–372. 2nd ed. New York: Oxford University Press.

UNITE! Report. 2000. "Sweatshops behind the swoosh." New York: UNITE!.

United Nations Conference on Trade and Development. 2008. *World investment report 2008: Transnational corporations and the infrastructure challenge.* New York: United Nations.

Urban Community Mission. 1999. Cruel treatment working for Nike in Indonesia. Campaign for Labor Rights, December. www.clrlabor.org/alerts/1999/crueltreatmentworkingfornikeinindonesia.html.

Vamplew, Wray. 1988. Sport and industrialization: An economic interpretation of the changes in popular sport in nineteenth-century England. In *Pleasure, profit, proselytism: British culture and sport at home and abroad, 1700–1914,* ed. J. A. Mangan, 7–20. London: Frank Cass.

Wetzel, Dan, and Don Yaeger. 2000. *Sole influence: Basketball, corporate greed, and the corruption of America's youth.* Boston: Grand Central Publishing.
Wilson. 2010. About Wilson. Wilson. www.wilson.com/wilson/home/index .jsp.
Zieger, Robert H., and Gilbert Gall. 2002. *American workers, American unions: The twentieth century.* 3rd ed. Baltimore: Johns Hopkins University Press.

CHAPTER 5

GLOBAL SPORT AND GLOBAL MASS MEDIA

> The study of the ways in which media and sport interact
> crosses boundaries and can be found in literature con-
> cerned with the sociology of sport, history of sport, gen-
> der studiers, cultural studies, journalism, leisure studies
> and beyond.
>
> —Alina Bernstein and Neil Blain, *Sport, Media,*
> *Culture: Global and Local Dimensions*, 2003, 1.

Sport endorsements and sponsorships are part of the array of methods
employed in the promotion of global sports, and since these tools of sport
promotion are closely linked to the production of sporting goods and
equipment, the previous chapter examined these two parts of the sport-
industry segment model (Figure 1.1)—sport goods production and sport
promotion—together. However, mass communication forms the basis
from which all marketing and promotional strategies are launched in the
global sport industry. Thus, a separate chapter on sport and the global
mass media is warranted.

Mass Communication, Mass Media, and Media Sport

Mass communication is a process by which individuals or institutions
send and receive messages to and from large audiences that can extend

from a local community to the entire world. The term *mass media* refers to the technological tools used to transmit and receive the messages of mass communication. Although these distinctions are real, by written and spoken custom the term *mass media,* or just *media,* is commonly used to refer to the process as well as the technology of the industry of modern communications. What I shall call media sport is one division of this industry. Other major divisions are local, national, and international news, business news, and entertainment and cultural news. This sectoring of the mass media is exemplified by the four sections—News, Money, Sport, and Life—of the United States' self-proclaimed "Nation's Newspaper," *USA Today,* owned by Gannett Corporation, the largest newspaper chain worldwide (Hanson 2008).

Media sport is not isolated or self-contained; instead, it is an integrated part of global mass media commerce. Before turning to global media sport, the main topic of this chapter, I examine the social roles and global organization of the mass media in the contemporary world order. I do this to help readers understand and appreciate the large, vastly complex environment in which media sport operates and functions.

Social Roles of the Mass Media

Communication is the fundamental constituent of our social lives: We talk, listen, read, see, hear, watch, gesture, and so forth. It is a form of social glue bonding people together with common knowledge. Because of worldwide access to newspapers, magazines, books, films, television, and the Internet, the mass media have become a powerful cultural source of information and public debate on matters of national and international importance, as well as a rich source of entertainment. In North America alone there are about 1,450 daily newspapers, with a total paid circulation of some 55 million; Asia has some 2,500 dailies, and Europe, including the United Kingdom (England, Wales, Scotland, and Northern Ireland), has more than 1,400.

Of all North American homes, 98 percent have television sets, and *households* watch more than eight hours of television a day; there are some 11,000 radio stations, and radios (home and automobile) are turned on for over six hours per day. The Internet is now the most frequently used and important source of news in the United States, outweighing newspapers, television, and radio. With digitalization and more than 125 communications satellites sending television signals to every inhabited continent of the world, and with the number of TV sets now exceeding 1.5 billion, both the developed and developing countries of the world are rapidly adopting modern mass media (Nachison 2009).

Two fundamental social roles of the mass media are to communicate information about people and events and to provide entertainment to consumers. In performing these two roles, the media serves two less obvious, but nevertheless important, functions: social integration and social change. To the extent that the media promote shared values and norms, they contribute to social integration. The narrative and broadcast imagery accompanying significant events have the ability to integrate and unify people—however momentarily. Take media usage in the aftermath of September 11, 2001, for example, or the recurring celebrations in countries after media broadcasts of victories in the World Cup and Olympic Games.

The media are not neutral communicators of messages in any of their forms. Instead, they comprise an industry involved in the everyday production and marketing of mass cultural products. This industry's values, norms, and practices interpret and promote mainstream culture and consciousness, thus promoting social integration. Furthermore, advertiser- and stockholder-conscious editors and publishers filter information through a profit motive when making major decisions about media content. A careful analysis of the news pages and broadcast programs reveals lamentably little outside the mainstream of public discourse (Graber 2009; Hanson 2008).

Although the mainstream media tend to be biased toward maintaining the status quo and promoting conventional norms and values, they also print and broadcast information about cutting-edge research, new social practices and values, and critiques of contemporary attitudes and behaviors; thus, they support social change as well. Mere communication about new ideas and events serves as a stimulant for reinterpreting the world and promoting changes in many spheres of life. Nevertheless, calls for fundamental political and economic change go largely unreported or, if reported, are treated as extremist and therefore unacceptable. In every country of the world, however, small media organizations promote progressive, even radical, social change.

Global Organizations and the Mass Media

Each nation in the world has its own system of mass media. In some countries the mass media are solely under the jurisdiction of the government and thus are publicly financed; others have a commercial system in which media organizations are privately owned and operated. Still others have a mixed public and private system of mass communications. Media in dictatorships and one-party countries tend to be under governmental control. Democratically based countries tend to have commercial or mixed systems of mass communications. For example, both Great Britain and Australia have mixed communications systems that began as publicly financed systems but have added commercial sectors. In the United States, with the exception of the Public Broadcasting System and National Public Radio, all of the major mass media outlets are for-profit companies (Banerjee and Seneviratne 2006; Griffin 2005; Turow 2008).

The trend in most countries has been toward an increasing domination of commercial over public control of the mass media. In the early 1990s the trend in British broadcasting was a shift from a public service system toward a predominantly commercial system. Public broadcasters play a large role in the German media landscape, while media ownership in France is shared between the state and other commercial companies. The state is very prominent in broadcasting, while private companies dominate print media. Of the world's major political and economic global powers, the People's Republic of China has the most prominent government involvement in the media; many of the largest media organizations are agencies of the government. Several media scholars have argued that an expanding concentration of global media power is built on systemic commercialism and an accompanying decline in the relative importance of public broadcasting and the applicability of public service standards (Herman and Chomsky 2002; McChesney 2008).

Conglomerate Media Ownership

Accompanying the trend toward private ownership of media organizations, a small group of very large transnational organizations now dominate the global media market, and they have a significant cultural and economic presence worldwide. Massive corporate conglomerates—mostly American based—own newspaper, radio, and television networks and Internet websites. See Box 5.1 about the newspaper industry.

The *Financial Times* identifies the five hundred largest corporations in the world by industry sector each year. Table 5.1 lists the eleven largest corporations in the media sector for 2009. General Electric and Microsoft are two transnational corporations not listed in the *Financial Times*

Box 5.1 Conglomerate Ownership in the Newspaper Industry

At the beginning of the twentieth century, wherever private ownership existed, individuals or partnerships owned most newspapers, and publishers were not particularly wealthy. By mid-century, more than 80 percent of the daily newspapers were still independently owned in Western countries. By 1999, however, less than 20 percent were independently owned. Presently, the prevailing pattern for newspapers is corporate ownership. Indeed, fifteen large newspaper chains own and control more than 50 percent of roughly 1,450 U.S. daily newspapers. The Gannett Corporation, publisher of *USA Today*, is the largest newspaper chain in the world; it publishes 85 daily newspapers, nearly 850 nondaily publications, and *USA WEEKEND*, a weekly newspaper magazine. The company also owns twenty-three television stations, as well as 130 Internet sites in the United States and 80 in the United Kingdom. Operating in the United Kingdom as Newsquest, the second-largest regional newspaper publisher in that nation, it publishes seventeen daily newspapers and more than two hundred weekly newspapers, magazines, and trade publications. Along with each of its daily newspapers, the *USA Today* company operates Internet sites offering news and advertising customized to the market served and integrated with its publishing operations. USAToday.com is one of the most popular news sites on the Web.

In 2006 the McClatchy Company bought Knight-Ridder, at that time the second-largest newspaper chain, with around thirty-five dailies. After selling a dozen Knight-Ridder newspapers, McClatchy now owns thirty dailies and is the second-largest newspaper chain in the United States. Other large chains include Scripps Howard and the Tribune Company. Of course, these are small compared to Rupert Murdoch's News Corp., which owns over 135 daily papers, including the *Wall Street Journal*, and weeklies, including Australia's only national paper, the *Australian*, and the *Times* of Great Britain.

Concentration of power in the newspaper industry is reflected in another way. Behind most of the news in our hundreds of newspapers are but a few highly centralized organizations that feed stories to the local papers—the wire services of the Associated Press, United Press International, Reuters, the *New York Times*, the *Los Angeles Times*, and the *Washington Post*.

media sector, but they are often considered media corporations because a significant part of their operations involve media and communications. Both are larger than any of the corporations listed in the media sector of the *Financial Times* Global 500.

General Electric is the twenty-third-largest nonfinancial corporation in the world (in terms of market value), but it is classified as a general industrials company rather than a media corporation, even though it has ownership in the NBC, CNBC, and MSNBC cable channels. Microsoft, the sixth-largest corporation in the world, is involved in digital media and games, but its industrial sector is classified as software and computer services (*Financial Times* 2009).

Table 5.1 shows Comcast to be the largest firm in the media sector; the company classifies its operations in two reportable segments: cable, which develops, manages, and operates its broadband cable systems, including video, high-speed Internet, and phone services; and programming, which consists primarily of its consolidated national programming networks, including E!, The Golf Channel, VERSUS, G4, and Style. Walt Disney Corporation is the second-largest firm in the media sector; it operates the ABC television network and owns ten television stations, the ESPN Radio network, the Radio Disney network, and forty-six radio stations. Its parks and resorts segment owns and operates the Walt Disney World Resort in Florida and the Disneyland Resort in California. Its studio entertainment segment produces and acquires live-action and animated motion pictures for global distribution.

Table 5.1 World's Largest Media Corporations, 2009

Sector Rank	Global Rank	Company	Country	Market Value (U.S.$ millions)	Net Income (U.S.$ millions)
1	101	Comcast	US	38,539.2	2,547.0
2	115	Walt Disney	US	33,711.0	4,427.0
3	129	Vivendi	France	30,957.4	3,422.8
4	191	DirecTV	US	23,184.1	1,521.0
5	192	Time Warner	US	23,081.5	13,402.0
6	223	Thomson Reuters	Canada/UK	20,695.4	1,405.0
7	268	News Corporation	US	18,165.8	5,387.0
8	329	Reed Elvsevier	Neth/UK	14,992.7	697.0
9	432	Liberty Media	US	11,611.5	4,852.0
10	457	BritishSky Bdcst	UK	10,891.4	−185.9
11	473	Viacom	US	10,611.6	1,251.0

Notes: Sector rank—among media corporations in *Financial Times* Global 500 corporations; global rank—among all corporations in *Financial Times* Global 500 corporations.
Source: Financial Times 2009.

Because the News Corporation has been more globally involved with sports for the past eighteen years than any of the third- through sixth-largest media firms, I shall skip them and comment on News Corp., the seventh-largest media corporation. Billionaire Rupert Murdoch's News Corporation is a transnational media conglomerate, owning the FOX network and several pay satellite services, such as British Sky Broadcasting (BSkyB) and Hong Kong–based STAR TV, which broadcasts over forty program services in seven languages to an estimated 300 million viewers in fifty-three countries across Asia. News Corp. has operations in seven industry segments: filmed entertainment, television, cable network programming, direct-broadcast satellite television, magazines and inserts, newspapers, and book publishing. It is engaged in the production and acquisition of live-action and animated motion pictures for distribution and licensing in all formats in all entertainment media worldwide, as well as in the production and licensing of television programming worldwide. News activities are conducted principally in Asia, Australia, Continental Europe, the Pacific Basin, the United Kingdom, and the United States.

Table 5.1 illustrates that collectively the global media sector is dominated by U.S.-based transnational conglomerates. Below the top eleven media firms are another thirty to forty very large, mostly North American and western European firms, occupying what are called niche and regional markets.

The most obvious consequence of corporate conglomerate ownership of the global media is that control of what people see, read, and hear flows from this powerful cluster of corporations. Speaking about the United States, media analyst Ben Bagdikian (2004) has asserted that most media firms are owned by giant corporate conglomerates, just five of which now supply most of the nation's media fare. Although ownership of newspaper, magazine, book-publishing, radio, and TV organizations is, in theory, available to all, in reality ownership of mass media communication businesses is restricted to those who have the financial means to afford the costs involved.

In the present era those who have the necessary financial resources are a few extremely wealthy individuals and, increasingly, large corporate conglomerates. It is they who are the power holders of the media, and it is they who fashion the daily discourse through that ownership (Flew 2007). Beyond that, media and communications scholars Robert McChesney and Dan Schiller argue that "a transnational corporate-commercial communication" system was "crafted and a new structural logic put in place" as media and communications "became subject to transnational corporate-commercial development" (2003, 6).

Media scholar Terry Flew argues that the media industry plays a central role in globalization processes in three ways. First, media organizations have been among the leaders in globalizing their operations. Second, they have played a significant role in developing the infrastructure of global communications that facilitates global information flows and cross-border commercial transactions. Third, global media are the main conduit through which "we make sense of events in distant places, and the information and images that they carry are central to the development of shared systems of meaning and understanding across nations, regions and cultures" (Flew 2007, 72).

The Global Media Sport Complex

One of the dominant forces accompanying the growing political, economic, and cultural interdependence among the world's nations is an increasing global media/sport-production complex. The development of the global sport "system" is closely linked to the emergence of the global media industry, thus intertwining sport with global media actions. This complex consists of several key groups: media corporations and their personnel, notably broadcasters and journalists; transnational product, marketing, and advertising organizations, such as Coca-Cola, Anheuser-Busch, and IBM; and sport organizations.

Ownership and control of global media/sport communications is in the hands of the same few transnational corporations that dominate mass communications in United States, as Tables 5.1 and 5.2 clearly illustrate. News Corporation's Rupert Murdoch, owner of the FOX television network and a leading player in international sports television, was chosen the most powerful person in sports by *Sporting News* four times in the six years between 1994 and 1999; the same publication also judged him the seventh-most-powerful person in sports during the twentieth century. His power and influence have been maintained through the first decade of the twenty-first century. In a 2007 special report by *Business Week* that listed the most influential people in the world of sports, Murdoch was ranked tenth (Gietschier 1999; *Business Week* 2007).

Several examples will illustrate how the global media/sport/transnational corporate complex works and how it shapes global consumer attitudes, values, and behavior. First, the global media/sports-production

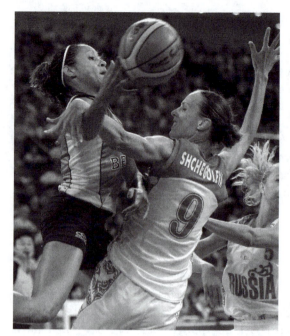

Russia's Tatiana Shchegoleva fouls Brazil's Adriana Pinto during a women's basketball game at the Beijing 2008 Olympics. The Russian team took the bronze medal at these Olympics. (Associated Press Photo/Dusan Vranic)

Joyce Silva, left, of Brazil's Rio de Janeiro Vôlei team, spikes the ball against Jelena Alajbeg, right, of Romania's Metal Galati team during the Women's Top Volley International tournament in Basel, Switzerland, December 2009. Rio de Janeiro Vôlei won the 2009 championship. (Associated Press Photo/Keystone/ Georgios Kefalas)

The Leverkusen team celebrates their first goal during the German first-division Bundesliga soccer match between Bayer Leverkusen and Borussia Moenchengladbach in Leverkusen, Germany, December 2009. (Associated Press Photo/ Mark Keppler)

Francios Beauchemin, right, of the Toronto Maple Leafs elbows Jarome Iginla of the Calgary Flames during an NHL hockey game in Calgary, January 2010. There is a fine line between legal and illegal violence in the NHL. (Associated Press Photo/The Canadian Press, Jeff McIntosh)

The International Association of Athletics Federations (IAAF) is the world governing federation for track and field (internationally known as athletics). Female interest in the events of this sport has skyrocketed. Young women throughout the world train to become Olympians. (iStockphoto)

Brazil's President Luiz Inacio Lula da Silva, second left, Brazilian soccer icon Pele, right, celebrate after the announcement that Rio de Janeiro has won the bid to host the 2016 Summer Olympic Games during the International Olympic Committee session at the Bella Center in Copenhagen, October 2, 2009. Chicago, Madrid, and Tokyo were the other top contenders for the right to host the 2016 Summer Olympic Games. (Associated Press Photo/Charles Dharapak)

USA forward Chris Bosh (12) defends China center Yao Ming during their basketball game at the Beijing 2008 Olympics. Yao Ming plays professional basketball for the NBA Houston Rockets. He has been named to the All-NBA Team five times. (Associated Press Photo/Eric Gay)

A popular part of the pageantry of international sporting events is the flags of the participating countries flying over the venues. Collectively, these symbols of nations illustrate the globalized nature of contemporary sport. (iStockphoto)

process spreads American sports around the world, with the commercials accompanying televised events advertising nonsport commodities (i.e., Coca-Cola, McDonalds, Nike, and Visa). The growing global popularity of American sports, such as American football, baseball, and basketball, in countries throughout the world is partially attributable to the various corporations whose television advertising is associated with those sporting events.

Second, when British television began showing American football games on a regular basis in 1982, the programs attracted an average viewer audience of 1.1 million. By 1990 the viewing audience had more than doubled to 2.39 million. The marketing strategies of the National Football League (NFL), Anheuser-Busch, and a British television company were instrumental in this growth and in the emergence of an American football subculture in English society (Maguire 1999).

Third, in describing two studies of sport heroes among New Zealand youth, sports scholar David Andrews and his colleagues reported that Michael Jordan was by far the number one choice. According to the researchers, New Zealand teens' "knowledge of Jordan appears dependent upon sports highlight programs, news, and the myriad of television commercials that reveal his corporate alliances"; they add that "perhaps the most important finding was simply that all [respondents] could identify Jordan as an athlete or, at least, as an American corporate icon" (1996, 433).

Fourth, Eurosport, a European sports cable and satellite network owned and operated by a French media company, the TF1 Group, broadcasts in over fifty countries in twenty different languages. It is the largest European sports network, and its programs are broadcast in most countries across Europe, usually in the local language. Although most European countries also have domestic sports channels, Eurosport is the only pan-European sports channel.

There are conflicting interpretations of the role of the global media/sport complex on the world order. As I said in Chapter 1, several sport-studies scholars have suggested that the social process of global sport development produced what they call "Americanization," which suggests a one-way process by which American cultural products, forms, and meanings are imposed on other nations and their cultures. Thus, Americanization is envisioned as a process involving the political, economic, and cultural diffusion of American methods, values, and social forms at the expense of domestic cultures.

I shall not repeat the arguments for and against the Americanization thesis here because I summarize them in Chapter 1, except to say that analysts generally agree that during the last half century there has been a strong American presence in many aspects of Asian, European, and Middle Eastern economies and cultures, especially through American transnationals (e.g., Coca-Cola, Esso, Ford, Heinz, Microsoft) that sell their products, marketing strategies, and advertising around the world.

In terms of cultural pursuits, American mass media, especially television and increasingly the Internet, has had some impact on cultural thought and lifestyles throughout the world. Televised American sports, since they are widely distributed globally, have obviously played a role in shaping some attitudes and values. More specifically, America's global sports presence has taken several forms: the spread of American sports forms, the adoption of sports marketing strategies along American lines, and the migration of American sports personnel.

Some thus consider the United States a major influence on the production and distribution of a globalized sports model, along with the practices and values that accompany it. But a statement by sport sociologists Steven Jackson and David Andrews, based on their study of the National Basketball Association (NBA) and its corporate and intertextual alliances in New Zealand, eloquently synthesizes the cultural role of American global media sport. They assert that the worldwide circulation of American sporting practices "is not only contributing to the flow of global cultural products and practices, it is also leading to the rearticulations of national and local cultural identities.... Hence, rather than causing the dissolution of local identities through the establishment of a homogeneous global culture, the NBA may actually play a role in energizing multiple popular and local cultures" (1999, 40). In effect, they view the Americanization thesis as an oversimplification of popular-culture transmission.

Articulations Between the Mass Media and Sport

The global media and sport have become mutual beneficiaries of one of the world's most lucrative associations. Information, communication, social integration, and social change, the four social roles of the media, are manifested in their association with sports. First, the media supply information about sports—for example, sports events results and statistics about individual players and teams. Second, they communicate that in various ways. Reading about, listening to, or watching sporting events gives individuals opportunities to escape temporarily the burdens and frustrations that bind them to reality. Media sport has the perfect combination for communicating entertainment, including controlled violence, excitement, and lots of audio and visual power.

Social integration, one of the media's subtle roles, is often played out through conversations about sport. One can ask almost any stranger about sports or well-known sporting events, and he or she will likely know the relevant information from having read about it, heard about it, or seen it in the media; consequently, the conversation can be sustained and sometimes transformed into a more enduring social relationship. Media sport, then, provides a communal focus whereby large segments of the population can share common norms, rituals, ceremonies, and values.

Finally, media play a significant role in social change as it relates to sports. The media have played a role in the creation of some sports, the popularity of others, and rule changes in others; media sports has also been on the forefront of social changes through clothing fashion, language, and entertainment preferences.

Media Technology and Commercial Sport Evolve Together

Little did the inventors of advanced technical means of communication realize how their inventions would become associated with sport. The rise of modern commercial sports and technologically based media evolved simultaneously and symbiotically. Each supplied the other with the essential resources for development: capital, audiences, promotion, and content. Media sport emerged to communicate sports information through the print media and, later, through broadcasting about sports via the electronic media.

Print Media. Johannes Gutenberg invented movable type in the mid-fifteenth century. As his invention was refined during the following centuries, the ability of the printing press to produce reading material quickly and cheaply increased and made possible the growth of the publishing industry. According to some historians, newspaper coverage of sport can be found as far back as the eighteenth century. Michael Harris found that "cricket was drawn into the content of the London newspapers" by the mid-eighteenth century as part of the "widening circle of commercialization within what might ... be described as the leisure industries" (1998, 19, 24). In the mid-nineteenth century, newspapers began periodic coverage of sports events, but not until the 1890s did the first sports sections become a regular feature in newspapers. In the United States, William Randolph Hearst, publisher of the *New York Journal,* is often credited with developing the first modern sports section. Newspaper sports sections began to appear at about the same time in England and Europe.

Over the past hundred years, the association between the newspaper and sport has become so well established that in popular newspapers throughout the world, sports coverage often constitutes almost 50 percent of each issue. Furthermore, newspaper sports sections have not been curtailed by the growth of either radio or television; instead, these have strengthened rather than replaced newspaper sports sections.

Even before the advent of the sports section, magazines and books chronicled the activities of athletes and teams. In 1820 Pierce Egan, a British journalist, started publishing a monthly journal titled *Life in London,* which regularly included sporting topics. Between the late 1770s and mid-1900s, there arose a widespread interest in journals of all kinds, and magazines cropped up everywhere to exploit the popular interest in horse racing, hunting, fishing, and athletic sports. The momentum of sports literature accelerated in the 1830s, and the first prominent sports journal in the United States, *Spirit of the Times,* began publication in 1831. This journal featured horse racing in particular but also reported on other sports and indirectly helped to establish what was to become "the national pastime"—baseball (Brake and Demoor 2009).

Magazines specializing in sports have been standard fare in the publishing business for the past one hundred years, with almost every sport having its own publication. Indeed, one indication that a new sport is rising in popularity is the appearance of a magazine describing its techniques and strategies, profiling its best players, and advertising equipment and accessories for playing or watching the sport. *Sports Illustrated,* founded in 1954 and currently the best-selling sports magazine, is read by over 25 million adults each week.

Books on field sports, horse racing, and popular games have been published for over two hundred years. Among the most famous of these is Joseph Strutt's *Sports and Pastimes of the People of England,* published in 1801. This volume of over three hundred pages describes everything from children's games to an incredible variety of adult games and sports. The same Pierce Egan who published the journal *Life in London* also wrote one of the first full-length books about sports in the early nineteenth century, *Pierce Egan's Book of Sports and Mirror of Life: Embracing the Turf, the Chase, the Ring, and the Stage* (1836).

Newspaper sports sections, sport magazines, and books about sports continue to have significant linkages to sport, but the electronic media—radio, motion pictures, television, and the Internet—have made dramatic inroads into the traditional information and entertainment functions of the printed media.

Radio. Wireless telegraphy, invented at the end of the nineteenth century, served as the technological foundation for radio, television, and the Internet. In 1897 the inventor of wireless telegraphy, an Italian by the name of Guglielmo Marconi, obtained a patent for his invention in England, and within a year he had used that technology to send a wireless telegraph account of a sporting event, the 1898 Kingstown Regatta, a rowing race on the Thames in England, to the *Dublin Daily Express* (Smith 2001). Only a few years separated the invention of wireless technology and the advent of radio sportscasts. From the mid-1920s to the early 1950s, radio reigned supreme in broadcasting sports news and live sports events.

Radio's popularity as a medium for sports information and entertainment declined with the advent of network television in the 1950s. Nevertheless, today some 11,000 radio stations in North America broadcast more than 700,000 hours of sport annually. Sports call-in shows, interviews with sports celebrities, and play-by-play game reporting are popular throughout the world and have sustained the role of radio in sports.

Sirius Satellite Radio initially began operating in 2002 in the United States and Canada, but it quickly globalized its broadcasting with extensive programming on multiple channels that cover a variety of genres. One feature of Sirius's business strategy has been to cover global sports content. Currently, Sirius has exclusive satellite radio broadcasting rights to most North American professional sports teams and several major college sports teams. It also broadcasts select English Premier League soccer matches and Union of European Football Associations (UEFA) Champions League matches in Europe, which in 2008 included the UEFA European Football Championship—Euro 2008.

In the past decade twenty-four-hour, all-sports radio stations have created excitement about sport in many countries. In the United States there are now more than 435 all-sports radio stations, as well as 7 in Canada, devoted almost solely to discussion, debate, and analysis of athletes and teams by both hosts and callers.

In Europe, *Talk on Sport* with Steve Gilmour and Mat Court is Talk Radio Europe's premier sports show. The hosts focus on the latest sporting news, results, opinions, and gossip (Dempsey 2006; Owens 2006). The United Kingdom's national commercial sports radio station, talkSPORT, is that country's number one sports talk radio station. The hosts broadcast the latest scores and breaking news from the world of football (soccer), as well as keep listeners up-to-date with everything else in the world of UK sports.

Motion Pictures. As popular as movies are with the general public, movies about sports have been rather rare. However, in recent decades several sports films have received critical acclaim; *Rocky* and *Chariots of Fire* won Oscars for best picture. In 2009 two of the most acclaimed movies had sport themes—*The Blind Side*, about American football, and *Invictus*, about rugby in South Africa. Increasingly, sports films are transcending mere entertainment and attempting to explore broader social issues of power, race, masculinity, and gender relations.

Television. The technology to produce telecasts was developed during the 1930s, but World War II delayed the large-scale growth of commercial television for nearly a decade. When commercial television did start to grow, the rate was staggering. In 1950 less than 1 percent of households in the world had television sets. In 2009 over 2 billion television sets are in use worldwide. That is three televisions for every ten people. The most television sets in use are in China, with 500 million. There are forty televisions for every one hundred people there. In the United States, with the second-highest television count of 280 million televisions, there are about ninety-six televisions for every one hundred people, or nearly one per person. According to Nielsen Media Research, on average, North American households watch more than 8 hours of television per day, and the average individual watches 4.5 hours per day (Colvin 2007).

Sport made a union with television while the tube was still in its infancy. The first live television coverage of a sporting event took place in Germany at the 1936 Berlin Olympic Games. The German post office broadcast over seventy hours of live television coverage to special viewing rooms throughout Berlin, where the public could view the events live. Technological limitations prevented the local Olympic organizing committee from selling the international broadcast rights. The British Broadcasting Corporation (BBC) made the first sports television broadcast in 1937 when it telecast the Wimbledon tennis championships to 20,000 British households with television sets (Barney, Wenn, and Martyn 2004; Genova 2009).

Before discussing the role that television plays in contemporary global media sport, I explain the overlap of ownership in media organizations and sport organizations. I believe this is important to understanding the structural foundation for governance and decision making in both of these industries.

Overlapping Ownership of Media and Sport Organizations

The financial association between the media and commercial sports is a classic example of business interdependence. This is especially evident in terms of cross-ownership; the media and sports have intimate ownership relationships. Several owners of media corporations are also owners, or shareholders, of professional sport teams. In 2000 twenty-nine North American major-league teams were wholly or partially owned by media corporations. In France, Greece, Italy, the United Kingdom, and most European countries, media firms have ownership in soccer teams (Kilbride 2000; see also Gerrard 2004). Table 5.2 illustrates the cross-ownership between sport organizations, media corporations, and individuals with media ties.

Rupert Murdoch is the media mogul with arguably the broadest experience in global sport. In the mid-1990s, when Murdoch was making his first forays into sports ownership, he called sports the "cornerstone of our worldwide broadcasting" efforts (Bellamy 1998, 77). Two sport-studies researchers confirmed Murdoch's judgment, saying, "There is no one in the media world who has a greater commitment to the commercial exploitation of sport than Murdoch" (Rowe and McKay 1999, 191).

Murdoch's portfolio of sports acquisitions and sales is too extensive to list in detail here, but the following provides examples of several of his sport ownership positions:

- In 1990 Murdoch's News Corp. acquired control of BSkyB, a leading subscription television service in Ireland and the United Kingdom. In 1992 BSkyB paid £191 million (approximately $355 million)[1] for a five-year deal to televise live games of the newly founded English Premier Football (soccer) League. Then, in 1997 Murdoch agreed to pay £670 million (approximately $1.1 billion) for another four years of televising English Premier League games. In its most recent contract, BSkyB retained its share of live Premier League broadcast rights in the United Kingdom for 2010 to 2013 for £1.7 billion (approximately $2.5 billion).

Table 5.2 Examples of Media/Communications Corporations with Whole or Part Ownership in Professional Sports, 2000 to 2009

Owners/Corporations/Industry	Teams
Arturo "Arte" Moreno	
Radio/News/Talk Sports	MLB's Los Angeles Angels of Anaheim
Liberty Media Group	MLB's Atlanta Braves
Rogers Communication	MLB's Toronto Blue Jays
Comcast/Spectacor	NBA's Philadelphia 76ers, NHL's Philadelphia Flyers
Madison Square Garden LP	NBA's New York Knicks, NHL's New York Rangers
Silvio Berlusconi	
Media Properties	AC Milan European (Italian) Soccer Club
Ackerley Group	NBA's Seattle Supersonics
News Corporation	National Rugby League, the top league of professional rugby league clubs in Australia; ownership stakes in five English Premier League soccer clubs
Anschutz Entertainment	Major League Soccer's Los Angeles Galaxy, Houston Dynamo (50 percent), Los Angeles Kings, Colorado Rapids; American Hockey League's Manchester Monarchs; Germany's Eisbären Berlin and Hamburg Freezers (ice hockey); New Los Angeles Lakers (minority interest), WNBA's Los Angeles Sparks (49 percent); Sweden's Hammarby IF (soccer)
Nintendo (Japan)	MLB's Seattle Mariners
AOL Time Warner	NBA's Atlanta Hawks
Cablevision Systems	
Corporation	NBA's New York Knicks
Paul Duffen	
Various Media	English Premier League's Hull City Association Football Club
Walt Disney	NHL's Anaheim Ducks
Paul Allen	
Telecommunications	NFL's Seattle Seahawks; NBA's Portland Trailblazers; MLS's Seattle Sounders

- In 1998 BSkyB bid to buy ownership in Manchester United, one of the most successful and popular soccer clubs in the world, triggering a public outcry against the acquisition. As a result, the United Kingdom's Monopoly and Mergers Commission ruled against Murdoch's bid on the grounds that it decreased broadcasting competitiveness and was not in the public interest. However, partial ownership of Premiership teams is permitted, and BSkyB acquired ownership stakes in several Premier League teams, including Manchester United, Leeds United, Sunderland, and Chelsea.

- In 1993 Murdoch's FOX network stunned the media sport world by outbidding CBS for the rights to broadcast NFL football for four years. FOX's coverage started in the 1994 season. In 1998 a new eight-year contract for NFL television rights was signed for $17.6 billion, divided between ABC/ESPN, FOX, and CBS.
- In 1997 Rupert Murdoch bought Major League Baseball's (MLB) Los Angeles Dodgers for $350 million. Murdoch planned to use his sports holdings for overseas broadcasts, noting that the Dodgers in particular had a globally recognizable brand name. In 2004, News Corp. sold the team.
- Presently, Murdoch jointly (with the Australian Rugby League) owns the National Rugby League (NRL), the top professional rugby league in Australasia. NRL competition is contested by sixteen teams, fifteen based in Australia and one based in New Zealand, and is the Southern Hemisphere's elite rugby league championship.
- Besides sport-team and league ownership and various sports broadcasting rights, Murdoch's News Corp. also owns FOX Sports Net (FSN), a conglomeration of U.S. cable TV regional sports networks. In 1996 Murdoch cobbled together several other media affiliates and created FOX Sports Net, renamed simply FSN in 2004. Most FSN networks attempt to acquire the play-by-play broadcast rights to major sports teams in regional markets. In addition to local play-by-play coverage, FSN networks create pre- and postgame programs and weekly magazine shows about teams to attract viewers. FSN's *The Best Damn Sports Show Period* and *Final Score* are staples for dedicated fans.

For more details about Murdoch's experiences in sports ownership, see Michael Wolff (2008) and Neil Chenoweth (2001).

The other media-related owner with a large stake in sport-team ownership is Philip Anschutz (oil, railways, telecommunications), who founded the Anschutz Corporation in 1965. The enterprise was initially involved in oil and gas drilling, but over the years Anschutz diversified his interests into media and entertainment, which today includes a subsidiary, the Anschutz Entertainment Group (AEG). Table 5.2 provides a sample of AEG ownership of sports teams; additionally, the corporation owns some of the world's most profitable sports and entertainment venues.

The Symbiosis Between Television and Sport

Sport and television have been growing "side by side for half a century, profiting from both the convergence and the complementarity of their interests: sport is a pool of programmes and audiences for television, which is itself a financial pool and a vehicle for the promotion of sport" (Bolotny and Bourg 2006, 112). In the beginning, television needed sport more than sport needed television. Sport was perfect content for the networks, first as a means of selling more television sets—NBC and CBS were both involved in the business of making and selling them—and then as a way of increasing audiences. Sport broadcasting was a means for networks to attract large audiences, as well as an ideal way to raise the profile of sports events and build team and league recognition.

Spectators consume sport to a far greater extent through television than through personal attendance at events. Garry Whannel, director of the Centre for International Media Analysis at the University of Bedfordshire, synthesizes the salience of sport for television, saying that "in a world dominated by and in many ways defined by media imagery, it is in no small part sport that drives television—it is one of the primary forms pushing the commodification of television ... [and] the only viable pay-per-view form of television" (2008, 200).

The most dramatic programming trend in television has been the enormous increase in sports coverage. French researchers at the Centre for the Law and Economics of Sport argue that "the increasing penetration of 'sporting' events in different areas of the world, on the one hand, and the increase in the number of [television] channels, on the other, makes it possible to understand the exponential growth in the number of hours devoted to sport on television" (Bolotny and Bourg 2006, 115). To provide an example of this growth, they say that the amount of sports programming on French television multiplied by more than 140 times between 1968 and 1999, from 232 hours in 1968 to 32,640 hours in 1999. In the United States in the early 1980s, about 1,200 hours of televised sports were broadcast annually, and free-to-air television was the dominant platform. Today, more than 60,000 hours of sports are televised annually by four major free-to-air networks as well as pay-TV platforms, such as cable, pay-per-view (PPV), and satellite television, along with various digital channels and local sports cable networks (Hiestand 2009). Table 5.3 displays the variety of sports TV that make up the TV menu.

Table 5.3 The Sports Television Menu

Original major networks	ABC—Wide World of Sports (1961) NBC—Olympic Games (1980) CBS—Sunday afternoon football
New major networks	FOX—FOX Sports, formed in 1994 NFL Network
Regional sports networks	Team-owned channels: YES Network, Altitude Sports Regional cable networks: Comcast Sports Net Chicago, FOX Sports Net Pittsburgh
Cable sports networks	ESPN, Versus (previously called OLN)
Superstations that broadcast sports	TBA, WGN
Single sports channels	NFL Network, Golf Channel, NBATV, Tennis Channel
Satellite TV	NFL Sunday Ticket (by DirectTV; subscriptions give viewers access to NFL games)

Initiative Worldwide, an advertising service, reported that Italy's soccer World Cup final win over France in July 2006 was television's most-watched sports event of that year, drawing more than twice as many viewers as any other program. More than 600 million viewers watched some part of the Berlin match in which Italy claimed its fourth title. The championship game relegated the Super Bowl to second spot in the 2006 ratings (Cone 2006).

The Associated Press (2008) reported that 4.7 billion viewers—more than two out of three people worldwide—tuned in for the Beijing Olympics for at least some of the seventeen days of television coverage. This viewership was one-fifth larger than the 3.9 billion who watched the 2004 Olympic Games in Athens. Nielsen TV Ratings said China, the host nation, had more viewers than any other nation, logging an audience reach of 96 percent among its population of 1.3 billion. NBC reported that 215 million Americans—more than 70 percent of the population—tuned in on that network to the 2008 Beijing Olympics, which took the record as the most-viewed event in American television history.

PPV television has been a growing reality throughout Europe and North America since the mid-1990s. In 1992 BSkyB secured its first contract with the English Premier League (soccer), giving it exclusive rights to live broadcasts of Premier League matches on pay-TV. A series of new contracts have been concluded up to the present. In Germany, Italy, and Spain, soccer was used as bait to establish pay-TV, which seems poised to become an increasingly popular form of sports telecasting (Szymanski and Zimbalist 2005).

Some TV analysts believe PPV will become the norm for sports broadcasting of major sporting events. Indeed, in a way it already has. NFL Sunday Ticket, available on satellite or cable, costs approximately $300 per season; for that subscribers get every out-of-market nonnationally televised NFL game. Baseball has the MLB Network, basketball has the NBA Network, ice hockey has the NHL Network, and intercollegiate athletics has the CBS Sports Network. ESPN GamePlan is the ultimate college football PPV package. Available on cable, satellite, and the Internet, it provides access to a handful of games per week and provides a nice alternative to the local game of the week.

The U.S. Olympic Committee (USOC) made a surprising announcement—surprising even to the International Olympic Committee (IOC)—during the summer of 2009 that it was launching a U.S. Olympic network that would premiere in 2010 with availability to about 10 million digital-cable subscribers. Just as surprising, within two months of the first announcement, the USOC postponed plans for its own television network after the IOC expressed objections to it.

All sports news channels are the newest innovation in sports television. ESPNews and CNN/SI began this form of twenty-four-hour sports coverage in the fall of 1996. They do not carry live sports events. Instead, they telecast only sports news.

Despite the many problems encountered by the infant television industry, it grew enormously in a short time, and television is now by far the most popular and most time-consuming leisure activity in the United States.

In a global context, televised sports programs are attractive to media marketers who take part in the financing of important sporting events because it provides their firms with worldwide public exposure and is a significant source of indirect commercial revenue.

Enhancing Sport Revenue via Television

Prior to the advent of television, professional sport throughout the world was only a skeleton of what it would become, and most professional teams, clubs, and leagues that did exist were struggling financially. Television-rights deals were the major force behind the expansion and affluence of today's commercial sports. For example, in England the Football League was the top-level league in that sport from its founding in the 1888 until the late 1980s. For a variety of reasons, mostly revolving around financial instability, a radical restructuring was needed to take advantage of expanding opportunities for television revenue. In 1992, the top twenty-two clubs split away to form the Football Association Premier League, leaving it free to organize its own broadcast and sponsorship agreements. As I noted above, the Premier League negotiated television-rights contracts with BSkyB worth £191 million ($355 million) over five years. While that was viewed as a huge contract at the time, under the current contract, from 2010 to 2013, BSkyB and Setanta, a sports broadcaster based in Ireland, have paid a staggering £1.7 billion ($2.5 billion) to televise the matches.

Another example: There were only sixteen MLB teams in the 1950s, and no new teams had been added in more than fifty years; now there are thirty teams. This expansion and baseball's prosperity have been largely due to television. Similar patterns can be seen in American professional football, basketball, and hockey. All of these sports entered the 1950s as struggling enterprises with fewer than ten franchises each, and neither the owners nor the players made much money. These sports now have more than twenty-five franchises each, and all have expansion plans. Television contributes a substantial portion of every league's revenues. Professional golf, tennis, soccer, and other professional sports either did not exist or were inconsequential prior to the infusion of large sums of television money.

The extent to which professional sport has become dependent upon television revenue is captured in remarks frequently made by sports executives, comments like, "There is no way we could survive without television" or "If sports lost television revenues, we'd all be out of business." Indeed, so many pro sports organizations have built their budgets around TV income that if television ever did withdraw its money, the entire pro sports structure in its present form would collapse (Gorman and Calhoun 2004; Fort 2006).

Professional sports owners have not been the only beneficiaries of this windfall. Television money has increased athletes' incomes as well. Pro athletes' salaries have tripled or even quadrupled; television money has largely made it possible for them to command their enormous salaries and endorsements. Table 5.4 lists the highest-earning athletes in the world in 2009 according to SI.com (Freedman 2009a, 2009b).

These spectacular incomes of contemporary professional athletes have a very high correlation with the increases in broadcast television rights. Television supports sports. TV networks move in with their money and

Table 5.4 The Highest-Earning Athletes in the World in 2009

Name	Sport	Country	Pay (US$ millions)
Tiger Woods	Golf	United States	100
Phil Mickelson	Golf	United States	52
David Beckham	Soccer	England	45
LaBron James	Basketball	United States	42
Kimi Raikkonen	Formula One auto racing	Finland	40
Manny Pacquiao	Boxing	Philippines	40
Lionel Messi	Soccer	Argentina	40
Alex Rodriguez	Baseball	United States	39
Fernando Alonso	Formula One auto racing	Spain	35
Shaquille O'Neal	Basketball	United States	35

Sources: Freedman 2009a, 2009b.

support sports in a style that would have been unbelievable just a generation ago.

The Market for Broadcast Rights

The first objective of private media corporations is profit, and profit comes from selling the published or broadcast product to consumers and advertisers. Because people throughout the world read about, listen to, and watch sports in huge numbers, the sport industry is a lucrative means of making profit for the media industry. For newspapers and magazines, sport coverage helps sell these publications because many people enjoy reading about sports. The situation is different for radio and TV; sporting events—such as NFL games or Manchester United soccer matches—are the product being sold.

Sports organizations sell their sports events to radio and television networks in the form of "broadcast rights." Indeed, television-rights fees have become the main source of income for many sports, and sports are a key factor in attracting television audiences. In fact, the search for broadcast-rights revenues has come to dominate the revenue-seeking structure of the professional sport industry (Mondello 2006). Two European economists have declared, "In Europe, football rights have been the driving force in the development of pay-TV, and in Britain the acquisition of exclusive rights for live Premier League matches was a key element in

Sky's strategy to dominate the satellite television industry" (Jeanrenaud and Késenne 2006, 7).

In Europe, broadcasting rights often make up 30 percent or more of a soccer club's total revenue. In Germany, television-rights fees account for about 40 percent of the total income of professional soccer clubs (Parlasca 2006). In Italy's Serie A league, a professional soccer league at the top echelon of the Italian soccer-league system, television rights account for 37 percent of a club's revenue. In the United Kingdom, television income is particularly important for soccer: On average, it accounts for 42 percent of revenue for an English Premier League club (Smith 2009). In the United States the NFL derives about 50 percent of its revenues from its long-term national television, cable, and satellite broadcasting contracts (Leone 2008).

Once media organizations have bought the rights to broadcast specific sports events, they then sell advertising time to corporations wishing to advertise their products. Corporations that have bought the advertising time use it to advertise their products during "commercial breaks" that periodically interrupt broadcast sports events. Some media analysts claim that radio and TV networks are actually selling advertisers *audiences*—the listeners and viewers. In this view, radio and TV audiences—based on their predicted size and demographic characteristics—are assigned a monetary value by media organizations and sold to corporate advertisers.

Regardless of how the practice is viewed, media organizations sell billions of dollars worth of advertising for broadcasting sporting events worldwide. Indeed, wherever corporate advertising during sports events is popular, it accounts for a substantial amount of radio and TV network revenues and abundant profits for the media industry. Realizing the popularity of broadcast sports, sport organizations have been successful at negotiating large contracts with media organizations for the rights to broadcast events. This, in turn, helps make commercial sports profitable.

TV networks have been able to charge astonishing advertising fees because sports events are extremely popular; and the larger the anticipated audience for a sports event, the larger the broadcasting-rights fees charged by the networks, and telecasting fees have escalated dramatically. For example,

- NBC and the European Broadcasting Union television broadcast-rights fees for the Winter and Summer Olympic Games rose from $1.5 billion in 1998 and 2000 to $2.7 billion for 2010 and 2012.

- World Cup broadcasting rights increased from $126 million in 1998 to 1.4 billion in 2006 to $2.8 billion for the 2010 World Cup final in South Africa.
- Broadcast revenue for the UEFA football (soccer) championship rose from $403 million for UEFA Euro 2004 to $576.5 million for UEFA Euro 2008. UEFA comprises fifty-three national football associations and is itself recognized by the Fédération Internationale de Football Association (FIFA) as one of six continental federations.
- Table 5.5 lists the sports broadcasting-rights contracts for two consecutive World Cup and Olympic Games.

Major television networks, superstations, cable sports stations, and local TV stations have bankrolled commercialized global team sports with a veritable bonanza of dollars. Contracts like these have made the commercial sports industry very profitable, resulting in expanded franchises, higher salaries, and all-around plush lifestyles for many in the global sport industry. In exchange for the broadcast-rights fees, the networks gain credibility as the copromoters of sporting events, secure "must-buy" programming for advertisers, and limit competitors' access to major sports events.

In addition to the broadcasting-rights fees paid by media organizations, corporations in other industries—from breakfast cereals to automobiles—spend extravagantly on advertising during sports events in order to create a demand for their products. Broadcast sporting events are immensely popular and attract large audiences because many people are interested in the beauty and drama of sports events, which are more exciting and suspenseful than most other broadcast programming. Thus, audiences who hear and see the broadcast commercials become consumers of the

Table 5.5 Sports Broadcasting-Rights Contracts for Two Consecutive World Cup and Olympic Games

Sporting Event	Broadcasting Rights
World Cup	
1994 and 1998	€157 million (approximately $190 million)
2002 and 2006	€1.84 billion (approximately $1.73 billion)
Olympic Games	
2006 (winter) and 2008 (summer)	$1.057 billion
2010 (winter) and 2012 (summer)	$2.004 billion

products and help the advertisers realize a profit. So sports are a natural setting for corporate advertising.

The major U.S. national TV networks that dominate sports broadcasting offer pay-TV (cable subscription) broadcasts of top commercial sports events. In Europe the majority of the top national-league-soccer championship sports broadcast rights have gone to pay-TV. On the other hand, in France, Germany, and the United Kingdom, live sports events of national soccer tournaments are shown exclusively on pay-TV, usually on PPV. Pay-TV broadcasting in Italy began in 1993, and by the end of that decade, all league matches had become PPV. Spain has some broadcasting of live national-league matches on free television, but most of the live broadcast rights to the national league in Spain had migrated to pay-TV by 2000.

The UEFA Champions League has a mix of free-to-air and pay-TV programming. For example, in the 2009 Barcelona versus Manchester United UEFA Champions League final, FOX Soccer Channel (subscription pay-TV) broadcast seven hours of coverage but did not broadcast the actual game. ESPN (cable TV) broadcast the game to 115 nations using fourteen commentators in three languages with pregame segments scattered throughout its programming on ESPN and ESPN2. In 2009 ESPN acquired the rights for the first time to broadcast 115 English Premier League games live in Britain over the next four seasons.

Transnational Corporate Sport Sponsorships

In Chapter 4, I described sponsorships in which sporting goods manufacturing companies sponsor sports teams and sporting events. But sporting goods manufacturers are not the only corporations that sponsor sports events. In fact, in the sports-sponsorship business, sporting goods manufacturers play a relatively small role. It is the giant, transnational corporations in a whole array of industries—Coca-Cola, McDonalds, Sony, Toyota, Visa—that are the major sport sponsors of global sports.

Globally popular sporting events are ideal instruments for corporate sponsors to boost the global profile of their brands. They transcend cultural differences and offer access to consumers globally in a distinctive way that most other social and cultural practices cannot. Thus, they offer sponsors a unique global promotional platform for exposing consumers throughout the world to corporate advertising and marketing (Smart 2007).

Astute corporate executives understand the value of sponsoring sports, and this is reflected in their expenditures. The global sport sponsorship market grew from $10 million in 1993 to $27 billion in 2003; by 2009 its value had increased significantly to $45 billion. Sponsors are expected to pay $1.3 billion collectively for the 2010 World Cup in South Africa.

Globally popular sporting events, most notably the World Cup and the Olympic Games, are among the few cultural phenomena able to attract global audiences to broadcast programming. Commercial sponsorship in sports first appeared with the rise of professional sports in the early twentieth century, but it was with the growth of the television industry and the widespread popularity of televised sports during the last four decades of that century that corporate sponsorship of sporting events became an established form of corporate marketing. Because they are the two sporting events with the most global appeal, the World Cup and the Olympic Games are the most significant sports events for corporations seeking ways to market their products to global consumers.

In Chapter 2, I identified FIFA as the international governing body of association football (soccer). Its major sports event, the World Cup, held every four years, became the first global sports event to attract lucrative global commercial sponsorship contracts. For the 1978 World Cup in Argentina, the FIFA leadership negotiated contracts with six corporate sponsors, such as Coca-Cola, Gillette, and Seiko, that set the framework for subsequent World Cups (Sugden and Tomlinson 1998; Smart 2007).

Over the next thirty years, FIFA continued to expand its corporate sponsorship program. In 2007 FIFA embarked on a new commercial-sponsor-hierarchy lineup called the FIFA Sponsorship Programme, which covers the period from 2007 to 2014 and will include its flagship FIFA World Cups in 2010 and 2014. This program puts prospective marketing partners into three categories: there are six FIFA Partners, eight FIFA World Cup Sponsors, and six National Supporters. The six members of the FIFA Partners category are Adidas, Coca-Cola, Emirates Airline, Hyundai, Sony, and Visa. Only one slot is left for second-tier FIFA World Cup Sponsors alongside Anheuser-Busch, Castrol, Continental Airlines, McDonalds, MTN, Yingle Solar, and Satyam. BP Africa, FNB, Neo Africa, Prasa, and Telkom have claimed five of the six National Supporter slots, and negotiations were underway to confirm the remaining one (August 2010) (FIFA 2010).

A representative for MasterCard, a long-time FIFA sponsor, asserted, "There is no sponsorship platform anywhere in the world that rivals the FIFA World Cup in terms of the global reach and breadth of penetration it affords sponsors.... The only sponsorship platform that even comes close to the FIFA World Cup is the Olympics" (Viscusi 2006, 2).

The Olympic Games, a multisport event that reaches billions of people all over the globe and thus commands the focus of the media and the attention of the entire world, is one of the most effective international sponsorship marketing platforms in the world. However, the IOC was slower to commercialize the Olympic Games than FIFA. During the 1950s commercial television was spreading rapidly throughout the world. As it did, it became clear that televised sports events would play a major role in its growth and popularity, but the IOC showed little interest in televising the Olympic Games. However, by 1960 the prospect of TV as a revenue source became obvious to many in the IOC leadership, even though Avery Brundage, the IOC president, resisted what he considered an unwelcome commercialization of the games. At the 1960 Winter Olympics, the IOC agreed to sell CBS the television broadcast rights, marking the beginning of corporate sponsorship and the sale of television rights to the games (Moretti 2005).

Through the 1960s revenue generated by broadcast-rights fees and corporate sponsorship increased. By 1972, at the Munich Summer Olympics, revenues from sponsorship and licensing contracts generated more than 10 percent of games revenues for the first time. At those games, Brundage, the main impediment to everything commercial for the Olympics, retired. He was replaced by Lord Killanin, who was then replaced by Juan Antonio Samaranch in 1980.

Beginning with Killanin and continuing under Samaranch, a major shift in ideology took place among the IOC members about commercializing the games through corporate sponsorships (Senn 1999; Pound 2004). The importance of maximizing corporate sponsorships and TV broadcast rights became inescapably clear with the financial success of the 1984 Summer Olympics in Los Angeles, when a surplus of $227 million was created for the IOC. Indeed, the IOC considers the 1984 games as having launched the most successful, and profitable, era of corporate sponsorship in Olympic history.

From 1924, when the first Winter Olympics were held, until 1994, the Winter and Summer Games were held in the same year. But with the enormous revenue that had begun flowing in during the 1980s from corporate sponsorship and TV broadcasting-rights fees, the IOC and its consultants determined that staggering the Summer and Winter Games by two years would maximize revenue potential. So the 1994 Lillehammer games were the first Winter Olympics held in this new format. Of course, other reasons for staggering the Summer and Winter Olympics had been under review for some time, but it was the potential to increase income from corporate sponsorships that tipped the scales in favor of the idea.

During the 1980s the IOC became fully supportive of the move toward an all-out commitment to commercialization in view of the huge sums of money corporate sponsorships produced. IOC members were open to all innovations that would expand corporate sponsorships. Under the leadership of Richard Pound (2004), a member of IOC's executive board, The Olympic Partner Program (TOP) was established in 1985. Based on a four-year operations cycle, it is the highest level of worldwide sponsorship for the IOC. Corporations selected to join TOP are designated as global Olympic partners and granted exclusive worldwide marketing opportunities for their products, technologies, and services.

The partnership also covers the organizing committees hosting the Olympic Games as well as more than two hundred national and regional Olympic committees and participating delegations. The period from 2005 to 2008 was the sixth generation of TOP. The IOC raised $866 million from twelve TOP sponsors for the four years that ended after the 2008 Beijing games. To illustrate the escalation of rates, $603 million was raised in the period ending with the 2004 Athens games, and the first TOP, which ended with the 1988 Seoul games, generated $95 million (IOC 2008). Richard Pound's understanding of the crucial role of sponsorships is illustrated by this statement: "Take away sponsorship and commercialism from [the Olympics] today and what is left? A large, sophisticated finely-tuned engine developed over a period of 100 years—with no fuel" (quoted in Bernstein and Blain 2003, 40).

Media As Public Relations Tool for Global Sport

Beyond the direct financial association between the mass media and global sport, there are several indirect financial linkages between them. Commercial sport receives an enormous amount of free publicity via the media. Media coverage of sports itself tends to promote them—their leagues, teams, athletes, and coaches. Furthermore, the typical sports coverage is blatant boosterism, designed to hype interest in the athletes and teams.

Newspaper sports sections are, in subtle ways, advertising sections for commercial sports. Radio and television segments dealing with sports news essentially provide advertising for commercial sports. Indeed, many sports news announcers act like cheerleaders for their local professional sports teams, often referring to them as "our team." No other privately owned, profit-making industry—which the commercial sport industry is—receives as much free publicity for its product. Of course, the reciprocal business aspect of this is quite clear: The more interest is generated in commercial sports, the greater the profits for the mass media.

New Media and Global Sports

The mass communications forms that began with wireless technology have evolved from radio and television broadcasting to computer technology and the Internet. Comparative studies scholar David Leonard asserts that *new media,* the term now used for the latest forms of mass communications, is a "catch-all phrase that includes everything from the Internet and e-commerce, to the blogosphere, video games, virtual reality, and other examples in which media technologies are defined by increased accessibility, fluidity, and interactivity" (2009, 2).

The Internet

The current cutting edge in communications is the Internet (or the Web). Its explosive development in the last decade of the twentieth century was a quantum leap beyond previous forms of communication because it makes possible the inexpensive transmission of messages and images throughout the world in seconds. The Internet had its origins in U.S. Defense Department research done in the late 1960s, but by the mid-1990s it was almost entirely funded by private communications conglomerates, some of them originally founded as Internet firms and others originally founded as print or broadcast corporations.

According to Internet World Stats, the number of people who use the Internet was nearly 1.5 billion worldwide as of March 2009. Table 5.6 shows the top seven countries in terms of Internet users; some of the numbers are rounded. Although these figures are impressive, it is necessary to keep in mind that only between 15 and 22 percent of the world's population uses the Internet.

Table 5.6 Top Seven World Internet Users

Country	Users (millions)
China	298
United States	220
Japan	94
India	81
Brazil	67
Germany	55
United Kingdom	44

Source: Internet World Stats 2009.

The potential of the Internet as a source of sports information of all kinds has created a fundamental change in the delivery of media sports. Some media analysts predict that some time in the next twenty-five years, the Internet will surpass all other forms of mass communication as a source of sports information and entertainment. Currently millions of websites supply sports information to consumers. In September 2009, a Google search using the keywords "sports AND websites" produced a list of 110 million websites. In the short history of the Internet, sports websites regularly are among the leaders in terms of traffic and commercial activity. Table 5.7 lists the top five U.S. sports websites in November 2008.

Because of the popularity of many sporting events, full-motion video of sports events became inevitable. However, to protect their television-rights contracts, most sports organizations have placed limitations on websites' coverage. As the technology was developed to make the Internet respect geographical borders, sports organizations began offering its television-rights holders the option to show video of sports events on their websites. In 2007 Turner Broadcasting System, for MLB.com, produced live online coverage of first-round MLB playoff games and the National League Championship series. Even bigger, several broadcasters, including NBC, BBC, and European Broadcasting Union, posted on the Internet thousands of hours of free live-video coverage of the 2008 Beijing Summer Olympics. In addition, broadcasters worldwide streamed on the Web 2,200 hours of free online Beijing Olympic action that grew exponentially with highlights and replays. ESPN360.com, ESPN's signature 24/7 broadband sports network, is an online website for live sports programming that streams 3,500 hours of live sports coverage from a broad selection of global sports events each year.

Table 5.7 Top Five U.S. Sports Websites in November 2008

Rank	Website	Unique Visitors (millions)	Percentage Change versus November 2007
1	Yahoo! Sports	22.788	2
2	ESPN	22.198	12
3	NFL Internet Network	14.072	0
4	FOX Sports on MSN	13.766	−10
5	CBS Sports	12.939	− 7
	All U.S. sports websites	78.499	5

Source: Google.

Video Games

Video games are a form of communication that grew out of the integration of television and computer technologies. The video game industry has had a rapid and sustained global growth and is now a $10 billion industry that rivals the motion picture industry as producing the most profitable entertainment medium in the world.

A sports game, Tennis for Two (1958), was one of the first video games. Over the past fifty years, a video game has been developed for virtually every sport played in the world. Like the auto industry, the sports video game industry brings out a new version of its products annually to prime the pump for profits. The processing power of the new generation of video game equipment—Microsoft's Xbox 360, Sony Computer's PlayStation 3, and Nintendo's Wii—has brought the real world into play.

Wii Sports's unique wireless, motion-sensitive remote allows players to make the physical body movements involved in playing a sport. Originally bundled with sports from tennis to bowling, the 2009 version, Wii Sports Resort, enables players to engage in over a dozen activities and is expected to generate $400 million in revenue.

As with other forms of entertainment, especially television, questions have arisen about the effects of video game playing on users' habits, behaviors, and social development. For example, how does playing sports video games affect the play habits of children and youth? Do the games influence attitudes and behaviors in terms of sportsmanship, violence, and morality? Does prolonged sports video game playing affect physical fitness, weight management, and social interaction with peers? At this time there has been little research into these questions, and many others, but undoubtedly this will be a rich area for psychological and sociological scholarship in the coming years (Crawford and Gosling 2009; Wolf 2007).

Twitter, Facebook, MySpace, and YouTube

Sport organizations throughout the world are employing direct communications with customers—mostly fans—through social-media tools such as Twitter, Facebook, MySpace, and YouTube. These popular communications technologies have helped professional sports teams to quickly and inexpensively respond to customers and tailor services for fans. It is the younger fans who flock to Twitter and make it a useful social-media tool.

Twitter is a social-networking application that has taken "immediacy" to new heights; it is rapidly becoming a staple in businesses customer service, and that includes sport organizations (see Box 5.2). In the spring of 2009, during a Stanley Cup play-off game between the Philadelphia Flyers and Pittsburgh Penguins, television sets suddenly went blank. Many cable subscribers Twittered to find out why. One subscriber said, "I did a search on Twitter as soon as the game went off the air. The mystery was resolved in minutes. Before Twitter, it would have been a nightmare trying to find out on the phone what happened" (Swartz 2009, 1B). In the summer of 2009, MLB used Twitter to its maximum advantage leading up to—and during—its 2009 First-Year Player Draft. MLB.com launched the first online "social community" integration of the draft by integrating Twitter into its expanding live interactive media experience, the Draft Caster, and its searchable draft database, the Draft Tracker (Winston 2009).

Other social-media tools, such as Facebook, YouTube, and MySpace, are fostering sports fans service through online communities to exchange comments, ideas, and questions (see Box 5.3). Through their respective services they can offer massive bulletin boards for consumers to weigh in on major issues about athletes and teams.

Online Sport Gambling

Gambling is an economic activity with a history that dates back to antiquity. Betting on sports events was popular with the ancient Greeks five hundred years before the birth of Christ, and it was very popular in all of their Pan-Hellenic Games—one of which was the Olympic Games. Gambling reached some incredible extremes at the Roman chariot races, with rampant corruption and fixed events. Histories of sport over the past two hundred years are replete with accounts of gambling. It is often claimed that wherever you find sport you find gambling. Internet online wagering is the fastest-growing new form of gambling and has become a major force in the global gambling industry. According to *60 Minutes* host Steve Kroft, online gambling is currently an $18 billion industry and growing each year.

Internet gambling is illegal and unregulated in many countries of the world, but bans are almost impossible to enforce since the Internet sites and computers that randomly deal the cards and keep track of the bets are located offshore, beyond the jurisdiction of law-enforcement agencies. Moreover, with the enormous increase of interest in spectator sports over the past thirty years, there has been a corresponding explosion in sports gambling, with online venues being the most convenient. As media analyst Michael Real has observed, "Offshore online sites can be

Box 5.2 Twitter and Global Social Networking in Sports

Hey there! NBA is using Twitter
    Hey there! FIFA World Cup is using Twitter
   Hey there! Japanese MLB (mlbjapan.com) is using Twitter
      Hey there! SportsFanLive is using Twitter
    Hey there! Sports Illustrated is using Twitter
  Hey there! Professional athletes are using Twitter

Not only are leagues, teams, sporting events, and athletes using Twitter; since its creation in 2006, Twitter has gained global popularity.

Twitter is a free social-networking service that enables users to send and read messages known as "tweets." Tweets are text-based posts sent to the author's subscribers, who are known as "followers." Senders can restrict tweet delivery to those in their circle of friends, or they can allow open access, and they can send and receive tweets via the Twitter website, Short Message Service (SMS), or external applications.

The 140-character limit on message length was initially set for compatibility with SMS messaging and has brought to the web the kind of shorthand notation and slang commonly used in SMS messages. The 140-character limit has also spurred the usage of URL shortening services such as tinyurl, bit.ly, and tr.im, and content-hosting services, such as Twitpic and NotePub, to accommodate multimedia content and text longer than 140 characters.

It is sometimes described as the "SMS of the Internet" since the use of Twitter's application programming interface for sending and receiving short text messages by other applications often eclipses the direct use of Twitter.

Twitter emphasized their news and information network strategy in November 2009 by changing the question it asks users for status updates from "What are you doing?" to "What's happening?" Although estimates of the number of daily users vary because the company does not release the number of active accounts, a February 2009 Compete.com blog entry ranked Twitter as the third-most-used social network based on their count of 6 million unique monthly visitors and 55 million monthly visits. Twitter had a monthly growth of 1,382 percent, Zimbio of 240 percent, followed by Facebook with an increase of 228 percent. However, only 40 percent of Twitter's users are retained.

Still, in March 2009 Twitter was ranked as the fastest-growing site in the member communities category. By early 2010 Twitter was ranked as one of the fifty most popular websites worldwide.

The Twitter homepage (www.twitter.com) declares that in countries all around the world, people follow the sources most relevant to them and access information via Twitter as it happens—from breaking world news to updates from friends. Join the conversation.

Box 5.3 Facebook and Global Sports Applications

Facebook is a global social-networking website launched in 2004. Users select friends and post messages and personal profiles to notify their friends about themselves. More than 350 million active users are reported for Facebook, about 70 percent of whom are outside the United States. A 2009 study ranked Facebook as the most used social network worldwide by active users.

Over 300,000 applications have been developed for the Facebook platform, with hundreds of new ones being created every month. Many of these allow users to join networks organized by city, workplace, school, and special interests, like sports (even specific sports), to connect and interact with other people with similar interests.

SportsFanLive.com is a premier content and global social-networking site for sports fans. In effect it is its own Facebook. The customizable interface provides easy access to sports information throughout the world. The home page content has a plethora of sports stories about games, athletes, leagues, and so forth. Users can customize the site to highlight the teams and players they are devoted to, and they regularly receive copious amounts of updated news aggregated from over 4,000 sources.

In addition, users of SportsFanLive.com can send articles to like-minded friends on the site through the My FanFeed feature. With an application called FanFinder, which has a ZIP code– and map-based function, they can search for a specific place to watch a game or alert buddies about the sports bar where they are cheering on their team. SportsFanLive users are not just limited to being spectators. Their opinions can be expressed, allowing them to contribute to the daily sports conversation.

To experience this new wave of sports on the Web, log on to www .sportsfanlive.com.

readily accessed by casual betters, children, gambling addicts, and even athletes" (2006, 189).

A study by the Annenberg Foundation reported that more than 27 percent of young Americans ages fourteen to twenty-two bet on sports events at least once per month. Even more troubling, sports gambling is rampant and prospering on university campuses throughout the world, and the majority of bookies are students. One writer referred to this phenomenon as "the dirty little secret on university campuses"; another referred to it as a "silent addiction" for many university students. Studies of sports betting by American college students have reported that between

35 and 50 percent of male college students and between 10 and 20 percent of female students have bet on sports events.

There are far too many sports-betting websites to list, and they are being constructed and dismantled weekly, so I will list a few to illustrate their global spread. The European online sports-betting industry is made up of operators that are established, licensed, and regulated in the European Union, some of which are grouped under the European Gaming and Betting Association, the leading industry body representing online gaming and betting operators in Europe. Eurobet claims to be Europe's leading bookmaker; it offers sports betting, easy withdraw methods, and online casinos, poker, bingo, and games. The European Sports Security Association (ESSA) was established in 2005 by the leading online sports book operators in Europe to monitor irregular betting patterns or potential insider betting from within each sport. ESSA has signed a memorandum of understanding with FIFA and several European sports leagues and has established close relations with the IOC.

In the United Kingdom, BetUK.com advertises itself as the leading online sports-betting bookmaker. But more than that, BetUK.com offers an array of online sports-betting lines for betting on UK events, as well as provides subscribers with a range of sports betting, the latest bets, tips, strategies, and the latest online sports-betting markets from all sports.

Sports Fantasy Leagues. Sports fantasy league "play" is a form of sport gambling, even though at its most local level it is played by a group of friends for very small stakes. At the upper extremes online sport fantasy leagues are huge businesses in which players pay up to several hundred dollars to play by selecting a team of professional athletes from a "draft" and then working the team through the season. Large sums of money can be attained by winning a sports fantasy league championship. A survey by the Fantasy Sports Trade Association (FSTA) indicates that some 30 million individuals actively participate in fantasy sport in the United States alone, spending $800 million yearly on products related to fantasy sports (FSTA 2009). According to its website, in 2008 the National Fantasy Football Championship paid out over $850,000 in prizes—bringing the total payout since 2004 to over $5 million. In the United Kingdom the Fantasy Football Premier League enables players to manage their own teams of players from that league.

Sport fantasy players have an enormous variety of online information sources to help them make good choices in selecting players for their fantasy teams. As Real notes, "The quantity and depth of information available on the Web enables a fantasy league player to be the well-informed general manager of a complex, seemingly realist virtual team" (2006, 178).

Media Sport and Deterritorialization of Fans

Media sport analysts frequently say, "There are no displaced sports fans anymore." They are suggesting that with the cascading media sequence of broadcast television, then cable, then satellite, then the Internet, and now professional teams and leagues creating premium-TV sports packages and their own TV networks, the horizon for sports fans has become global. Before all of these media technologies, fans were pretty much restricted to adopting local athletes and teams as their own; they were loyal hometown fans. Because of the new technologies fans can become familiar with athletes and teams hundreds or even thousands of miles away—they may even be located in another country.

The process of "deterritorialization," creating what some call "the long-distance fan," has similarities to the migration of athletes, the subject of Chapter 3. Just as athletes have migrated all over the world to ply their trade, sports fans are migrating to athletes and teams globally. They can watch televised events on premium-TV sports channels and obtain scores, records, standings, and thumbnail accounts of favorite athletes and teams on the Internet or their cell phone, Blackberry, or iPod. According to *Wall Street Journal* reporter Sam Walker (2003), research has found that 55 percent of MLB fans do not live near their favorite team. Michael Real provides an excellent scenario of the opportunities that globalization of the Internet creates: "Soccer fans in South Africa follow European teams closely, Japanese fans track the careers of their heroes performing in American baseball, franchises buy Chinese players to get access to that huge market, media moguls buy teams and leagues to provide content for their global satellites—distance disappears" (2006, 180).

Global Media Sport and Gender

In the world of organized sport, females have systematically been marginalized. It is not too extreme to say that throughout most of the twentieth century, sport was considered an exclusively male domain. Thus, as there was little in the way of female sport for the mass media to cover, sports-women were rarely seen in either print or broadcast media. When they were, their achievements were denigrated: The women were framed in terms of women's traditional private roles (e.g., girlfriend, wife, mother) and objectified in ways similar to those employed by soft-core pornography, and their sports records were often compared to men's deliberately to belittle their achievements. Arguably the worst form of discrimination that continues into the twenty-first century against female involvement in sport takes place in Islamic countries.

Studies of the contents of newspapers and magazines in a dozen or more countries have consistently found that stories and photos of women's sports constitute a minority of the coverage; stories and photos of men's sports dominated the print media. The percentage of feature print media stories involving females in sport roles has been increasing, but many such stories still reveal a conventional and restricted view of female sport participation, typically framing female athletes in terms of sexual appeal, homosexuality, and sports achievements that do not measure up to those of males.

As for televised treatment of women, several of the major findings of a 2005 report on gender in televised sports were as follows:

- Women's sports were underreported in the six weeks of early-evening and late-night television sports news on three network affiliates sampled in the study.
- Men's sports received 91.4 percent of the airtime, women's sports 6.3 percent, and gender-neutral topics 2.4 percent.
- On ESPN's nationally televised program *SportsCenter* and on FOX's *Southern California Sports Report,* the proportion of stories and airtime devoted to women's sports was even lower than on the local Los Angeles sports news shows. Whereas on the Los Angeles news, men's sports reports outnumbered women's sports stories by 9:1, FOX's male-to-female ratio was 15:1, and *SportsCenter*'s ratio was a whopping 20:1.
- All of the *SportsCenter* programs, all of the FOX programs, and 96.2 percent of the network affiliate sports news shows in the sample began with a men's sports topic as the lead story.
- Many broadcasts in the sample contained no coverage of women's sports whatsoever. Well over half (58 percent) of the network affiliate news shows included no women's sports stories, and 48 percent of the FOX and ESPN highlights shows included no women's sports

stories. Meanwhile, 100 percent of the 279 news and highlights broadcasts in the sample included coverage of men's sports (Duncan and Messner 2005).

The television programs in this study were all on American networks, but the legacy of media negligence of women athletes is confirmed in non-American media outlets. British sport sociologist Christopher King examined the coverage in two national British newspapers, the *Times* and the *Daily Mail*, of male and female athletes competing in the Olympic Games from 1948 to 2004. King (2007) found that, compared to men, female athletes were underrepresented until the 2004 Athens games (see also Markula, Bruce, and Hovden 2009).

Another relevant study compared coverage in newspapers from three countries—the United Kingdom's *Times*, the United States' *New York Times*, and Canada's *Globe & Mail*—of female and male tennis players competing in the 2004 Wimbledon Championships. It found that male players received significantly more total coverage than female players, with significantly more articles and photographs (Crossman, Vincent, and Speed 2007). Finally, Ping Wu (2009), an analyst of sport journalism who studied the subject in China for several years, reported that Chinese female athletes are belittled by the media, which prefer to emphasize their personal characteristics and appearance rather then their sport skills (see also Yu 2009).

The status quo is yielding to the future. During the last quarter of the twentieth century, considerable progress was made in opening up opportunities for females and giving them access to sporting activities, from the recreational level to the world-class elite level. This progress has come about via typical globalization-from-below tactics: combinations of coalitions, diverse global campaigns, and assorted activist events and local struggles. Progress has occurred in how media sport represents females, even though women's sports have not achieved parity with men's in any of the media forms.

One of the most promising trends toward increasing women's sports coverage is the emergence of magazines and websites devoted exclusively (or almost exclusively) to women's sport and fitness. These print and Internet outlets provide comprehensive coverage of women's sport activities, focusing on individual female athletes, women's teams, and women's sport organizations; they also examine issues and problems in women's sports.

Until 1996, no women's professional team-sport league had ever secured a contract with a major national television network. No doubt there were several reasons for this, but certainly a major one was that advertisers were not convinced that viewers would watch women's sport. Advertisers buy time slots during sports programming to reach a target audience, so they did not buy time during women's sports events. This pattern was broken in the fall of 1996 when the new American Basketball League (ABL) secured a national cable-network contract; in 1997, when the Women's National Basketball Association (WNBA) began play, a national-network-television contract was in place. The ABL went out of business, but the WNBA's network coverage remained in place, and several WNBA teams negotiated local TV contracts with regional sports networks. In 2007, a major breakthrough came through for the WNBA when the organization reached an eight-year, multi-million-dollar TV deal that, for the first time, pays broadcast rights to the WNBA. Furthermore, network radio and TV contracts for other women's sports organizations are gradually increasing.

In the past thirty years, there has been a significant social transformation in opportunities for females to engage in sports of every kind at every level. Accompanying this trend, significant strides have been made to include women in media sport, but sportswriters and broadcasters still have yet to accord them the respect and coverage their achievements in sports deserve. Ironically, as women strive for parity with men in media sport, they are being co-opted by the forces of commercialism in subtle ways that make them just another commodity to be sold to media sports audiences (Creedon and Cramer 2007).

Summary

Media sport is one division of the mass communications industry and an integrated component of global mass media commerce. Worldwide access to the wide variety of mass media that now exist enables that industry to be a powerful cultural source of information and entertainment. In some countries the mass media are a division of the government and are publicly financed; in other countries media organizations are privately owned and operated.

Private ownership of media is more common globally, and there is a concentration of ownership by large, transnational conglomerate corporations that dominate the global media market. Their size and the product they distribute—mass communications—enables them to control what people see, read, and hear and thus positions them at the apex of globalization from above.

Ownership of global media sport is concentrated in the same few transnational corporations that dominate global mass communications. During the past two decades, Rupert Murdoch, owner of News Corporation and a large group of newspapers, radio, and television networks, has also been a leading figure in media sport ownership. Several times he has been ranked as the most influential person in the world of sports.

Modern sports have evolved simultaneously with advances in media technology. The two are often said to have a symbiotic relationship. Newspapers, radio, and television have depended upon sports to advance and popularize their industry; likewise, sport, especially professional sport, has depended upon these media for their popularity and financial support. This financial association is an example of business interdependence, and it has extended to frequent overlapping ownership of media and sport organizations.

Television remains at the center of professional sports and big-event sports, both economically and culturally. It continues to wield enormous influence over almost every facet of global sports. Sports television broadcasting has helped networks—commercial free-to-air, cable, and satellite—to enhance their status as global media. Television broadcast-rights fees have become the main source of income for many sport organizations. Beyond the direct financial benefits, sport receives a great deal of free publicity via televised broadcasts.

The new media, including everything from the Internet and e-commerce, to video games, to YouTube, MySpace, Facebook, Twitter, and the blogosphere, is the cutting edge in communications and is creating a fundamental change in the delivery of media sports.

Females have systematically been marginalized in global media sport, just as they have in other sectors of social life. A significant social transformation toward a goal of gender equity in global media sport has taken place during the past quarter century, but there is much to be accomplished before that goal is achieved.

Notes

1. All dollar currency conversions in this chapter reflect values during the year in which the contracts were made.

References

Andrews, David L., Ben Carrington, Steven J. Jackson, and Zbigniew Mazur. 1996. Jordanscapes: A preliminary analysis of the global popular. *Sociology of Sport Journal* 13: 428–457.

Associated Press. 2008. 2 out of 3 people worldwide tuned in for Olympics. *USA Today*, September 5. www.usatoday.com/sports/olympics/2008-09-05-2248757259_x.htm.

Bagdikian, Ben H. 2004. *The new media monopoly.* Boston: Beacon Press.

Banerjee, Indrajit, and Kalinga Seneviratne, eds. 2006. *Public service broadcasting in the age of globalization.* Singapore: Asian Media Information and Communication Centre and Wee Kim Wee School of Communication and Information, Nanyang Technological University.

Barney, Robert K., Stephen R. Wenn, and Scott G. Martyn. 2004. *Selling the five rings: The International Olympic Committee and the rise of Olympic commercialism.* Salt Lake City: University of Utah Press.

Bellamy, Robert V., Jr. 1998. The evolving television sports marketplace. In *MediaSport*, ed. Lawrence A. Wenner, 73–87. New York: Routledge.

Bernstein, Alina, and Neil Blain. 2003. *Sport, media, culture: Global and local dimensions.* London: Frank Cass.

Bolotny, Frédéric, and Jean-François Bourg. 2006. The demand for media coverage. In *Handbook on the economics of sport*, ed. Wladimir Andreff and Stefan Szymanski, 112–133. Northampton, MA: Edward Elgar.

Brake, Laurel, and Marysa Demoor, eds. 2009. *A dictionary of nineteenth-century journalism in Great Britain and Ireland.* London: British Library.

Business Week. 2007. The power 100: The most influential people in the world of sports. *Business Week*, September 25. www.businessweek.com/table/07/0926_power100.htm.

Chenoweth, Neil. 2001. *Rupert Murdoch: The untold story of the world's greatest media wizard.* New York: Crown Business.

Colvin, Geoff. 2007. TV is dying? Long live TV! *Fortune*, January 23, 43.

Cone, James. 2006. Soccer World Cup final had sport's largest TV audience of 2006. Bloomberg.com, December 19. http://bloomberg.com/apps/news?pid=20601077&sid=aOYdMOmxoV4c&refer=intsports.

Crawford, Garry, and Victoria K. Gosling. 2009. More than a game: Sports-themed video games and player narratives. *Sociology of Sport Journal* 26: 50–66.

Creedon, Pamela J., and Judith Cramer, eds. 2007. *Women in mass communication.* 3rd ed. Thousand Oaks, CA: Sage Publications.

Crossman, Jane, John Vincent, and Harriet Speed. 2007. "The times they are a-changing": Gender comparisons in three national newspapers of the 2004

Wimbledon Championships. *International Review for the Sociology of Sport* 42, no. 1: 27–41.

Dempsey, John Mark. 2006. *Sports-talk radio in America: Its context and culture.* Binghamton, NY: Haworth Half-Court Press.

Duncan, Margaret Carlisle, and Michael A. Messner. 2005. *Gender in televised sports: News and highlights shows, 1989–2004.* Los Angeles, CA: Amateur Athletic Foundation of Los Angeles.

Egan, Pierce. 1836. *Pierce Egan's book of sports and mirror of life: Embracing the turf, the chase, the ring, and the stage.* No publisher.

Fantasy Sports Trade Association (FSTA). 2009. Welcome to the official site of the FSTA. FSTA. www.fsta.org.

Fédération Internationale de Football Association (FIFA). 2010. Marketing affiliates. FIFA.com. www.fifa.com/worldcup/organisation/partners/index .html.

Financial Times. 2009. FT global 500. *Financial Times.* http://media.ft.com/ cms/5f933498-4c41-11de-a6c5-00144feabdc0.pdf.

Flew, Terry. 2007. *Understanding global media.* New York: Palgrave Macmillan.

Fort, Rodney D. 2006. *Sports economics.* 2nd ed. Upper Saddle River, NJ: Prentice Hall.

Freedman, Jonah. 2009a. The 50 highest-earning American athletes. SI.com. http://sportsillustrated.cnn.com/more/specials/fortunate50/2009.

———. 2009b. The top-earning non-American athletes. SI.com. http:// sportsillustrated.cnn.com/more/specials/fortunate50/2009/index.20 .html.

Genova, Tom. 2009. 1936 German (Berlin) Olympics. Television History—the First 75 Years. www.tvhistory.tv/1936%20German%20Olympics%20TV% 20Program.htm.

Gerrard, Bill. 2004. Media ownership of teams: The latest in the commercialisation of team sports. In *The commercialisation of sport,* ed. Trevor Slack, 247–266. New York: Routledge.

Gietschier, Steve. 1999. 20th century ad. *Sporting News,* December 20. http:// findarticles.com/p/articles/mi_m1208/is_51_223/ai_58411314.

Gorman, Jerry, and Kirk Calhoun. 2004. *The name of the game: The business of sports.* New York: Wiley.

Graber, Doris A. 2009. *Mass media and American politics.* 8th ed. Washington, D.C.: CQ Press.

Griffin, Jeffrey. 2005. The United Kingdom. In *Global entertainment media: Content, audiences, issues,* ed. Anne Cooper-Chen, 39–57. Mahwah, NJ: Lawrence Erlbaum.

Hanson, Ralph E. 2008. *Mass communication: Living in a media world.* 2nd ed. Washington, D.C.: CQ Press.

Harris, M. 1998. Sport in the newspapers before 1750: Representations of cricket, class and commerce in the London press. *Media History* 4, no. 1: 19–28.

Herman, Edward S., and Noam Chomsky. 2002. *Manufacturing consent: The political economy of the mass media.* New York: Pantheon.

Hiestand, Michael. 2009. In TV sports, more is more. *USA Today,* December 31, 3C.

International Olympic Committee (IOC). 2008. *Marketing Media Guide.* IOC. http://multimedia.olympic.org/pdf/en_report_1329.pdf.

Internet World Stats. 2009. Internet usage statistics: The Internet big picture. www.internetworldstats.com/stats.htm.

Jackson, Steven J., and David L. Andrews. 1999. Between and beyond the global and the local: American popular sporting culture in New Zealand. *International Review for the Sociology of Sport* 34: 31–42.

Jeanrenaud, Claude, and Stefan Késenne. 2006. Sport and the media: An overview. In *The economics of sport and the media,* ed. Claude Jeanrenaud and Stefan Késenne, 1–25. Northampton, MA: Edward Elgar.

Kilbride, Kieron. 2000. Comparing media ownership of football clubs in England and Europe. In *Euro Football Finance 2000 Conference Documentation.* London: SMi.

King, Christopher. 2007. Media portrayals of male and female athletes: A text and picture analysis of British national newspaper coverage of the Olympic Games since 1948. *International Review for the Sociology of Sport* 42, no. 2: 187–199.

Leonard, David. 2009. New media and global sporting cultures: Moving beyond the clichés and binaries. *Sociology of Sport Journal* 26: 1–16.

Leone, Marie. 2008. NFL runs up the score. CFO.com, January 30. www.cfo.com/article.cfm/10600845?f=search.

Maguire, Joseph. 1999. *Global sport: Identities, societies, civilizations.* Cambridge, UK: Polity Press.

Markula, Pirkko, Toni Bruce, and J. Hovden. 2009. Key themes in the research on media coverage of women's sport. In *Sportswomen at the Olympics: A global comparison of newspaper coverage,* ed. Toni Bruce, J. Hovden, and Pirkko Markula, 1–19. Rotterdam, Netherlands: Sense Publishers.

McChesney, Robert. 2008. *The political economy of media: Enduring issues, emerging dilemmas.* New York: Monthly Review Press.

McChesney, Robert, and Dan Schiller. 2003. *The political economy of international communication: Foundations for the emerging global debate about media ownership and business and society,* United Nations Research Institute for Social Development, Technology, Business and Society Program Paper No. 11, October.

Mondello, Michael. 2006. Sport economics and the media. In *Handbook of sports and media,* ed. Arthur A. Raney and Jennings Bryant, 277–294. Mahwah, NJ: Lawrence Erlbaum.

Moretti, Anthony. 2005. The Olympics. In *Global entertainment media: Content, audiences, issues,* ed. Anne Cooper-Chen, 221–236. Mahwah, NJ: Lawrence Erlbaum Associates.

Nachison, Andrew. 2009. WeMedia/Zogby poll: Who will lead us to a better future? WeMedia, February 25. http://wemedia.com/2009/02/25/betterfuturesurvey.

Owens, John W. 2006. The coverage of sports on radio. In *Handbook of sports and media,* ed. Arthur Raney and Jennings Bryant, 117–129. Hillsdale, NJ: Lawrence Erlbaum.

Parlasca, Susanne. 2006. Collective selling of broadcast rights in team sports. In *Handbook on the economics of sport,* ed. Wladimir Andreff and Stefan Szymanski, 719–729. Northampton, MA: edward Edgar.

Pound, Richard. 2004. *Inside the Olympics: A behind-the-scenes look at the politics, the scandals, and the glory of the games.* Etobicoke, Canada: John Wiley & Sons Canada.

Real, Michael. 2006. Sports online: The newest player in mediasport. In *Handbook of sports and media,* ed. Arthur A. Raney and Jennings Bryant, 171–184. Mahwah, NJ: Lawrence Erlbaum Associates.

Rowe, David, and Jim McKay. 1999. Field of soaps: Rupert v. Kerry as masculine melodrama. In *SportCult,* ed. Randy Martin and Toby Miller, 191–210. Minneapolis: University of Minnesota Press.

Senn, Alfred E. 1999. *Power, politics, and the Olympic Games.* Champaign, IL: Human Kinetics.

Smart, Barry. 2007. Not playing around: Global capitalism, modern sport and consumer culture. In *Globalization and sport,* ed. Richard Giulianotti and Roland Robertson, 6–27. Malden, MA: Blackwell.

Smith, Alexander. 2009. COLUMN-debts mount up in Premier League. ESPN.com, June 9. http://sports.espn.go.com/espn/wire? section=soccer&id=4245151.

Smith, R. A. 2001. *Play by play: Radio, television, and big-time college sport.* Baltimore: Johns Hopkins University Press.

Sugden, John, and Alan Tomlinson. 1998. *FIFA and the contest for world football.* Cambridge, UK: Polity Press.

Swartz, Jon. 2009. Businesses get cheap help from a little birdie. *USA Today,* June 26, 1C–2C.

Szymanski, Stefan, and Andrew Zimbalist. 2005. *National pastime: How Americans play baseball and the rest of the world plays soccer.* Washington, D.C.: Brookings Institution Press.

Turow, Joseph. 2008. *Media today: An introduction to mass communication.* 3rd ed. London: Taylor & Francis.

Viscusi, Gregory. 2006. The high price of World Cup exposure. *Business Report,* June 20. www.busrep.co.za/index.php?fSectionId=553&fArticleId=3299772.

Walker, Sam. 2003. The long-distance fan. *Wall Street Journal,* July 18. http://online.wsj.com/article/SB105847497140986200.html.

Whannel, Garry. 2008. *Culture, politics and sport: Blowing the whistle, revisited.* New York: Routledge.

Winston, Lisa. 2009. Fans can share draft takes on Twitter. MLB.com, June 7. http://mlb.mlb.com/news/article.jsp?ymd=20090607&content_id=5197482&vkey=draft2009&fext=.jsp.

Wolf, Mark. 2007. *The video game explosion: A history from PONG to PlayStation and beyond.* Westport, CT: Greenwood.

Wolff, Michael. 2008. *The man who owns the news: Inside the secret world of Rupert Murdoch.* New York: Broadway Books.

Wu, Ping. 2009. From "iron girl" to "sexy goddess": An analysis of the Chinese media. In *Olympic women and the media: International perspectives,* ed. Pirkko Markula, 70–86. New York: Palgrave Macmillan.

Yu, Chia-Chen. 2009. A content analysis of news coverage of Asian female Olympic athletes. *International Review for the Sociology of Sport* 44, nos. 2–3: 283–305.

CHAPTER 6
GLOBAL POLITICS AND SPORT

> To seek to isolate sport as an activity that stands alone in
> human affairs, untouched by "politic" or "moral consid-
> erations" and unconcerned for the fates of those deprived
> of human rights, is as unrealistic as it is (self-destructively)
> self-serving.
>
> —Des Wilson, "Cricket's Shame:
> The Inside Story," 2004, 28.

The statement above contradicts commonly heard mantras like "Keep
politics out of sport" or the reverse, "Keep sport out of politics." But
these mantras do not correspond at all with reality. A more realistic point
of view is that expressed by UK journalist and sport administrator Des
Wilson. For anyone who might be skeptical about Wilson's statement,
examples of the ties between sport and politics are plentiful. A few are
described below:

- At the 1972 Munich Summer Olympic Games, Palestinian terrorists
  attacked Israeli athletes, killing eleven of them.
- The United States (and other nations) boycotted the 1980 Summer
  Olympic Games; the Soviet Union (and other nations) boycotted
  the 1984 Los Angeles Summer Olympics.
- South African sport was isolated worldwide from international sports
  events from the 1960s through the 1980s because of its apartheid
  governmental policies.

- In the 1993 World University Games in Buffalo, New York, federal agencies, such as the Departments of Defense, State, and Transportation and the U.S. Information Agency, collectively contributed $10 million.
- Some countries threatened to boycott the 2010 World Cup if South Africa continued to ignore human rights abuses in Zimbabwe.

All of these examples illustrate the intermingling of sport and politics, and all involve international sporting events because this book is about global sport. But before continuing with the global perspective, I want to emphasize that sport-political connections are present at all levels of sport and politics, from the local to the national to the international. For example,

- A decision by the city council of a town to build (or not to build) a public community football stadium is a political decision.
- A decision by a city metropolitan district to seek public funds to build a baseball field for a Major League Baseball team is a political decision.
- The decision by former U.S. president Gerald Ford to create the President's Commission on Olympic Sports, committing the U.S. government to a continuing role in international sport, was a political decision.

Political Intervention in Sports

The word "politics" brings forth considerations about government, politicians, and public policies or about corruption and dirty tricks. Politics is, of course, involved in all of these, but the network of administrative and bureaucratic agencies that make up a national political system is often referred to by social scientists as "the state" (which is not to be confused with one of the fifty United States, each of which is a form of regional government). The state encompasses the national government and the elected officeholders in all its branches. Beyond that, the state is an organized power structure comprising a great variety of organizations, including hundreds of appointed officials, the military, the legal system, and the many public bureaucracies and agencies involved in public policy making, opinion shaping, and ideology formation.

Governments have intervened in the play, games, and sports of its citizens in a variety of ways, although such interventions have never been a dominating feature of government legislation and policy making. But political intervention to control or prohibit domestic sporting practices actually has a lengthy history. British sports history is replete with various prohibitions that monarchs placed on sporting activities over the centuries. For example, in 1457, the Scottish parliament of King James II banned "futball"—a ball-kicking game that ultimately became soccer—and golf, a ban that was reaffirmed in 1470 and 1491, although people largely ignored it (Leibs 2004). In the New England colonies of what is now the northeastern United States, Puritan influence resulted in laws prohibiting boxing, wrestling, and cockfighting for their violence and play and games in general because they were often performed on the Sabbath. Even today, professional boxing has been illegal in Sweden since 1970. It is also banned in Cuba and North Korea.

In the early twentieth century, U.S. President Theodore Roosevelt threatened to abolish intercollegiate football unless changes were made to reduce the brutality of the game. More recently, gender discrimination in U.S. high school and college sports programs was made illegal when the federal government passed Title IX of the Educational Amendments Act of 1972, which specified, "No person in the United States shall, on the basis of sex, be excluded from participation in, be denied the benefits of, or be subjected to discrimination under any education program or activity receiving Federal financial assistance."

Sport and the Promotion of Political Ideology

One of the traditional roles of the state is that of fostering and preserving social harmony. States have enforcement agencies, such as the police force, to ensure social order is maintained, but they typically try to avoid using them because this often involves violence, which has the potential of antagonizing citizens and causing resentment and rebellion. Instead, social harmony is shaped through a common system of goals, values, and beliefs, and from this system a consensus is built that supplies the cohesion on which nation-states stand.

Social cohesion is formed and maintained through ideological inculcation, which socializes people to internalize and accept, even embrace, the prevailing social order. On this point, the state does not enshrine and reproduce political domination solely through repression, force, or violence; instead, it employs ideology to shape and legitimize a consensus of the social order.

Formal education is a primary avenue for the transmitting the state's ideology, as it socializes people to accept the existing social formation and to see "their" government and all its branches as right and true. Two notions underlie the use of the educational system to promote the state's dominant ideology: First, citizens must be taught loyalty and patriotism so that they will support their political leaders and willingly fight to defend their country if it becomes necessary. In the school systems of most countries, the subjects through which these ideas are primarily taught are history and government (or civics), and both are typically required by law. Second, schools, through their own organization and social milieu, tend to sustain and reproduce the existing national social values and relations. Of course, ideological work is not just found in the schools. It is actually carried out in several social institutions. The political system has a leading role, but the economic system and mass media also play decisive roles in the ideological sphere.

Advancing National Unity and Recognition Through Sport

Sport in modern societies has also become one of the means by which nation-states socialize their citizens, transmitting the symbolic codes of the dominant culture and inducing citizens toward conformity with beliefs and values that prevail in the wider society. At the same time, sport is one of the most salient molders of national unity and collective identity.

The beliefs that sport, especially international sport, promotes a sense of national unity, builds national identity (often called nation building), and projects a positive reputation internationally have served as political tools of foreign policy for governments throughout the world. They enable governments to intervene in sport to advance values and norms that promote national unity and pride, thus uniting their own citizens and impressing those of other countries (Whannel 2008).

National loyalty and patriotism are fostered through sport rituals and ceremonies that link sport and nationalism. Probably nothing provokes stronger nationalistic emotions than activities tied to patriotism. National symbols and pageantry are often woven into sport events. Singing the national anthem, performing patriotic pageants, and displaying emblems and insignias like flags all ideologically celebrate national identity and the legitimacy of the current social order.

The achievements of athletes in international competition serve as symbols of national unity and excellence, thus providing temporary emotional surges of national passion. Important national and international events like the Olympic Games and World Cup are incorporated into a panoply of patriotic rituals that serve to remind people of their common destiny (Jackson and Haigh 2009).

A specific example of seemingly obligatory patriotic symbolism at the Olympic Games occurs when a victorious athlete (or team) is handed the flag of his or her country, which is then held aloft or wrapped around the athlete's body as he or she parades around the sports venue. For a few minutes spectators' estimation of themselves and their country will be bound up with this display. The athletes' victory will be a victory for their nation, the embodiment of their nation's strength. Spectacles like this help to create and support national cultures because they convey messages about norms, values, and dispositions that serve as an index of national superiority—in military might, in political economics, and in culture.

The institution of sport, just like other social institutions, is conservative, so it tends to preserve and reinforce the existing social order. Most sport organizations and officials foster national loyalty and patriotism, and in almost every political controversy, the sports establishment lines up behind the reigning political leaders. Their stands on social or political issues typically support the government, claiming that this is in the "national interest." Coaches, athletic directors, broadcasters, and so forth limit the exposition of ideological perspectives to those supportive of the prevailing political-economic system. Anything not in agreement with the reigning authority is censured; all that is seditious is removed or explicitly condemned.

Sport As an Instrument of International Politics and Diplomacy

The high visibility of international sport events has fostered a favorable climate for state intervention. Nations have increasingly forged direct propaganda links between sport triumphs and the viability of their political-economic systems. In this strategy, sport is an instrument of state policy that ties achievements of the nation's athletes to the country's political-economic system to promote the system's superiority. This has been called sports diplomacy, and the athletes used for this purpose have been labeled diplomats in sweat suits.

Promoting Nazism: The 1936 Olympic Games

The first blatant international example of the use of sport as a platform for demonstrating political superiority was Adolf Hitler's exploitation of the 1936 Olympic Games to fortify his control over the German people and to display Nazi culture to the entire world. The games were a stunning charade that reinforced and rallied the hysterical patriotism of the German masses (Hilton 2008; Large 2007).

The success of the German Olympians at those games was spectacular. They won eighty-nine medals, twenty-three more than U.S. Olympians and more than four times as many as any other country won. For Hitler, these sports achievements were "proof" of the superiority of the Aryan race (blue eyes, blond hair).

Promoting Communism: The Soviet Sport System

It was the Soviet Union that pushed the principle of achieving national recognition and prestige, while uniting a broad range of ethnicities under a Soviet identity, through victories in international sport. In doing this it actually became the global model for this approach through the last half of the twentieth century. Until 1952 the Soviet Union shunned the Olympic Games as a Western capitalist creation, which the Communists disapproved of, so it was not until the Helsinki Olympics in 1952 that the Soviet Union first participated. The Cold War between Western and Communist countries was beginning, and the Soviet Union saw the importance of using sport as a political tool for enhancing the reputation of Communist states. The Soviets also grasped the potential of sport victories to advance their political cause.

A system of specialized sports schools was first established in the 1930s in the Soviet Union, and by the 1940s dozens of them were functioning in the USSR. By the time the USSR took part in the 1952 Olympics, specialized youth sports schools were preparing young athletically gifted athletes for elite international competition. The number of these sports schools grew, some of them training students only in Olympic sports. By 1991, some 6,000 sports schools existed in the USSR.

Beyond the sport schools Soviet adult elite athletes who continued to compete successfully in international sports events received well-paying government positions and well-appointed housing. Upon retirement from sport, they were accorded "sport-hero" status and were well taken care of.

This system achieved its goal of garnering victories in international sport competition. Before it was dismantled in 1991, the Soviet Union had competed at the Summer Olympic Games nine times, and at seven of these its national team ranked first in the total number of medals won; it ranked second in the other two. Furthermore, the USSR ranked first in the medal count seven times and second twice in nine appearances at the Winter Olympic Games. Soviet leaders touted each victory as confirmation of the superiority of communism over Western capitalism (Riordan 1980).

Like it or not, the Soviet Union's system of elite sport development became the model globally for countries wishing to compete with any chance of success in international sport or to use sport as a tool for national identity.

East Germany and the People's Republic of China: Adopting the Soviet Sport Model

At the end of World War II, Germany was divided into two countries. The western part became the Federal Republic of Germany and was under the control of the United States, the United Kingdom, and France. An eastern zone was held by the Soviet Union and became the German Democratic Republic. Before the reunification of Germany in 1990, East Germany (German Democratic Republic), perhaps more than any other country, created a deliberate elite sports program modeled after the Soviet Union's. Its main purposes were to gain international acceptance as a sovereign state, demonstrate the superiority of the Communist way of life, and create a specific East German identity (Johnson 2008).

A nation of only 17 million people (about two-thirds the population of California at that time), it developed an elaborate system of sport schools for the most promising athletes, at which they received intense training and expert coaching, in addition to academic schooling. A sophisticated regimen of performance-enhancing drugs was part of the overall sport system to win victories, medals, and international recognition and respect (Ungerleider 2001). Most impressively, East Germany placed among the top three nations in Olympic medals won throughout the 1970s and 1980s (East Germany did not take part in the 1984 games). Each victory by East German athletes in international competition was proof of "their better socialist system," claimed the East German general secretary (quoted in Rosellini 1992, 51).

After the death of Communist leader Mao Tse-tung in 1976, the People's Republic of China, the most populous country in the world, gradually began to revise its national sport policy from "friendship first, competition second," once advocated by Mao, to an all-out quest for global recognition and status. China's political and sport officials openly acknowledged that they viewed sport as one instrument for promoting national pride and identity while boosting the stature of the Chinese political and social system worldwide.

These are the motivations behind the current Chinese government's huge expenditure of hundreds of millions of dollars annually for sports. An estimated six million young athletes are trained at sport schools, with those at the highest levels subsidized by the state. Training athletes in the four years leading up to the 2008 Olympic Games cost China roughly $400 million to $500 million (MacLeod 2007; Worden 2008; Xu 2008).

The United States: Joining Other Countries in Sport Politics

Compared with most countries of the world, the United States has always had a more limited direct involvement in international sport. Many countries have a minister of sport (or an official with a similar title), who has access to the country's top political leadership, just as the other ministers do, and has a direct funding source from the national treasury. As the accounts above illustrate quite vividly, in these countries, the government supports international-level sports directly. Nevertheless, the U.S. government and its many branches and agencies are committed to supporting sport for the advancement of the American political-economic system.

The major geopolitical dispute from the end of World War II until the early 1990s was between the two superpowers, the United States and the Soviet Union. They confronted each other throughout the world in what was called the Cold War. By the early 1970s it had become clear that the successes of Soviet and East German athletes in international sport competition were having favorable worldwide political significance. Each new victory was seen as irrefutable proof of the superiority of those Communist nations over the non-Communist states.

At about this time, editorial writers, politicians, and various sport organizations began advocating that American athletes be subsidized and receive the best coaching and facilities to keep up with the Soviet Union and East Germany in order to regain international sport supremacy. Those pleas reached Congress, which as a result appropriated funds for the U.S.

Olympic Committee (USOC) to establish permanent training sites for Winter and Summer Olympic sports. Also, the USOC was allowed to gradually loosen the eligibility rules for participation, which meant expanding the rules about amateur status.

Meanwhile, concern about America's international image became the motivation behind former president Gerald Ford's creation of the President's Commission on Olympic Sports. The commission's recommendations resulted in the Amateur Sports Act of 1978, reorganizing amateur sport and committing the government to a continuing investment in international sport. At the same time, the report strongly recommended that private-sector firms provide the major funding for American sports, suggesting that it was in their interests to promote American athletes and teams competing around the world.

By the mid-1980s, U.S. athletes were being subsidized by corporations like Nike and Reebok, yet still being allowed to compete in the Olympic Games. That is, athletes were permitted to retain their "amateur" status while they were receiving money for sport performances, appearances, and endorsements; thus, world-class American athletes could make hundreds of thousands of dollars, some surpassing $1 million, without losing their eligibility. As I have previously explained, in the late 1980s, the International Olympic Committee (IOC) relaxed its amateur rule, opening the Olympic Games and all Olympic-sponsored sports to professional athletes. The USOC and national sport federations began to give more and more funds to elite athletes. Between 2004 and 2008 the USOC and various national Olympic committees (NOCs) spent approximately $250 million to prepare the United States team for the 2008 Beijing Olympic Games.

No specific American governmental agency funds America's international-level sports, but federal, state, and local governments contribute public money to support elite sports in various ways. A few examples will suffice to illustrate this point:

- Federal and state governments have contributed land, buildings, personnel, and support services to all the U.S. Olympic training centers. In 2008 the city of Colorado Springs offered the USOC $27.2 million in public money to keep the Olympic Training Center in that city.
- In all Olympic Games held in the United States, federal government money has been used in support of the venues and for security. Although the 1996 Atlanta Summer Games were privately funded,

the federal government contributed an estimated $227 million for security, transportation, and so forth.

- The state of Georgia spent $150 million on public buildings that were used during the Atlanta games. Atlanta and other local governments spent approximately $90 million on projects related to the Olympics.
- For the 2002 Salt Lake City Winter Olympic Games, the Utah state government and local governments contributed in excess of $250 million, and the federal government contributed an estimated $1.5 billion in taxpayer dollars.
- The U.S. government utilizes high-profile elite athletes to cultivate international goodwill and to enhance America's image in foreign countries. For example, the State Department sponsors tours of athletes and teams to foreign countries for these purposes. In 2007, President George W. Bush appointed ex–Major League Baseball player and Hall of Famer Cal Ripken Jr. as special envoy for the State Department.

These examples represent a small fraction of the total public support for America's international-level sports. It is actually impossible to determine how much government money is spent because much of it is spread out and hidden deeply in the labyrinth of hundreds of agencies' and bureaucracies' budgets.

New and Smaller Nations Adopt the Model

For the smaller, sometimes new, nations, triumphs in international sport competition can also bring national pride, recognition, and respect in the world community. A relatively unknown country can gain worldwide attention when one of its athletes or teams wins an important international sporting event. For a few days at least, a country can bask in the limelight of the world's attention. Invariably, such achievements become a focus of conversation within a country, and feelings of national pride are enhanced as people sense a common bond, a collective identity, among the athletes, themselves, and their nation.

Canada and Australia are two countries with small populations that invested heavily in sport during the 1960–1990 era by creating systematic programs to produce elite athletes for international competition with the aim of developing symbols of national identity. Their governmental actions began as efforts to provide greater opportunities for mass sport and physical fitness but turned rather quickly toward the promotion of high-performance sport because of its perceived potential for much more attractive political payoffs, especially in unifying nationalist needs.

Sport Canada, a federal agency under the jurisdiction of a minister of state for sport, and similar organizations at the provincial level promote sports excellence in elite athletes. A federal Athlete Assistance Program provides living and training grants to outstanding athletes. There is also a group of national training centers staffed with professional coaches. A special project, called Podium Canada and consisting of the Own the Podium and Road to Excellence programs, aims mainly to improve Canada's performance at the Olympic Games and Paralympics.

In a book about sport and politics in Canada between 1960 and 1990, the authors describe the massive federally funded sports program as an instrument "to promote national unity" (MacIntosh, Bedicki, and Franks 1988, 4). Canadian sport-studies scholar Bruce Kidd maintained that the purpose of Canada's program was to "enhance Canadian nationalism and [international] legitimacy" (1991, 182; see also Macintosh and Whitson 1990).

Cuba, another small country in population, makes a serious effort to intervene in and promote sport for national unity and international recognition. Even though Fidel Castro has relinquished the reigns of leadership in Cuba, his decree that sport is a right of the people remains in place. No admission fee is charged at sporting events. Promising young athletes are given the best coaching and training. Approximately 3 percent of Cuba's national budget is provided to the sports ministry for selecting, training, and providing living expenses for elite athletes.

Cuba has dominated the Pan American Games, winning nearly fifteen times more medals, on a per capita basis, than the United States. Castro often proclaims to his Latin American neighbors that these sports achievements are proof of the superiority of the Cuban people and the Cuban political system (see Tables 6.1 and 6.2 for an analysis of how nations ranked in the 2008 Summer Olympics, taking population and gross domestic product into account).

Developing Countries and National Unification Through Sport

The use of sport as an instrument of national policy has not been limited to the developed countries of the world. Many political leaders in developing countries have seriously pursued sporting success for national-unification

Table 6.1 Medal Standings per Country by Population, Beijing Olympics, 2008

Rank	Actual Rank	Country	Population (millions)	Actual Medal Totals
1	13	Jamaica	2.7	11
2	65	Bahamas	0.3	2
3	71	Iceland	0.3	1
4	41	Slovenia	2.0	5
5	21	Norway	4.7	10
*				
11	28	Cuba	11.3	24
*				
22	4	Great Britain	61.0	47
*				
30	10	France	61.7	40
*				
32	5	Germany	82.3	41
*				
36	3	Russia	141.6	72
*				
44	2	United States	301.6	110

Notes: Column 1 shows rank according to weighted per capita total. Column 2 shows the actual rank according to actual medals.
Source: Mitchell 2008.

and nation-building purposes. Some 90 percent of developing countries have a cabinet-level post related to sport. A primary task of sport ministers in these countries is the development of elite sport—athletes, coaches, sport medicine, sport science, sport facilities—for success in international sporting competitions. Rather than identifying and discussing national sport policies across the globe, I shall focus on one region: sub-Saharan Africa. As I will concentrate only on black African states, I will not include South Africa.

The African Continent and African States

The industrial and technological development in Asian political economies since the 1970s and in many South American countries since the 1980s has, unfortunately, not been replicated in African countries. Despite their inability to establish stable regimes, several sub-Saharan national leaders

**Table 6.2 Medal Standings per Country
by Gross Domestic Product (GDP), Beijing Olympics, 2008**

Rank	Actual	Country	GDP 2007 (US$ millions)	Actual Medal Totals
1	33	North Korea	2,220	6
2	38	Zimbabwe	3,418	4
3	31	Mongolia	3,894	4
4	13	Jamaica	10,739	11
5 *	27	Georgia	10,176	6
7 *	28	Cuba	45,100	24
18 *	46	Estonia	21,279	2
34 *	26	New Zealand	129,372	9
37 *	3	Russia	1,291,011	72
44 *	1	China	3,280,053	100
61 *	5	Germany	3,297,233	41
72	2	United States	13,811,200	110

Notes: Column 1 shows rank according to weighted per capita total. Column (2) shows the actual rank according to actual medals.
Source: Mitchell 2008.

have attempted to utilize sport to create a unifying symbolism, via various internationally renowned African athletes, for political gain and to bring some credibility to their failing rules.

Some were briefly successful. Between the 1960s and 1980s, several national leaders attained international recognition, stature, and national unity through sport. They did this by establishing a national sport system similar to the ones in developed countries under the direction and control of a sports council or commission with authority to organize and finance sport nationally.

African achievements in international sport had been minimal until Ethiopian Abebe Bikila won the 1960 Rome Olympics marathon race (running barefooted!) to become the first black African Olympic champion. Another African, a Moroccan, Rhadi Ben Abdesselam, took second place. Bikila's victory brought just the kind of worldwide recognition to

Ethiopia that Emperor Haile Selassie sought for his nation. When he awarded Bikila the Order of the Star of Ethiopia for his Olympic marathon victory, Selassie said, "To win the laurel of world victory ... is a significant event that brings global reputation to our country" (Maraniss 2008, 399).

During the 1960s and 1980s, a wave of excitement for sport spread across Africa, fueled by a group of African athletes who captured the world's attention with victories at various international sports events, including the Olympic and Commonwealth games. In Kenya President Jomo Kenyatta astutely recognized that the international achievements of a group of Kenyan middle- and long-distance track stars, led by two-time Olympic gold medal champion Kip Keino, had established their nation's worldwide domination of distance running. He used these international sports achievements by Kenyan athletes to promote national unity and pride in a country with a history of deep political divisions based on family and tribal loyalty. Using the sports victories of Kenyan runners as diplomatic lubrication, Kenyatta briefly managed to establish stability in Kenya and attract foreign investment. Unfortunately, his regime drifted into domestic dissent and tribal rivalries.

From the 1960s through the 1990s, other African political leaders attempted to follow Kenyatta's precedent in exploiting the sporting triumphs of African athletes to create a single consciousness among their diverse peoples, promote their own political ambitions, and build national pride and international prestige. Political leaders in Cameroon, Ghana, Libya, Morocco, and Zaire were some of the most ardent in pursuing sport successes for political gain. Most African nations did make some progress in gaining national and international recognition through their athletes, but many floundered with corrupt governments, civil conflicts, and political coups. Consequently, whatever geopolitical success they had experienced through sports was largely lost. As sport-studies scholars Lincoln Allison and Terry Monnington say, "The great promise of the early years of independence has for many African countries evaporated as natural disasters, economic mismanagement, corruption and poor leadership have crippled their economies and political systems.... Sport can only bring temporary respite and transient pleasure for a beleaguered society. Sporting success and the associated prestige for all concerned, including the political 'hangers on,' cannot hide the consequences of a collapsing, corrupt economy" (2004, 23).

Moreover, from the mid-1970s right up to the present, many of the best African athletes have been lured to professional soccer teams throughout the world and to the United States by athletic scholarships to compete on university sports teams.

National Embarrassments Through Sport

When nationalistic emotion gets wrapped up in sports triumphs, sporting failures can generate national embarrassment. The Brazilian World Cup teams' poor showing during the past two decades has caused hand-wringing among political and sports officials and led to numerous mass media diatribes characterizing Brazil's soccer as a national disgrace. Even more embarrassing to the United States, though, was the ignominious disclosure that Marion Jones, track and field winner of three Olympic gold medals and two bronze medals at the 2000 Sydney Summer Olympics (dubbed "America's darling" at those games), admitted she used steroids and had lied to federal investigators when she denied taking performance-enhancing drugs (Shipley 2007).

Some citizens in countries that spend huge sums of money on elite athletes, sport facilities, and plush training centers do not find these issues terribly embarrassing, while others find them socially troubling. In many of these countries, public investment in mass sport participation is redirected toward a narrow focus on elite sports. At one time Peru, certainly not an international powerhouse in sport, nevertheless spent 80 percent of its national sport budget on one sport—women's volleyball (Anthony 1991, 332).

Geopolitical Censorship in Sport: Nation-Led Boycotts

International sport has become a global public political forum. Countries can express disagreement with other countries' policies by refusing to compete with them, and sport organizations can refuse to compete with other sport organizations. Actions taken by nations against other countries gain worldwide attention; therefore, registering disapproval of a particular nation, either by attempting to isolate that country from international sporting competition or by boycotting particular events, pressures the offender into complying with the censuring nations.

Governments have increasingly used boycotting to penalize international behavior of which they disapprove. Because of their worldwide visibility and popularity, the Olympic Games have provided a unique stage upon which governments can take a political stand, and indeed the Olympics have been plagued by threats of boycotts from the very beginning. But no major boycott of the Olympics occurred until 1956—sixty years after the first modern Olympic Games were held. See Box 6.1 for descriptions of Olympic boycotts instigated by national government actions.

Box 6.1 lists only the major Olympic boycotts; there have been dozens of others by small nations, territories, organizations, and even individuals wishing to secure Olympic membership or to protest the policies of nations that are Olympic members or of the Olympic Movement itself. Furthermore, other global sport organizations have been subject to intervention based on geopolitical issues. For example, in 2010, South Africa became the first African nation to host the World Cup. Some individuals and groups decided that if South Africa continued to ignore human rights abuses in Zimbabwe, the solution would be to boycott the 2010 event.

Global Politics Within Sport

Up to this point in this chapter, I have focused on ways in which national governments have used sport for their own political interests—for national-unity and national-identity creation, sport diplomacy, and geopolitical censure. It is important to understand that national governments are not the only sites of political action in sport. Much of the politics of sport occurs outside the purview of state politics.

Early in this chapter I emphasized that sport-political connections exist at all levels of sport and politics. Sport organizations, like organizations of any kind, have conflicts about the division of power; rules and policies; the selection of leaders; and class, race, ethnicity, and gender discrimination; they also have interorganizational disputes. Finally, issues arise about the ways in which an organization uses power to pursue its own interests at the expense of other groups and organizations.

The Politics of Gender Inequality in Global Sport

Gender and racial prejudice and discrimination are intensely political insofar as they can have a profound impact on individual choices and career opportunities, as well as on social justice in general, for those subject to these forms of inequity. The feminist movement popularized the slogan

Box 6.1 Boycotts of the Olympic Games

Melbourne 1956. The first Olympics to be boycotted by a government decree was the 1956 Melbourne Summer Olympic Games. Three countries, the Netherlands, Spain, and Switzerland, boycotted because of the Soviet Union's repression of the 1956 Hungarian Revolution. Also Cambodia, Egypt, Iraq, and Lebanon boycotted the 1956 Olympics because of a military attack by several countries when Egypt nationalized the Suez Canal. The People's Republic of China (PRC) refused to participate because of the presence of the Republic of China (Taiwan), which the PRC has never recognized as a sovereign nation.

Montreal 1976. Twenty African countries were joined by Guyanna and Iraq in a Tanzania-led boycott of the 1976 Montreal Summer Olympics, in an effort to force the IOC to ban South Africa and Rhodesia because of their apartheid policies. The African nations also boycotted because the IOC did not suspend New Zealand for its continuing contacts with South Africa. Taiwan also boycotted these games over issues having to do with a dispute about the name under which the nation would compete.

Moscow 1980. In 1980 the United States and sixty-four other nations boycotted the Moscow Olympic Games because of the Soviet Union's military intervention in Afghanistan. This boycott reduced the number of nations participating to only eighty-one, the lowest number since 1956.

Los Angeles 1984. In retaliation, the Soviet Union and fourteen Eastern Bloc supporters (not including Romania) boycotted the 1984 Los Angeles Summer Olympics, arguing that anti-Soviet hysteria was rampant in the United States, so the sport delegations from these countries would be unable to guarantee the safety of their athletes.

Seoul 1988. In 1988, North Korea, still officially at war with South Korea and unhappy about its unsuccessful cohosting bid for that year's games, boycotted the Seoul Olympics. Cuba, Ethiopia, and Nicaragua joined the boycott.

Beijing 2008. There were calls for a boycott of the 2008 Olympics in Beijing in protest of China's human rights record and in response to the recent disturbances in Darfur, Taiwan, and Tibet. Ultimately, no nation withdrew before the games.

"The personal is political" during the late 1960s and early 1970s to rebut critics who accused women of "playing politics" when they sought equal treatment and opportunity in the economic, political, religious, educational, social, and sporting sectors of their lives. The slogan was meant to inspire women to be politically active in the issues that affected their lives, to make sure that decision makers at all levels paid attention to women's lives, and to be aware of how laws, policies, and practices throughout the world ignored women.

Few international sport federations or other global sport organizations have taken a prominent stand on gender equity in their policy agendas beyond ritual condemnation of gender discrimination. Here we have another example of globalization from above. One of the main reasons for the lack of equity is that modern sport emerged within a historical global culture of male dominance and female subordination. At the global sport organization (GSO) level, gender equality has had a low priority in the IOC and other major GSOs as illustrated by the general reluctance of most international sports bodies to adopt a clear policy about women's status in these organizations. Thus, GSOs and their affiliates continue to be bastions of male dominance.

As one might expect, opportunities for women to engage in sports at the highest levels have been severely restricted historically, and differential rewards have been the norm. Gender inequality has prevailed in the Olympic Games since the modern games began in 1896. The statements of modern Olympics founder Pierre de Coubertin, which I cited in Chapter 2, make quite clear his belief that females did not belong, and there were no sporting events for women in the first modern Olympic Games in 1896. A few women participated in the second Olympics in 1900; their participation increased in subsequent Olympics, but in 1924 they still constituted only 4 percent of the total participants. Even by 1964 women competitors made up only 25 percent of the total athletes competing.

Events for females have gradually been added to both the Summer and Winter Olympic Games over the past forty-five years, but vast gender inequities remain. For example, in the 1992 Barcelona Summer Olympics 286 events were open to men, but only 86—30 percent—were open to women. The situation was not much better at the 1994 Winter Games in Lillehammer, Norway. That year, 1,302 men and 542 women—42 percent—competed. By the 2004 Athens Summer Olympic Games, there were over 120 women's events and more than 170 men's events (about a dozen were mixed); some 41 percent of the total participants were women, and 59 percent were men. Thus, there were more women's events than ever before, and the gap between the number of men's and women's events narrowed to an all-time low. At the 2008 Beijing Olympics, the all-time highest percentage of females participated, 43 percent; still, men outnumbered women as Olympic athletes.

Accompanying the increase in female competitors, new opportunities are opening up for women in the Olympics. Women's ice hockey was added for the 1994 Winter Games in Lillehammer, and women's softball and soccer were part of the 1996 Summer Games in Atlanta.[1] In 2000 and 2004, several new sports and more than twenty new events for women were added to the Summer Olympic Games. In 2008 in Beijing women competed in the same number of sports as in 2004 (26) but in two more events (137). New women's sports events have been added to recent Winter Olympic Games, and the percentage of female athletes participating rose from 27 percent in the 1992 Winter Olympics in Albertville to 40.5 percent in 2010 at the Vancouver Winter Olympics (IOC 2010b).

Although a clear pattern is evident of an increasing number and percentage of women in every Olympiad for the past fifty years, there is wide variation in the percentage of women representing each country at each Olympic Games. In the 2004 Athens Summer Olympics, more than twenty countries sent no women to the games; about half of these all-male Olympic teams were from Islamic countries. On the other hand, at the 1996 Atlanta Olympics, for the first time Canada had more women than men on its team; of the 307 Canadian athletes, 154 were female, and 153 were male.

Coaches are an indispensable part of organized sports. Thousands of coaches coach national Olympic teams, and thousands more coach teams that play for other GSOs, but the fluid movement into and out of those positions makes it difficult to determine the percentage of male and female coaches with any accuracy. One generalization is possible, however: The overwhelming majority of coaches are men. Wherever elite and professional sport is played internationally, men coach almost all of the men's sport teams, and males also coach many of the women's teams as well. Where the head coach of a women's sport team is a woman, men often hold positions as assistant, or special-position, coaches.

As I reported in Chapter 2, leadership positions in GSOs have been, and continue to be, filled predominantly by men. In 2007 only 29 percent of the USOC management staff and only 27 percent of the board of directors were female. Not until eighty-seven years after the IOC was formed was the first woman elected to membership in this GSO—in 1981. In 1990, for the first time in the history of the IOC, a woman, Flor

Isava Fonseca, was elected to the executive board, and in 1997 another woman, Anita L. DeFrantz, became an IOC vice president. In 2010 16 out of 108 active IOC members were women (three women are honorary members) (IOC 2010a).

In recognition of a need to provide greater opportunity for women's leadership in the Olympic Movement, in 1997 the IOC established targets for women's membership on NOC executive committees. Women were to hold at least 10 percent of executive decision-making positions in NOCs by December 2001, rising to at least 20 percent by December 2005. In 2004 the findings were published of a research project by the Institute of Sport and Leisure Policy at Loughborough University and the International Olympic Committee that evaluated the progress of the implementation of the IOC target policy in relation to women's leadership on the executive committees of NOCs. The final report, *Women, Leadership and the Olympic Movement,* concluded,

> Perhaps the most obvious point to make is that the introduction of minimum targets has had a clear and positive impact on the proportion of women in NOC Executive Committees. The rapid growth of the numbers of women is such positions, from a very low base, immediately after the announcement of the minimum targets is clear both in numeric terms from the questionnaire data, and also from the observations made by women and the Secretary Generals during the interviews. Thus the target approach can be said to have had success in raising awareness of gender inequalities, in bringing talented women into the Olympic family, and of improving Olympic governance by setting an example and providing moral leadership to the world of sport in terms of equity in representation. (White and Henry 2004, 7)

Despite the lengthy history of discrimination against women's sport and women in sport at the top levels of sport, and notwithstanding the slow pace of change and the degree of inequality that remains, progress has been made throughout the world toward expanding opportunities for females during the past three decades. That being said, significant progress remains to be made.

The Politics of Racial Inequality in Global Sport

Unlike the patriarchal and religious ideologies that historically barred most women from sport, the ideology underlying racism has been less restrictive for black athletes' sport involvement. In some situations, however, it has dictated that black athletes be subordinated to, and in other times and places be totally segregated from, white athletes and teams. Still, despite pervasive and systematic discrimination against black athletes in many countries where the majority of the population is Caucasian, blacks have played a significant and continuing role in every era of modern sport.

Rather than recounting individual incidents of racism that have occurred in global sport, I shall explain how the politics of South African apartheid affected sport in that country. Then I shall explain how athletes, coaches, and sport organizations played a pivotal political role in persuading the South African government to abolish the apartheid regime.

South African Apartheid and Sport. Racial segregation in South Africa began during its colonial era, but its government enforced apartheid—a system of legal racial segregation—between 1948 and 1994. In this system of institutionalized racism and white domination, people were classified into racial groups (black, white, colored, and Indian). Blacks were barred from citizenship, residential areas were segregated by means of forced removals, and the government segregated education, medical care, and other public services, all of which provided black people with services vastly inferior to those for whites (Clark and Worger 2004; Martin and Martin 2006).

Not surprisingly, apartheid unleashed widespread internal resistance. Popular uprisings and protests were prevalent but were met with the government's banning opposition and imprisoning antiapartheid leaders. As resentment spread, it became more violent, so the African government responded with increased repression and state-sponsored violence. However, the international community avowed opposition to apartheid in a variety of ways. Political, economic, military, and cultural sanctions were brought against South Africa. Increasingly, it was isolated from the rest of the world. Providing an account of the domestic and international struggle to abolish the apartheid system is beyond the scope of this book, so I must narrow the focus to an outline of those developments (Clark and Worger 2004; Martin and Martin 2006).

Before turning directly to South Africa, it is useful to examine how sport organizations respond when they want to sanction other sport organizations for one reason or another. When athletes and teams agree to compete athletically against each other, this is interpreted as recognition of and respect for the athletes and teams and even the country they represent. Conversely, refusing to engage in sport events with another country's athletes and teams or denying them visas or travel documents has become equivalent to severing sporting relations. The history of international sport, especially the Olympic Games, is filled with examples of this tactic. Austria and Germany were denied participation in the 1920 Olympics at Antwerp because of their role in World War I. Germany, Italy, and Japan were banned from the 1948 Olympics because of their actions in World War II.

At first, South Africa's ruling National Party dismissed all demands to integrate sport. Apartheid prohibited multiracial sport, meaning foreign teams with multiracial athletes could not play in South Africa, thus depriving South Africans from seeing many of the world's best athletes and best teams in action. So in 1962 the South African Non-Racial Olympic Committee (SAN-ROC), an organization attempting to obtain the rights of all athletes and teams in international sports (but not officially recognized by the IOC), was launched and successfully orchestrated a public debate on sports apartheid, revealing the immorality of that system. It was also instrumental in persuading the IOC to evict South Africa from the Olympic Movement. The work of SAN-ROC and other antiapartheid groups prompted the IOC to issue a warning to the South African National Olympic Committee (SANOC), the official South African representative to the IOC, that if there were no policy changes, South Africa would be barred from the 1964 Summer Olympic Games in Tokyo. When the South African minister of the interior Jan de Klerk asserted the team would not be racially integrated, the IOC withdrew its invitation to South Africa to the 1964 Olympics, in effect barring the country from the Tokyo games (Booth 1998). No South African team went to Tokyo (or to any other Olympics until the 1992 Barcelona Olympics).

As the 1968 Mexico City Summer Olympics approached, based on a vote of IOC members, the IOC was prepared to readmit South Africa because of assurances that South Africa's team would be multiracial. What followed was massive outrage. In advance of the IOC's decision to invite South Africa to the 1968 games, more than twenty-five countries threatened to boycott, led by black African nations. After the decision, other nations made the same threat. In the face of this opposition, the IOC reversed its stand, and South Africa was again not invited to the 1968 Olympics.

Finally, in 1970 recognition was withdrawn from SANOC, in effect formally expelling South Africa from the Olympic Movement. The IOC adopted a declaration against all "apartheid in sport" in June 1988 and for the total isolation of apartheid sport. Olympic historian Christopher Hill declares, "The isolation of South African sport is an exceptionally stark example of the use of sport for political ends, and the Olympic Movement was naturally involved from the earliest days" (1996, 198).

The IOC was not the only GSO that acted against South Africa's apartheid system; South Africa was also suspended by the Fédération Internationale de Football Association (FIFA) in 1963. When FIFA's president attempted to negotiate the country's reinstatement, the South African Football Federation proposed entering an all-white team in the 1966 World Cup and an all-black team in the 1970 World Cup. This proposal was rejected.

The actions of the Olympic Movement, FIFA, and other GSOs toward South Africa did not, of course, immediately affect its apartheid system; nor did these measures bring an end to international sport for South African teams. They did add, however, to the country's seclusion, while doing much to lift consciousness among many South Africans of the global condemnation of apartheid. Gradually, these sanctions and boycotts effectively created changes to apartheid policy, and weakened white South Africans' dedication to it. By 1990 President Frederik de Klerk had initiated negotiations to end apartheid, which concluded with multiracial democratic elections in 1994.

The African National Congress, under the leadership of Nelson Mandela, won the election, ending apartheid for all intents and purposes. The Olympic Movement ban was revoked in 1993, when conciliations with a democratic South Africa were well under way. Of course, the legacy of apartheid still shapes South African politics and society (Glaser 2001). Sport remains an integral element of postapartheid politics.

South African president Nelson Mandela and his government believed that sport can unite black and white South Africans and contribute to social and political change. Indeed, there have been moments, such as South Africa's victory in the 1995 Rugby World Cup, when unity through sport seemed possible. The 2009 film *Invictus,* based on John Carlin's book *Playing the Enemy: Nelson Mandela and the Game That Changed a Nation* (2008), illustrates Mandela's role in promoting sport as a means of social and political progress during the 1995 Rugby World Cup in South Africa. But through careful analysis, sport historian Doug Booth (1998) argues that sport will never unite South Africans except in the most fleeting and superficial manner.

The international campaign against apartheid in South Africa fashioned a perception of sport as a valuable political resource. The antiapartheid campaign raised the profile of the IOC, its international federations, and other GSOs as potential, if not actual, actors in international politics.

Other Incidents of Political Sport Rejection. Although the rejection is regional rather than global, Israel has faced hostile sport organizations with deep-seated objections to its status as a nation in what Arabs consider "their" region. Shortly after its creation in 1948, the state of Israel began sending athletes and teams to international sports events, one of which was the Asian Games, a regional sports competition regulated by the Olympic Council of Asia under the sponsorship of the IOC. These games are a multisport event held every four years in countries throughout Asia.

In 1962 the host country, Indonesia, opposed the participation of Israel (and Chinese Taipei too). Both the IOC and the International Association of Athletics Federations objected and threatened to cancel approval of the Jakarta Asian Games if the host country rejected the two countries. Nevertheless, Indonesia insisted on their exclusion and went ahead with the games. The same issue came up again in 1974, when Iran was the Asian Games host. Despite the opposition of Arab states, Iran allowed Israelis to participate in the games. However, Arab nations and athletes from other countries at the games refused to participate in several sports in which Israeli athletes and teams were competing.

In his account of these incidents, sport-studies scholar Barrie Houlihan suggests there were political motivations behind the lack of action by international sport organizations, such as the IOC, saying they "expressed their opposition to Israel's exclusion but backed away from expelling the countries supporting the boycott, thus avoiding a direct confrontation with Asian, and particularly Islamic, sports organizations" (2000, 218).

Political relations between Iran and Israel remain tense. At the 2004 Athens Summer Olympics, Iran took steps to avoid competition between Iranian and Israeli athletes. For example, Arash Miresmaeli, an Iranian judoka (a practitioner of judo), did not compete in a match against an Israeli. He was quoted in Iran as saying that he had refused to face his Israeli rival in sympathy with the "oppressed" Palestinian people. Although Miresmaeli was officially disqualified for excessive weight, this was merely a political face-saving action by Olympic officials. Miresmaeli was awarded the equivalent of $125,000 in prize money by the Iranian government, an amount usually paid only to Iranian gold medal winners (*BBC News* 2004).

As a consequence of the U.S. invasion and occupation of Iraq and the creation of a new Iraqi government, sport organizations within that country, as well as elite and professional sport teams, have been in a state of turmoil for several years. In July 2008, the IOC banned Iraq from taking part in the 2008 Beijing Summer Olympics due to "the government's political interference in sports" (Tawfeeq and Karadsheh 2008, 1). However, one week later the IOC reversed its decision after Iraq pledged "to ensure the independence of its national Olympics panel" by holding fair elections before the end of November; in the meantime, Iraq's Olympic organization was run by "an interim committee proposed by its national sports federations and approved by the IOC" (Jordans 2008, 1).

Politics Within the IOC and FIFA

The IOC and FIFA are the largest and most prominent GSOs. As I have mentioned several times, the IOC is the governance body for the Olympic Movement, which includes hundreds of subordinate sport bodies and, of course, the Summer and Winter Olympic Games. FIFA is responsible for the organization and governance of its major international tournaments, the best-known of which is the World Cup. In 2006, 198 nations challenged to qualify for the World Cup, and over 200 attempted to qualify for the 2010 World Cup.

IOC

The Olympic Movement has from the beginning recited, and continues to recite, the mantra "The Olympic movement is apolitical." Long-time Canadian IOC member Richard Pound recently asserted that "from the onset, the Olympic Games were conceived as an event that should be separate from political considerations.... The Olympic catechism regards the Games as a collection of individuals competing against other individuals" (2004, 88–89). However, several sport-studies researchers have convincingly documented the history of the centrality of politics in the Olympic Movement (Lenskyj 2000; Senn 1999). Australian Olympic scholars Kristine Toohey and A. J. Veal write, "From their inception to the present, the Olympic Games have been influenced by politics at individual, organizational, intra-national and international levels" (2007, 84).

Notwithstanding, the motto of the Olympic Games—"Citius, Altius, Fortius" ("Faster, Higher, Stronger")—and the often-repeated objective of the IOC "to cooperate with the competent public or private organisations and authorities in the endeavour to place sport at the service of humanity and thereby to promote peace" (IOC 2010c), the fundamental organizational feature of the Olympic Games is political. First of all, their very organization is political. Nations, through their NOCs (national organizations under the governance of the IOC), select all athletes who will participate in the Olympic Games. Thus, no athlete can compete without the sponsorship of his country. At the opening ceremonies of every Olympic Games, teams are publicly introduced with the country's name, and athletes march behind their country's flag. At the medal ceremony after each event is completed, the national anthem of the gold medal (first place) athlete is played, and the flags of the three medal-winning athletes' countries are raised at the awards ceremony.

Other activities by the IOC and its subordinate sport organizations are based on political considerations. Site selection for future Olympic Games is indisputably politicized. Cities, and the countries in which they are located, compete fiercely to win a bid to host an Olympic Games because of the potential economic, political, and cultural benefits they envision. High-level politicians, including prime ministers and presidents, usually lend their names to the bids because hosting an Olympics virtually makes the city and the nation the epicenter of world attention, while often legitimizing that nation's government.

The choice of Olympic sites is made by a vote of the members of the IOC and entails an elaborate system of site selection and decision making, involving applications, site visits, and multimedia presentations by applicants. While in theory the process looks impressive, objective, and nonpolitical, in practice it has historically been based on politics, corruption, and bribery—and in specific cases all three.

This is not hearsay or speculation. Andrew Jennings, one of Britain's best investigative journalists, and his colleagues published three remarkable books: *The Lord of the Rings: Power, Money, and Drugs in the Modern Olympics* (1992, with Vyv Simson), *The New Lords of the Rings* (1996), and *The Great Olympic Swindle: When the World Wanted Its Games Back* (2000, with Clare Sambrook). These volumes collectively report on the political corruption of the IOC and the Olympic Movement, including the use of bribery to buy votes for Olympic site selection. Respected *Sports Illustrated* writer Frank Deford praised *The Great Olympic Swindle*, saying, "Devastating disclosures so thorough they could have served, by themselves, as a prosecutor's brief" (quoted in Jennings and Sambrook 2000, back cover).

The revelations by Jennings and his colleagues were corroborated by the well-documented inducements made to IOC members by the organizers of the 1996 Atlanta Summer Games and the organizers of the 1998 Nagano Winter Olympics. More recently, Jennings and Sambrook's disclosures about the corruption and bribery involved in the awarding of the 2002 Winter Olympics to Salt Lake City are quite remarkable. Here the USOC spent $60,000 on favors for foreign sports officials to buy votes from IOC members to support Salt Lake City's bid. In addition $1.2 million was spent by the Salt Lake City Organizing Committee on college scholarships, shopping sprees, cash payments, free lodging, jobs, and other gifts for IOC members and their family members—those who would make the decision about the Salt Lake City bid (Brooke 1999; Drape 1999; Pound 2004, Chapter 8).

Richard Pound, an IOC member for over twenty-five years, accurately puts the Salt Lake City political machinations in historical context, saying, "The Salt Lake City disaster had been in the works for years. The IOC should have seen it coming much sooner" (2004, 225).

FIFA

The president of FIFA, Joseph "Sepp" Blatter, has been at the center of much of the political machinations within this global federation over the past decade, beginning with his election to the presidency of FIFA in 1998. Rumors circulated before his election about bribery and vote fixing, even that he paid several African delegates $50,000 each for their votes. Again, in 2002 Blatter's candidacy for president was marked by accusations of financial irregularities and corruption since his election in 1998. This time the charges were made by FIFA's general secretary, Michael Zen-Ruffinen, in a report he presented to the executive committee. However, Blatter claimed Zen-Ruffinen's allegations were politically motivated, and he went on to win reelection. Once his victory was assured, he immediately dismissed Zen-Ruffinen from the FIFA position he held. In 2007 Blatter was confirmed as president by acclamation for a third term (Jennings 2007; Sugden and Tomlinson 2005).

One of FIFA's statutes impinges on the politics of both its own associate and member organizations and the nations in which they function. If a national government interferes in the running of FIFA's associate or member organizations, FIFA suspends teams and associated members from international competition. For example in 2006, FIFA ruled that the Hellenic (Greek) Football Federation (HFF) did not meet the principles of FIFA policies about political independence, so it indefinitely suspended the HFF from international soccer competition. However, the Greek government quickly changed its sports law, granting the federation independence, and FIFA lifted its suspension.

Also in 2006, a similar suspension was imposed on the Kenya Football Federation (KFF) as a result of interference in the affairs of the federation by Kenyan governmental authorities, a violation of FIFA's rules. Consequently, Kenyan national teams and clubs were not allowed to participate in international competitive matches, all FIFA financial-assistance payments were frozen, and the KFF was deprived of its right to vote at congresses held by international soccer federations. The political pressure on the Kenyan government worked; it agreed to grant independent operations to the KFF, and the suspension was lifted in 2007 (FIFA 2009).

FIFA, like the IOC, has a decidedly Eurocentric bias, even though Africans have been wildly passionate about soccer for decades, and many of the world's top professional soccer players have come out of Africa for many years. GSOs, much like national governments and multinational corporations, have exploited African human labor and its natural resources. Because many of the black African countries are still developing, they have not been treated equitably by FIFA. Paul Darby, in his recent book *Africa Football and FIFA: Politics, Colonialism, and Resistance,* argues that political relations between soccer's national associations, international federations, and FIFA have been carried out on the basis of local, national, and regional allegiances rather than an attitude of internationalism. Darby asserts that this has been apparent in the relationship between FIFA and the African Football Confederation, the administrative and controlling body for African soccer. He convincingly describes how Africa's relationships within FIFA and other GSOs are linked to black African national political economies and how the balance of power within FIFA continues to favor European hegemony (Darby 2002).

Political Dissent at Global Sports Events

Regardless of the international sporting event (e.g., the Olympic Games, the Commonwealth Games, and the World Cup), nongovernmental activists wishing to advance their cause politically have often used sports events to gain worldwide recognition via various forms of protest. Almost every international sporting event in the past forty years has experienced activism for causes such as nuclear proliferation, world peace, Tibetan independence, AIDS, sweatshops, women's and race movements, human rights, the living wage, and so forth. There have been so many of these political dissents at sporting events, taking multiple forms, that it would be impossible to summarize them all. Therefore, I have chosen to describe only a few examples.

Because the Olympic Games are arguably the most prominent world sporting event, they have been the bull's eye for more political activism than any other international sporting event. Political protests, demonstrations, threats, and violence by dissenting groups have been a part of virtually every recent Olympiad. The most legendary sporting protest incident occurred at the 1968 Mexico City Summer Olympic Games. During the medal ceremony for the two-hundred-meter sprint race, two African American track and field athletes, Tommie Smith, the gold medalist, and John Carlos, the bronze medalist, raised gloved, clenched fists and bowed their heads during the playing of the national anthem in an attempt to call dramatic attention to pervasive racism in the United States. Silver medalist Peter Norman from Australia (who is white) wore an Olympic Project for Human Rights badge in support of Smith and Carlos. The photo of the three men on the podium has become an iconic Olympic image. But Smith and Carlos paid a heavy price for their commitment to racial justice. The U.S. Olympic Committee suspended them from the Olympic team, they were thrown out of the Olympic Village, and they were banned for life from competing in the Olympic Games.

Four years later, at the 1972 Munich Summer Olympics, a group of Palestinians went to the extreme of political protest by storming the living quarters of the Israeli team at the Olympic Village and capturing Israeli athletes. Their mission was to negotiate a trade whereby the Israeli athletes would be freed if Israel would release some 240 Palestinians held in Israeli jails. German commandos tried to free the captives, but one of the Palestinians ignited a grenade, killing eleven athletes and five kidnappers.

In just the past twenty years, there have been several actions by dissidents: The 1992 Barcelona Olympics faced Spanish Basque separatists, who threatened to use the Olympics as a vehicle for worldwide recognition of their demands. At the Atlanta Olympics in 1996, a bomb was exploded by an antiabortion activist who objected to legalized abortion. At the Sydney Olympics in 2000, Aborigines conducted peaceful demonstrations to showcase to the world the discrimination they face in Australia. At the Athens Olympics in 2004, protests against the Iraq War were held at the U.S. Embassy, protesting a visit by U.S. Secretary of State Colin Powell.

Preceding the 2008 Beijing Olympics, various protests centered on human rights issues such as the working conditions in Chinese factories (Play Fair 2008 2008), political prisoners, and the environment. The Olympic Flame relay protest attracted the most worldwide media coverage. The torch's twenty-nation global route attracted activists frustrated by China's human rights record—in particular, its grip on Tibet and its arming of Sudan's government (Goldman and Neary 2008). There were also calls for boycotts of the Beijing Olympics in protest against China's response to its disputes with Tibet and Taiwan. But ultimately no nation boycotted the Beijing Olympic Games.

China, in an effort to seem politically open, promised to provide specially designated zones for protesters during the 2008 Beijing Olympics, signaling that China's authoritarian government might allow some demonstrations during the games (ESPN 2008). However, of the more than seventy-five applications to hold protests in the designated zones, Chinese authorities approved none. This means that the demonstration zones existed in name only, so the promise of them was a charade (MacLeod 2007).

In contrast, protesters who converged on the 2010 Vancouver Winter Olympics with a myriad of causes—from opposition to the Olympic Movement to calls for Canada's withdrawal from Afghanistan—were permitted full public demonstrations for most every day of the Vancouver Olympics, in the spirit of the long history of free public expression in Canada (Johnson 2010).

Summary

It is often argued that sports should remain apart from politics or, conversely, that politics should be kept out of sport. In reality sport and politics have always been intermingled. Indeed, an office of minister of sport is often found in national governments. During international sporting events, like the Olympic Games, nationalistic displays of various kinds are ubiquitous.

Sport is used to promote national unity and build national identity and serves as a fundamental political instrument of foreign policy in many countries of the world. The fostering of national loyalty and patriotism through sport rituals and ceremonies is a global practice among governments. Direct propaganda connections between sports triumphs and the superiority of a political-economic system were forged prominently and globally during the fifty-year Cold War. But the use of sport as an instrument of national policy was not limited to that era. Actually, developing countries in Africa and Asia have also been adopting this method for nation building.

Because contemporary sport is so globally popular, it has become a public forum for censorship, either via the isolation of countries from international sports participation or the boycotting of sports events. The purpose is to pressure an offending nation into complying with the demands of the censuring ones. The Olympic Games have been boycotted several times by countries who wished to make a political statement about an issue.

Prejudice and discrimination are political in nature because of the effect they have on individual choice, occupational opportunities, and social justice. Gender and racial inequality have been pervasive in global sport organizations, not only in discouraging and limiting women and certain racial groups from competing as athletes and coaches, but also in the governing and administering of those organizations. The apartheid system of racial segregation in South Africa met global sport resistance, with many GSOs suspending South African athletes and teams from participation in their international events. Ultimately, actions by international sports bodies were instrumental in ending apartheid in South Africa.

Although the IOC and other sport organizations within the Olympic Movement have insisted that it stands apart from politics, convincing historical evidence suggests that politics has been central in the Olympic Movement at individual, organizational, and intra- and international levels since it was founded by Pierre de Coubertin. FIFA, the sponsor of the largest single-sport event, the World Cup, has been embroiled in internal political maneuvering, mostly involving its presidency, for over a decade.

Nongovernmental activists, as well as individual protesters, have found global sporting events an excellent site to advance their cause politically by obtaining worldwide publicity through media outlets. Most dissenters' actions are peaceful, but some turn violent. The most violent was the invasion of the Olympic Village at the 1972 Munich Olympics by Palestinians, which resulted in the deaths of eleven Israeli athletes and five kidnappers.

Notes

1. After being an Olympic sport for the 1996, 2000, 2004, and 2008 Olympic Games, softball was dropped from the 2012 London Olympics.

References

Allison, Lincoln, and Terry Monnington. 2004. Sport, prestige and international relations. In *The global politics of sport: The role of global institutions in sport*, ed. Lincoln Allison, 5–25. New York: Routledge.

Anthony, D. 1991. The north-south and east-west axes of development in sport: Can the gaps be bridged? In *Sport—the third millennium: Proceedings of the international symposium,* May 21–25, 1990, Quebec City, Canada, ed. Fernand Landry, Marc Landry, and Magdeleine Yerles. Sainte-Foy, Canada: Les Presses de L'Université.

BBC News. 2004. Mystery over Iran judo "protest." *BBC News,* August 15. http://news.bbc.co.uk/2/hi/europe/3562808.stm.

Booth, Doug. 1998. *The race game: Sport and politics in South Africa.* London: Frank Cass.

Brooke, James. 1999. Salt Lake City mayor quits as Olympic scandal grows. *New York Times,* January 12, A10.

Carlin, John. 2008. *Playing the enemy: Nelson Mandela and the game that changed a nation.* New York: Penguin Press.

Clark, Nancy L., and William H. Worger. 2004. *South Africa: The rise and fall of apartheid.* New York: Longman.

Darby, Paul. 2002. *African football and FIFA: Politics, colonialism, and resistance.* New York: Frank Cass.

Drape, Joe. 1999. Olympics; A plea of guilty in Olympic scandal. *New York Times,* August 4, D5.

ESPN. 2008. China to set up designated protest zones for Beijing Olympics. ESPN Olympic Sports, July 24. http://sports.espn.go.com/oly/news/story?id=3501456.

Fédération Internationale de Football Association (FIFA). 2009. About FIFA. FIFA.com. www.fifa.com/aboutfifa/federation/index.html.

Glaser, Daryl J. 2001. *Politics and society in South Africa.* Thousand Oaks, CA: Sage.

Goldman, Tom, and Lynn Neary. 2008. Continued protests plague Beijing Olympics. NPR, April 13. www.npr.org/templates/story/story.php?storyId=89598521.

Hill, Christopher R. 1996. *Olympic politics: Athens to Atlanta, 1896–1996.* 2nd ed. New York: Manchester University Press.

Hilton, Christopher. 2008. *Hitler's Olympics: The 1936 Berlin Olympic Games.* Charleston, SC: History Press.

Houlihan, Barrie. 2000. Politics and sport. In *Handbook of sports studies,* ed. Jay Coakley and Eric Dunning, 213–227. Thousand Oaks, CA: Sage.

International Olympic Committee (IOC). 2010a. Olympic Movement directory, IOC members. Olympic.org. www.olympic.org/en/content/The-IOC.

———. 2010b. Women make their way in Vancouver. Olympic.org, February 13. www.olympic.org/en/content/Olympic-Games/All-Future-Olympic-

Games/Winter/Vancouver-2010/?articleNewsGroup=-1&currentArticles PageIPP=10&currentArticlesPage=7&articleId=77001.

———. 2010c. The organization: Mission. Olympic.org. www.olympic.org/en/ content/The-IOC/The-IOC-Institution1.

Jackson, Steven J., and Steven Haigh, eds. 2009. *Sport and foreign policy in a globalizing world*. New York: Routledge.

Jennings, Andrew. 2007. *Foul! The secret world of FIFA: Bribes, vote rigging, and ticket scandals*. New York: Harper Collins.

Jennings, Andrew, and Clare Sambrook. 2000. *The great Olympic swindle: When the world wanted its games back*. New York: Simon & Schuster.

Johnson, Kevin. 2010. Free speech in Canada on display at the Games. *USA Today*, February 15, 4D.

Johnson, Molly. 2008. *Training socialist citizens: Sports and the state in East Germany*. Boston: Brill Academic Publishers.

Jordans, Frank. 2008. Olympic panel ends ban, says Iraq can go to games. *USA Today*, July 29. www.usatoday.com/news/topstories/2008-07-29-1527812812_x.htm.

Kidd, Bruce. 1991. How do we find our own voices in the "new world order"? A commentary on Americanization. *Sociology of Sport Journal* 8: 178–184.

Large, David Clay. 2007. *Nazi games: The Olympics of 1936*. New York: W. W. Norton.

Leibs, Andrew. 2004. *Sports and games of the Renaissance*. Westport, CT: Greenwood Publishing.

Lenskyj, Helen Jefferson. 2000. *Inside the Olympic industry: Power, politics, and activism*. Albany, NY: State University of New York Press.

MacIntosh, Donald, Tom Bedicki, and C. E. S. Franks. 1988. *Sport and politics in Canada: Federal government involvement since 1961*. Montreal: McGill-Queens University Press.

Macintosh, Donald, and Don Whitson. 1990. *The game planners: Transforming Canada's sports system*. Montreal: McGill-Queens University Press.

MacLeod, Calum. 2007. Chinese sports schools feel an urgency to find gold. *USA Today*, June 14, 1A, 6A.

———. 2009. Beijing games left a two-sided legacy. *USA Today*, April 16, 2C.

Maraniss, David. 2008. *Rome 1960: The Olympics that changed the world*. New York: Simon & Schuster.

Martin, Michael J., and Jennifer Martin. 2006. *Apartheid in South Africa*. San Diego, CA: Lucent Books.

Mitchell, Bill. 2008. Bill Mitchell's alternative Olympic Games medal tally—2008." BillMitchell.org, August 27. www.billmitchell.org/sport/medal_tally_2008.

Play Fair 2008. 2008. No medal for the Olympics on labour rights. PlayFair2008
.org. www.playfair2008.org/docs/playfair_2008-report.pdf.

Pound, Richard. 2004. *Inside the Olympics: A behind-the-scenes look at the politics, the scandals, and the glory of the games.* Etobicoke, Canada: John Wiley & Sons Canada.

Riordan, James. 1980. *Sport in Soviet Society: Development of sport and physical education in Russia and the USSR.* New York: Cambridge University Press.

Rosellini, Lynn. 1992. The sports factories. *U.S. News & World Report,* February 17, 51.

Senn, Alfred E. 1999. *Power, politics, and the Olympic Games.* Champaign, IL: Human Kinetics.

Shipley, Amy. 2007. Marion Jones admits to steroid use. *Washington Post,* October 5, A01.

Sugden, John, and Alan Tomlinson. 2005. Not for the good of the game: Crisis and credibility in the governance of world football. In *The global politics of sport: The role of global institutions in sport,* ed. Lincoln Allison, 26–45. New York: Routledge.

Tawfeeq, Mohammed, and Jomana Karadsheh. 2008. Iraq banned from Summer Games. CNN.com, July 24. www.cnn.com/2008/WORLD/meast/07/24/iraq.olympics/index.html.

Toohey, Kristine, and A. J. Veal. 2007. *The Olympic Games: A social science perspective.* 2nd ed. Wallingford, UK: CAB International.

Ungerleider, Steven. 2001. *Faust's gold: Inside the East German doping machine.* New York: Thomas Dunne Books.

Whannel, Garry. 2008. *Culture, politics and sport: Blowing the whistle, revisited.* New York: Routledge.

White, Anita, and Ian Henry. 2004. *Women, leadership and the Olympic Movement.* Loughborough, UK: International Olympic Committee and Institute of Sport and Leisure Policy, Loughborough University.

Wilson, Des. 2004. Cricket's shame: The inside story. *New Statesman* 133, no. 4717 (December 6): 27–29.

Worden, Minky, ed. 2008. *China's great leap: The Beijing Games and Olympian human rights challenges.* New York: Seven Stories Press.

Xu, Guoqi. 2008. *Olympic dreams: China and sports, 1895–2008.* Cambridge, MA: Harvard University Press.

CHAPTER 7

GLOBAL SPORT

FUTURE ISSUES AND TRENDS

> The future is here in global sport: In 2009 an Argentine
> won the Masters Golf Tournament, an American won the
> British Open, the PGA Championship was won by South
> Korea's Y. E. Yang, and eight countries were represented
> in the top nine at that tournament.

I conclude this volume with a chapter about the future of global sport. Throughout this book I have emphasized the interrelationship between the wider social world and global sport. As the social and physical conditions change across the planet, global sport will undoubtedly evolve in various ways as well.

Speaking before an audience, futurists often open with this tongue-in-cheek statement just to see if their audience is listening closely: "The future is before us." While there is some humor in this statement of the obvious, many people take futurists' predictions seriously—and for good reason. Business leaders look for predictions about population trends and shifts in consumer preferences; young adults seek information about trends in occupations, hoping that the career for which they are preparing will be a gateway to opportunity rather than a dead-end street; urban planners are attentive to future population composition and mobility trends; and average citizens worldwide realize that current trends may affect their lives in the years ahead.

Futurists, meaning groups of social forecasters and social scientists actively involved in predicting societal activity, study past and current trends and formulate analyses about the future. Private foundations and government agencies are the main sites for futuristic studies. Some of the best known include the following:

- The International Institute of Forecasters is a nonprofit organization founded in 1981 that analyzes insights gleaned from statistics, economics, psychology, and related disciplines for economic forecasting.
- The Trends Research Institute, founded in 1980, projects future global trends, how they will affect business, government, and industry, and what they will mean.
- The World Future Society, founded in 1966 as a nonprofit educational and scientific organization, studies and reports on how social and technological developments are shaping the future. It currently has 25,000 members in more than eighty countries.

Books on the future are often best sellers. Two such books, *Microtrends: The Small Forces Behind Tomorrow's Big Changes* (Penn and Zalesne 2009) and *Future Net: The Essential Guide to Internet and Technology Megatrends* (Ensor 2006), have garnered rave reviews in recent years. There are also several periodicals on futurism. Probably the best know is *The Futurist*, which has been published since 1966.

Global Population Trends and Sport

Changes in population characteristics have played a significant role in the transformation from the games and casual sports of the premodern era to the global sport organizations and their leagues, teams, and events that presently exist. Who plays and who watches sports, which sports are popular and which are not in certain regions and nations, and how sports popularity rises and declines are all related to population growth, composition, and location because they impact the social lives of people as participants and consumers of sports.

World Population Growth

The world's population continues to increase despite improved birth-control measures and campaigns in the developed world for zero population growth. Although it took several million years of human history to reach the first billion in population, it took only 130 years to reach the second. By 1999 world population had reached 6 billion people, doubling in size in only forty years (see Figure 7.1). World population is projected to grow from 7 billion in 2010 to 8.3 billion by 2030, an increase of roughly 19 percent in just twenty years (United Nations 2008).

Sport and Population Growth. The world's population growth is certainly a concern in terms of what it means for human life and the planet's physical condition. For sport it will likely lead to growth in the number of global sport organizations and in sports participation worldwide. Currently, China, with 1.3 billion people, and India, with 1.1 billion, dwarf other countries; together, they comprise 38 percent of the world's population. With the successful 2008 Olympic Games as a foundation, there is a

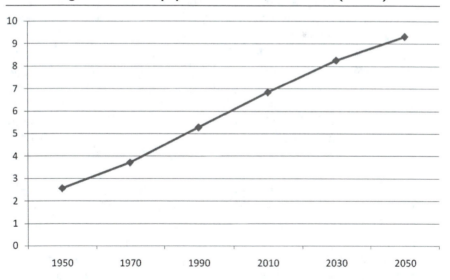

Figure 7.1 World population trends, 1950–2050 (billions)

Source: U.S. Census Bureau 2009.

strong likelihood that over the next twenty years China will displace North America and Europe as the epicenter of global sport dominance. If India adopts the culture of elite sport the way it has adopted the culture of computer technology, it has the population base to become a global sports power.

Population Composition

The age composition of the world's population has significant implications for current and future development in countries throughout the world. During the twentieth century most nations had a young population because the birthrate remained high for an increasing number of people of childbearing age. This condition is now changing rapidly because the long-term trends for birth and death rates are expected to decline. Thus, the proportion of young people will diminish, and the proportion of older people will increase, markedly affecting population composition.

In the first decade of the twenty-first century there were approximately 1.8 billion people under the age of fifteen in the world, which was just under 30 percent of the total population. The percentage of children was highest in sub-Saharan Africa, while it was generally lowest in the developed countries. Between 2010 and 2025, the population of those age zero to fourteen is projected to fall to about 25 percent of the total population. This trend is due in part to the substantial decline in fertility rates across the globe, but it is also due to increasing life expectancy worldwide.

In all parts of the world, there will be an increase in the percentage of people over the age of sixty-five. According to *World Population Prospects: The 2006 Revision,* by 2045 the number of older persons in the world will likely surpass, for the first time in history, the number of children (i.e., persons under age fifteen). This crossover is the consequence of the long-term reductions in fertility and mortality that are leading to the steady aging of the global population (Haub 2007). As Table 7.1 illustrates, there are, and will continue to be, wide variations in the percentage of older persons in different regions of the world.

In addition to age composition, the rapidly changing race/ethnic/religious composition of many countries of the world has significant political, economic, and social implications for the coming decades. North and South America are facing many challenges on the issue of immigration, and the racial and ethnic diversity it brings, especially for Canada and the United States. The United States is the largest immigrant-receiving country in the world. Many of the most recent immigrants or their descendents

Table 7.1 Percentage of Persons Age Sixty-Five and Older

World	2007	2025	2050
World	7	10	16
Industrialized countries	16	21	26
Developing countries	6	9	15
Europe	16	21	28
North America	12	18	21
Oceania	10	15	19
Latin America and Caribbean	6	10	19
Asia	6	10	18
Africa	3	4	7

Source: Haub 2007.

are from Mexico, Central and South America, and Southeast Asia. This trend is likely to continue.

Europe, including the United Kingdom, is also a magnet for immigration. Its nations are set to attract more than 1 million immigrants in 2010. Over the past thirty years, Europe's Muslim population has more than tripled. There are almost 25 million Muslims living in Europe today. London is often called "Londonistan." International immigration authorities expect these migration trends will continue to diversity the racial/ethnic/religious composition of countries into the foreseeable future.

Male-female composition worldwide will undergo only a small modification in the next forty years. In contrast to the first decade of the twenty-first century, in which males outnumbered females, females are likely to outnumber men in 2050. The differential is expected to be approximately 1 percent. The increase of females in the total population will be associated primarily with growth in the elderly population between 2010 and 2050 (U.S. Census Bureau 2009).

Sports and Aging and Diversifying Populations. Having a larger older proportion of the world's population, one that is older than ever before, will affect sport in a number of ways. Demographic trends that point to increasing life expectancy and a growing population of seniors who are healthy and active clearly indicate that sports of all kinds will grow in popularity, and especially in participation, among seniors. Indeed, sport planners claim that new sport organizations for seniors are where the action will be in the coming years.

The Senior Olympics has become the largest multisports event in the world for seniors. Its 2011 event in Houston, Texas, is expected to attract 15,000 top male and female senior athletes. The Masters Sports Tournaments and National Senior Games Association have become major forces in organizing competitive sports for senior men and women in the United States.

The increase in older people will form an infrastructure for the continued financial success of professional sports, and older fans will likely be seeing older professional athletes. Some of the biggest sports stories of the past few years have been about older athletes: Randy Johnson's continuing to pitch in Major League Baseball (MLB) well into his forties and golf pros Tom Watson and Gregg Norman captivating sports fans by continuing to play excellent golf way past their prime years. The senior tours of the Professional Golfers Association and the Professional Tennis Association illustrate quite well that older athletes can perform at high levels and that sports fans will pay to see them compete in their sport.

Historically, immigrants have always brought their preferred sports to their new countries. Although soccer is the most popular sport globally and has been for decades, historically the United States and Canada have been slow to adopt soccer as one of their "preferred" sports. But soccer popularity has soared in both countries in the past twenty-five years with the influx of immigrants from soccer-playing nations.

Increasing Global Urbanization

Increased urbanization has been one of the most dramatic demographic developments of the past forty years. As recently as 1970, only one in three persons worldwide lived in urban areas, with most living in areas with less than 1 million people. However, over the past four decades, the urban population has grown so that in 2010 more than half of the world's population is living in cities; approximately 37 percent live in cities with 1 million or more residents. Along with this overall urban trend is the emergence of urban areas with at least 10 million people, often called megacities. The number of megacities has mushroomed from three to twenty in the past forty years (United Nations 2008).

Global Urbanization and Sport. Urbanization, with its accompanying giant metropolitan areas, sometimes stretching out over hundreds of miles and engulfing many small communities as well as large cities, creates favorable conditions for commercialized spectator sports. At the same time industrialization and modern technology have gradually provided the leisure time and standard of living so crucial to the growth and development of all forms of sporting activity. In the developed countries, and more recently in the developing nations, towns and cities have been natural centers for organizing sports teams and leagues.

With growth in world population and the continuing concentration of that population in urban locations, the global sports world will have to adapt to the changing conditions. Indeed, professional sports managements and global sports organizations are already preparing for a future in which national and regional considerations will take precedence over local city loyalties.

Professional sport has been one of the most financially successful and growing industries of the past twenty years. Consumer-spectator interest appears to have no limit. New franchises, new leagues, new tournaments, and new championships spring up all over the world to be greeted by sold-out crowds. During the past two decades several sports have acquired global professional status—including cycling, triathlon, racquetball, distance running, beach volleyball, and lacrosse. With each sport comes leagues, tournaments, and world championship events. Within twenty years the total number of professional sports could double, and larger urban populations will be a key factor in this development.

Trends in urban characteristics, in conjunction with the expansion of sports opportunities for females, have created opportunities for women's professional sports to grow throughout the world. Sport entrepreneurs envision a global growth of women's sport organizations and leagues in a broad range of sports. Women's basketball, volleyball, and soccer have already established a worldwide base of leagues and championship events that undoubtedly will increase. But additional sports have the potential to follow patterns already established.

Professional men's and women's golf and tennis have extended their tour seasons, and both tennis and golf now have senior tours. In addition, a number of other professional sports (such as NASCAR racing, cycling, distance running, and lacrosse) are gaining a following in live attendance and television coverage. The future trajectory seems quite clear: Professional sports will become another global industry in the next two decades. They are already well on the way, with team franchises, tournaments, and championship events held around the globe.

The Future of Global Sport Organizations

The incredible worldwide expansion of commercial sport over the past fifty years has been accompanied by a global fragmentation of global sport organizations (GSOs). Numerous issues and problems—doping, violence, corruption, legal and financial woes—have challenged these far-flung sport organizations. The control GSOs have had over the development of international sport is coming under increasing criticism from various sources: national governments, global media interests, players' unions, even international governmental organizations such as the European Union and United Nations (Bourg and Gouguet 2006). A decade ago British political analyst Sunder Katwala, after an extensive study of global sport governance, concluded that "it is difficult to find anything else in the world quite so badly governed as international sport" (2000, 90). More recently, in their influential *The Political Economy of Global Sporting Organizations*, John Forster and Nigel Pope suggest what might be the outcome of the situation Katwala described; they argue that the GSOs' "continued existence cannot be taken for granted, either singly or as a group.... The GSOs face a set of challenges and potential threats to their existence" (2004, 135).

One challenge may come from national governments. Leaders of national governments—presidents, prime ministers, premiers—often complain about the powers that GSOs exercise over sports in their countries. As I noted in the previous chapter, national governments have intervened in sports in a variety of ways, and clashes between GSOs and government leaders have been frequent. Currently, most nations have some form of government agency, often called the Ministry of Sport or something similar, that has regulatory and policy-making powers. If commercial sport continues to play a larger and larger role in the global economy, national governments will likely seek more oversight—even jurisdictional control—over GSOs, professional leagues, and teams, and they will want to bring electronic media sport under national communications jurisdiction.

Calls for some form of umbrella, such as a global-level sport governing structure, is another form of transformation that could challenge the status of GSOs. One step in that direction is the recent creation of the World Anti-Doping Agency (WADA) and the Court of Arbitration for Sport (CAS). I have described WADA previously in this book as having been created to promote, coordinate, and monitor the struggle against drugs in sport. The role of the CAS is to adjudicate disputes that existing sport organizations have been unable to settle themselves. However, WADA and the CAS are small, single-purpose entities. A larger, more comprehensive body seems more appropriate for the future of global sport.

Swiss scholars Jean-Loup Chappelet and Brenda Kübler-Mabbott claim, "There is discussion, in some quarters, of a United Nations program for sport, similar to that created for the environment" (2008, 180). There is indeed some evidence for a future role in global sport because the United Nations is the largest and most comprehensive global governmental body, and it has been involved in global sport through one of its most important agencies, the United Nations Educational, Scientific and Cultural Organization (UNESCO).

In the mid-1970s UNESCO took steps to assume some leadership in sport when it adopted the International Charter on Physical Education and Sport. Several measures included support for promoting worldwide Sport for All, with special regard to the integration of the disabled and those with any form of social disadvantage and to the needs of women and girls.

By offering support for the voluntary efforts of national governments and nongovernmental organizations, UNESCO sought to combat excessive commercialization and the dangers of violence and drug taking. This global agency has also been very conscious of the need to extend the concept of sport beyond those competitive activities that are practiced internationally, so that traditional sports and games and all forms of physical exercise are adequately promoted for the well-being of all.

The United Nations General Assembly made an even more obvious bid for global leadership in sport when it proclaimed 2005 as the International Year of Sport and Physical Education. Numerous events were organized at the national, regional, and international levels to celebrate the international year. Conferences, seminars, workshops, and special sports events were sponsored by the United Nations, various governments, global sport organizations, and civil society. The media, academia, and other sectors cooperated to educate the public and instill the positive values of sport across the globe. Some examples of these activities include the following:

- Sporting events commemorating the international year were organized around the globe.
- A number of UN funds, programs, and specialized agencies used the year to highlight and encourage the use of sport in international development programs and projects.

- UNESCO played a key role during the international year as the lead agency for sport-related issues in the UN system, convening governments to advance the cause of sport and physical education.
- Roger Federer, a world-ranked tennis star, and Margaret Okayo, a marathon champion, were appointed as spokespersons to promote the objectives of the international year.
- The commemorative efforts undertaken during the year particularly took into account certain negative realities facing athletes, including child labor, violence, doping, early specialization, overtraining, and exploitative forms of commercialization.

Finally, the General Assembly requested that the secretary-general "elaborate an action plan that will expand and strengthen United Nations partnerships with Governments, sport-related organizations and the private sector, on the basis ... of an assessment of progress achieved, steps taken and difficulties encountered in realizing the potential of sport as a tool for development and peace" (United Nations 2006, 2).

The Olympic Movement: The IOC, the Preeminent GSO

In Chapter 2, I said that the Olympic Movement's International Olympic Committee (IOC) is not just another GSO; it is, in fact, the preeminent GSO. For that reason it has received the most attention in connection with all the other topics that have been addressed here. So it will come as no surprise that the IOC and the Olympic Movement will receive the lion's share of coverage in this section about the future of global sports organizations.

During a seminar on the Olympic Movement that I attended recently, there was a two-hour session titled "Future Problems Confronting the IOC." In his opening remarks at the beginning of the session, the moderator said, "I requested this session be scheduled for two *days*, not two hours." A knowing round of laughter from audience members showed they were well aware of the predicaments facing the IOC. In writing this section I, too, feel the attention I am devoting to the IOC's current and future issues and problems is inadequate. But it would take an entire book to cover all of them thoroughly.

Governance in the Olympic Movement. Governance of anything is political, and governance in GSOs is not just political, it is authoritarianly political. This especially applies to the largest GSO, the International Olympic

Committee. Australian Olympic researchers Kristine Toohey and A. J. Veal say that the IOC, "as a non-democratic, non representative international body ... has ... been particularly subject to criticism for its undemocratic, oligarchic and secretive nature" (2007, 50; see also Lenskyj 2008).

The IOC began with 13 members, all of whom were European; currently it may not exceed 115: 70 so-called independent members and 45 who are members through the office they hold within the wider Olympic structure. Independent members are elected by secret ballot for a term of eight years, with the possibility of reelection. However, their term ends if they are forced to resign or they reach the age of seventy. There have only been eight IOC presidents since the body's creation; five of the eight were European nobility, and only one was not a European: Avery Brundage, an American.

From its beginnings the IOC, and the Olympic Movement in general, has been criticized for its elitism, linkages to European nobility, and undemocratic structure. During the presidency of the two most recent IOC presidents, Juan Antonio Samaranch and Jacques Rogge, the IOC has taken steps to address its elitist reputation by dropping the "amateur" requirement for athletes and developing objectives for increasing the percentages of women in the IOC, international sports federations (IFs), and national Olympic committees (NOCs). Samaranch was under pressure to move the IOC toward enacting democratizing reforms by which most of the committee's membership would consist of individuals elected by IFs and NOCs. Although he seemed tempted, he stopped short of acceding to those demands.

Rogge has devoted his presidency to fighting the chronic problem of doping, strengthening the finances of the Olympics, limiting the size of the games, and overseeing the successful Beijing Olympics. Pressure has been mounting on him from within the Olympic Movement, from global sports outside the Olympics, and from the sport global media to institute democratic reforms in the IOC. Rogge has signaled that he is interested in initiating a movement of this kind, but with the IOC-mandated two-term, twelve-year limit facing him in 2013, he will have limited time to complete any kind of significant democratic reform.

Gender Inequity in the Olympic Movement. In Chapter 6, I noted that female involvement in the Olympic Movement has been an issue from its beginnings. Women's sports opportunities have increased to the point where 43 percent of the athletes participating in the Summer and Winter Olympic Games are female; women competed in about one half of the

2008 Summer Olympic sports and in all seven of the sports of the 2010 Winter Olympics.

Progress has definitely been made by the IOC, but gender equity has not yet been achieved, and conflicts over women in the Olympic Movement continue. For example, of the 302 sports events in the Beijing Olympics, only 127—42 percent—were women-only events. In addition, when only men's ski jumping was authorized by the IOC for the 2010 Vancouver Olympic Games, several Canadian female ski jumpers sought a Canadian court declaration ordering the IOC either to require that women's ski jumping be held at the Vancouver games or to cancel all ski-jumping events. British Columbia courts ruled that they did not have the authority to force the IOC to add women's ski jumping to the Vancouver program of events. At the same time that the women's ski-jumping controversy was occurring, the IOC voted to include women's boxing in the 2012 Summer Olympics in London. Of the sports contested at the 2008 Summer Olympics in Beijing, boxing was the only one that did not include women, a reflection of cultural beliefs that boxing is too dangerous for women (Clarey 2009).

Despite ongoing controversies like the two above, sports forecasters predict that by the 2020 Summer Olympics and 2022 Winter Games, men and women athletes will be competing in about the same numbers and in the same number of sports. All the recent trends point in that direction.

While the participation of women Olympic athletes has steadily increased, the same kind of progress toward gender equity and diversity of people of color has not been achieved in the governing and administrative bodies of the Olympic Movement. The percentage of women in these positions has been low throughout the modern Olympic era, and it remains low. I commented on this in Chapter 6. However, to its credit, in 1996 the IOC took steps to remedy this situation. Since the remedies will take place over time and will continue into the future, I only outline them briefly here.

First, NOCs, IFs, national federations, and the various other sporting organizations that are part of the Olympic Movement were required to establish an objective of reserving at least 20 percent of decision-making positions for women, especially those in executive and legislative bodies, within their organizations by the end of 2005. Based on information provided by NOCs, 32.3 percent had more than 20 percent women in their executive bodies by that target date. IFs of Olympic sports reported 29.4 percent having more than 20 percent women in their executive bodies by the 2005 target date. Information provided by Recognized

IFs indicates that 23 percent had more than 20 percent women in their executive bodies. Thus, a number of Olympic Movement organizations have shown their willingness to work on achieving parity between men and women. Improvement, yes, but these percentages of women in such positions are far below the established objectives; moreover, the target objectives represent only about half the percentage of women athletes competing in the Olympic Games.

As I stated in Chapter 6, the IOC did not have a woman member until 1981, and not until 1990 was the first women elected to the executive board. In 2010 only 15 percent of IOC members are women. The IOC's fifteen-member executive board still includes only one woman. This situation can only be described as blatant discrimination, and it is especially abhorrent, again, considering that over 40 percent of athletes competing in recent Olympic Games were women.

In cooperation with its Women and Sport Commission, the IOC has set up a women-and-sport policy group, which aims to promote and assist women's participation in sports activities and in the Olympic Games, as well as their involvement in the leadership and administration of sports organizations. Through this commission, the IOC has put in place a program of regional seminars for female administrators, coaches, officials, athletes, and sports journalists involved in the national or international sports movement.

The IOC is aware that its objectives can be attained only in successive stages. But momentum for achieving gender equity in leadership and administrative positions is under way in the Olympic Movement, and there is a broad expectation that during the coming decade major achievements will be made to close the current gender gap in those positions.

Racial Inequity in the Olympic Movement. Pierre de Coubertin desired to have every country participating in the Olympic Games represented on the IOC, even though the thirteen members he selected, which included himself, as the first IOC members were all Europeans. Throughout the more than 110-year history of the modern Olympics, de Coubertin's wish was never fulfilled, and with the current IOC policy limiting its membership to 115 and 203 nations participating in recent games, it is now impossible to achieve de Coubertin's aspiration.

Actually, the IOC has never made any effort to be a representative body of any kind. It is a self-perpetuating organization, with new members selected by the IOC itself, with virtually no specific criteria of qualifications for membership. Consequently, the possession of various types of social capital has served as the basis for invitation to membership in the IOC.

Several demographic patterns have been quite evident in the selection of
IOC members over the history of the modern Olympics. They have been
overwhelmingly male and European, about twenty have had royal or aristocratic titles, and most have been wealthy. The percentage of Europeans
has ranged from over 60 percent in the early decades to between 40 and
50 percent during the past thirty years. Since all the European members
were white, and those from North and South America have mostly been
white, adding Asians leaves room for very few black IOC members. Indeed, there have been few black IOC members in its entire history (see
Table 7.2). In 2010 there were only eight black members on the IOC. In
the same year there were five IOC members from Switzerland, a country
of less than 8 million people, while there are 150 million people in the
twenty-three countries that currently make up black Africa.

Black African athletes have been a significant presence in the Olympic
Games for the past forty years, winning medals at a rate far surpassing
that of socially and economically advantaged athletes from developed
countries. It is certainly time for the IOC to give greater recognition to the
continent of African in the future through a deliberate effort to increase
the number of African members. A future IOC with a more representative
racial composition would be something to be admired.

Geographical Location of the Olympics—Africa and Latin America. The
preamble to the Olympic Charter states that "the Olympic flag ... includes
the five interlaced rings, which represent the union of the five continents
and the meeting of athletes from throughout the world at the Olympic
Games" (IOC 2007, 10). The five rings represent the five major regions of
the world: Africa, the Americas, Asia, Europe, and Oceania. Unfortunately,
the IOC has not taken seriously the symbolic claim of the charter. There
are two entire continents on which no city has ever hosted an Olympic

Table 7.2 Geographical Residence of IOC Members (percentage)

Region	1988	1998	2010
Europe	42	41	43
Asia	15	16	23
Americas	20	18	16
Africa	19	19	15
Sub-Saharan Africa	—	—	7
Oceania	4		5

Sources: Alexandrakis and Krotee 1988; IOC 1998, 2010.

Games—South America and Africa—and there have been twenty-six Summer Games and twenty Winter Games.

It is also astounding that only two Olympic Games have been held in the Southern Hemisphere—both in Australia. The other forty-four Olympics have been held in the Northern Hemisphere. Figure 7.2 shows the sites of the Summer Olympic Games.

Figure 7.2 Host cities of the Summer Olympics, 1896–2012

North America	Europe	Asia
St. Louis–1904	Athens–1896, 2004	Tokyo–1964
Los Angeles–1932, 1984	Paris–1900, 1924	Seoul–1988
Mexico City–1968	London–1908, 1948, 2012	Beijing–2008
Montreal–1976	Stockholm–1912	
Atlanta–1996	Antwerp–1920	
	Amsterdam–1928	
	Berlin–1936	
	Helsinki–1952	
	Rome–1960	
	Munich–1972	
	Moscow–1980	
	Barcelona–1992	

South America	Africa	Oceania
Rio de Janeiro–2016		Melbourne–1956
		Sydney–2000

Note: The Olympics' five rings combine North and South America into one continent. In geographers' seven-continent classification of the world, North and South America are separate continents.

While the IOC has explained its reasons for these omissions, there is worldwide clamor for the IOC to open up to these two continents and to take the games to the Southern Hemisphere, where they are eagerly sought. Finally, South America will have an Olympic Games. Rio de Janeiro has been selected to host the 2016 Summer Olympics. Fédération Internationale de Football Association (FIFA) is showing the way for the IOC to give serious consideration to the Southern Hemisphere. Its 2010 World Cup will be held in South Africa, and Brazil will host the 2014 World Cup.

The IOC is not the only GSO with a Eurocentric leadership. This is the case in many international sport bodies (I will discuss FIFA later in this chapter). Only in recent years has there been recognition and resentment of geographically centralized leadership. Now that it has become transparent, these GSOs will have to make appropriate accommodations in the future or face growing resistance both within their own memberships and in world opinion.

The Future and Olympic Games Site Selection. Full-length books have been written on the bidding process, IOC members' voting patterns, and the selection of a host city for almost every modern Olympics. The reasons behind this outpouring of literature on the Olympic Games' site selection? Intrigue, secrecy, vote trading, influence peddling—actually, just about every imaginable unethical and corrupt practice. The books make fascinating reading, but they are devastating to the image that the Olympic Movement attempts to project through its Olympic Charter statement of Olympism as "a way of life based on the ... value of good example and respect for universal fundamental ethical principles" (IOC 2007, 11).

It was the campaign to bring the 2002 Winter Olympic Games to Salt Lake City that finally exposed the sordid practices that had become common in the site-selection process. Local Olympic officials made cash payments to members of the IOC during that city's bid to host the 2002 games. Individual payments ranging from $5,000 to $70,000 came from the Salt Lake City bid committee's privately financed $14 million operating budget. Some Salt Lake City Olympic organizers were charged with conspiracy to commit bribery, fraud, and racketeering related to the vote-buying scandal (Longman 1999).

In the aftermath of the Salt Lake City debacle, the IOC revived its long-dormant Ethics Commission and assigned it to develop a code of ethics to serve as a basis for monitoring complaints about IOC members,

NOCs, site bidding, and Olympic organizing committees. In 2009 the IOC's executive committee approved a document titled "Rules of Conduct Applicable to All Cities Wishing to Organize the Olympic Games." This seven-page document lays out in detail all the rules, regulations, and policies to which parties to an Olympic site bid must conform. The rules apply to the cities wishing to become applicant cities for the 2018 Olympic Games and beyond (IOC 2009).

It is tempting to hope that the rules in this document will be rigorously followed in the future, but given the history of the Olympic site bidding and selection processes, careful monitoring of all parties will be necessary. The legitimacy of the selection of applicant cities is an IOC function in which there will be a great deal of future interest.

Controlling Gigantism in the Olympic Games. The size of both Summer and Winter Olympic Games programs has been a subject of growing concern for the IOC and will likely remain a controversial issue for the foreseeable future. The number of both sports and events has been increasing since the modern Olympics began. At the first modern Olympics, competitions took place in nine sports with forty-three events. With each Olympic Games other sports sought recognition, and more and more were gradually added to the Olympic program. But growth was modest in the first half-century of the games. For example, in the 1932 Summer Olympics, athletes competed in only fourteen sports with 116 events.

After World War II the IOC was inundated with demands for sports to be added to the Summer Games. By the 1960 Rome Summer Games, the program consisted of seventeen sports and 150 events. Petitions for new sports and events multiplied to the point where the 1992 Barcelona Summer Games program had jumped to thirty-two sports and 286 events. Expansion of sports and events at the Winter Olympics was much more moderated, primarily because the Olympic Charter requires that all Winter Games sports must take place on snow or ice. Still, considerable increase, especially in sports events, has occurred. In 1960 there were four sports and twenty-seven events; in 1998 there were seven sports and seventy-two events; in 2010 there were seven sports and eighty-six events.

It was the 2000 Sydney Summer Games that became a watershed for size at the Olympics. With twenty-eight sports and three hundred events, "gigantism" became the buzzword in active discussion, and debate occurred, both within the Olympic Movement and in the global sport media, about the size of the Olympics. In 2002 the IOC decided to curb the growth of the Olympic program and to limit the number of sports in the Summer Games to twenty-eight and the number of events to 301. Over the past few years, the IOC and the Olympic Programme Commission have worked toward the goal of applying a systematic approach to establishing a stable Olympic program for each Olympic Games (IOC 2008).

The IOC's goal of containing the size of the Olympic program seems wise, but the future is likely to be very contentious. The committee successfully held the number of sports to twenty-eight and the events to 302 for the 2008 Beijing Olympics. However, by 2009 the International Amateur Boxing Association had petitioned for women's boxing to be included in the 2012 London Olympics. Boxing was the only Summer Olympic sport that did not include events for women. As I explained earlier in this chapter, in August 2009 the IOC approved adding women's boxing to the 2012 London Olympics. Baseball and softball, on the other hand, were denied admission to the 2012 Olympics, but both sports have undertaken aggressive campaigns to be added to the 2016 Summer Olympics. Rugby and golf have already been added to the 2016 Rio de Janeiro Summer Games. It seems clear that the IOC will likely have a future of agonizing decisions, as it attempts to contain gigantism.

Of course, the IOC is not just concerned about limiting the number of sports; it must also cap the number of events, which had risen to 302 for the 2008 Beijing Games. The Olympic Programme Commission has suggested dropping several of the wrestling events and some of the sports contested by weight, such as boxing. The interest here is not merely reducing the current number of events but in trading certain events now included for other worthier ones seeking to gain admission into the Olympic program. As I noted earlier in this chapter, women's ski jumping is striving to join the winter Olympics program since a ski-jumping event already exists for men.

Doping and Other Performance Aids in the Olympics. Newspaper and magazine headlines tell of substance abuse in sports: "Steroids Are Just a Click Away," "Drug-Free Sports Might Be Thing of the Past," "Tour de France's Downhill Slide: Doping Scandals Sully World's Biggest Bike Race." Some knowledgeable authorities believe that substance use by athletes is epidemic in scope, all the way from the youth-sport to the professional level (I include Olympic athletes as professionals).

The use of substances to enhance performance—"doping" as it is called outside the United States—has been present throughout the history of organized sports. The ancient Greek athletes consumed psychotropic mushrooms in the belief that they improved performance, and Roman gladiators used a variety of stimulants to hype themselves up and forestall fatigue. Athletes throughout the nineteenth century experimented with caffeine, alcohol, nitroglycerine, opium, and strychnine. Amphetamines and anabolic steroids have been popular drugs of choice for athletes for the past several decades.

IOC member Richard Pound recently asserted, "I regard doping as the single most important problem facing sport today" (2004, xiii). Pound is certainly eminently qualified to make such a statement. He has spent most of his adult life associated with the Olympic Movement. From a position as president of the Canadian Olympic Association, he was elected to the IOC in 1978. Except for perhaps the current president of the IOC, Jacques Rogge, Pound is arguably the most globally well-known member of the current IOC.

In 1999 the IOC took the initiative to form WADA, with Pound as the president. WADA was instrumental in the development of the World Anti-Doping Code, which provides the framework for antidoping policies, rules, and regulations within sport organizations, while harmonizing antidoping policies in all sports and all countries. Composed and funded equally by the sports organizations and governments of the world, WADA coordinates the development and implementation of the World Anti-Doping Code (Chappelet and Kübler-Mabbott 2008).

There is general support for WADA among global sport organizations, but there are objections as well, especially concerning athletes' privacy and human rights, such as

- random, short-notice, out-of-competition drug tests
- the "whereabouts" system requiring athletes to select one hour per day, seven days per week, to be available for no-notice drugs tests
- the Athletes' Passport system, which would provide testers with a lifelong "biological fingerprint" of an athlete to compare samples against

There is also a major future issue about implementation, that is, whether WADA and other global sport organizations will have the resources and persistence to sustain the project.

Obviously, these objections, and others that no doubt will arise, will make for a future beset with international controversy and wrangling. Legal challenges are probable in the future over methods of testing and testing results because there is much more criticism than WADA currently admits. Furthermore, as the technology becomes more advanced in genomics and other biosciences, sport technologists may turn to "genetic engineering" at some point in the future. Anticipating this, WADA has already asked scientists to help find ways to prevent gene therapy from becoming the newest means of doping. Eventually, however, preventing athletes from gaining access to gene therapy may become impossible.

The IOC, and all other GSOs, will confront other new technologies about which they will have to make decisions. One of these has already created a great deal of study, debate, and controversy: the eligibility of athletes with prosthetics. A South African track sprinter by the name of Oscar Pistorius who has carbon prosthetic Cheetah Flex-Foot legs and wished to try to qualify for the Olympics—not the Paralympics, the regular Olympics—was banned by the International Association of Athletics Federations (IAAF), contending that the prosthetic legs gave him an advantage over runners with natural legs. More broadly, the IAAF bans all athletes from using "any technical device that incorporates springs, wheels or any other element that provides the user with an advantage over another athlete not using such a device."

Progress in understanding the biological mechanisms of cell regeneration in mammals gives medical scientists hope that humans will be able to regrow organs and other parts of their bodies. Of course, sports medicine professionals become excited about the potential of this advance for the treatment of sports injuries.

Obviously, this is not the end of the issue regarding prosthetics, cell regeneration, and so forth. Moreover, many issues related to the application of new technologies to sport will undoubtedly challenge global sports regularly in the future.

Migration of Sport Labor in the Future

The future looks very promising for continued job opportunities in commercial sports for elite sports workers who wish to migrate for employment for one reason or another. Assuming there is no worldwide catastrophic economic depression, the trend appears to be toward an expansion of professional sports in the foreseeable future. Most sports forecasters predict that expansion will take place especially in sports, such as soccer, lacrosse, auto racing, and women's basketball.

Professional sports will also likely expand with leagues becoming more international. The four major North American team sports are played worldwide, and with air-travel speeds increasing, there seems little reason for these sports not to expand, giving some major U.S. sports leagues a truly global presence. The popularity of hockey and basketball in many locations have the National Hockey League and National Basketball Association best positioned to develop true European or Asian branches over the next decade or so, bringing jobs for athletes and coaches in those sports with them. These two sports are already global brands. It is just a matter of the competition catching up with the interest. Soccer is already a sport played worldwide, and it will likely not be too many years before North American soccer teams are incorporated into European and/or Asian soccer leagues.

In Chapter 3, I described the widespread migration of elite and professional athletes from team to team, nation to nation, and continent to continent. A pervasive migration of sports workers (mostly athletes) is already a prevalent pattern in all global sports. Because soccer is the world's most popular sport, and because professional soccer is played in more countries around the world than any other professional team sport, soccer has by far the most migratory sports workers. As I previously explained, the European Court of Justice's (ECJ) 1995 Bosman ruling allows professional soccer players to move freely from club to club, league to league, and country to country. It also removed restrictions on the number of foreign players a team could have from other European Union countries (Fordyce 2005).

The Bosman ruling came about because in 1990 a soccer player by the name of Jean-Marc Bosman, whose contract had expired with his Belgium team, attempted to transfer to a French team. His Belgian team refused to allow Bosman to play until it received compensation for him. Bosman sued the Belgian Football Association and the Union of European Football Associations, claiming the rules governing the transfer of players were unfairly restrictive. The ECJ agreed with Bosman, which was an important decision for the reasons I mentioned above. In effect, it legalized the free movement of sport labor within the European Union and thus had a profound effect on the transfer of soccer players. That, in addition to a ruling several years previously effectively nullifying MLB's reserve clause, has placed the legal system squarely on the side of free agency for professional athletes.

There has been a global free-flowing migration of athletes during the last twenty years because there have been few limits on the number of foreign players in the professional leagues. But the migration of professional team-sport athletes is affected by the free agency and transfer rules that professional leagues use to control athletes' mobility. The economics of unrestricted mobility for athletes disadvantages team owners and can lead to bidding wars, resulting in increased player salaries and decreased owner profits. Thus, team owners prefer restrictions on free agency, transfers, and other forms of player freedom of movement.

This issue promises to be contentious and to persist well into the future because professional athletes, their agents, and their unions will strive for the greatest freedom of migration because players want the right to have multiple teams bid for their services. Meanwhile owners and league administrators will strive for various limitations on player mobility.

Global Sport-Industry Production in the Future

The sporting goods and equipment industry is an integral part of the global economy, and the 2008–2010 U.S. recession had a global wavelike effect. Each nation attending the 2009 G-20 Summit on Financial Markets and the World Economy acknowledged economic challenges in its country, some much worse than others, and there was little agreement on a plan to fix the global economy. So the watch words for the global economy over the next several years seem to be "slow, steady recovery."

The World Federation of the Sporting Goods Industry (WFSGI), an independent association formed by sporting goods brands, manufacturers, suppliers, retailers, national and regional federations, and other industry-related businesses, and the Sporting Goods Manufacturers Association (SGMA), the premier trade association for more than 1,000 sporting goods manufacturers, retailers, and marketers in the sports-products industry, are both optimistic about a continued growth for their industry. They contend that many sporting goods manufacturers, looking past the weak global economy of 2008 to 2010, expect to see an increase in growth due to increased urban populations worldwide and more people entering retirement, living longer, and, presumably, buying more sporting goods and equipment.

Recent annual reports of the five sporting goods corporations I discussed in Chapter 4—Wilson, Adidas, Reebok, Mizuno, and Nike—corroborate the forecasts of the WFSGI and SGMA. So even with a weakened global economy, the sporting goods industry is still expected to expand industrywide during the 2010–2020 decade.

One factor that sporting goods manufacturers worry about—because it could affect levels of sports participation, thus slowing consumer spending on sporting goods and equipment—is the ongoing attraction of electronic devices, which are used mostly indoors and do not require vigorous physical activity, such as computers, iPods, Internet chat rooms, handheld games, computer games, and cell phones. Although these items are exciting technological innovations, they do consume large amounts of their users' time and, as a result, cut into time that could be spent in sports pursuits (SGMA 2008).

Another factor that seems problematic for the future is the stability of the ownership of these sporting goods companies. Corporate mergers, takeovers, and buyouts occur with regularity in the global economy, and three of these five sporting goods firms have been involved in these types of transactions in the past two decades.

Future Labor Issues in Sporting Goods and Equipment

The future conditions for the sporting goods and equipment labor force are not promising. Disputes concerning global labor practices are at the core of contemporary debates regarding globalization, and labor practices in sporting goods manufacturing in developing countries, especially in Asia and Latin America, have often been appalling. As I described in Chapter 5, based on a series of investigations of Nike's Asian footwear factories, little progress has been made in the ten years since Nike founder Philip Knight promised to eliminate sweatshop conditions there. Those conditions remain common, and major obstacles to their elimination persist. Similar manufacturing conditions exist for the other major sporting goods manufacturing firms.

In addition, Nike and other sporting goods and equipment corporations have not made significant progress on the question of a living wage. According to the SGMA's annual State of the Industry survey, more than 80 percent of manufacturers said they used factories in China, arguably the lowest-wage country in the world (SGMA 2008).

Will wages and working conditions improve in the next decade for those who make sporting goods and equipment? Global manufacturing is being challenged by a contentious transnational politics driven by alliances, advocacy groups, and coalitions of resistance that are confronting political and corporate elites and seeking global justice. We might speculate that the same dynamics that sociologist Frances Fox Piven (2006) described for bringing about political reform will also be effective for labor reform. She contends that when people exercise political courage, rise up in anger and hope, and defy authorities and the status quo, they bring about meaningful social reform.

Applying this principle to sporting goods manufacturing, it seems that improved wages and working conditions will only come about when a variety of initiatives are brought to bear on sporting goods manufacturers to abolish global sweatshop practices. It was the Nike Social Movement of the 1990s that led Nike's CEO to acknowledge during a 1998 National Press Club luncheon speech that "the Nike product has become synonymous with slave wages, forced overtime, and arbitrary abuse," then to promise significant reforms. Unfortunately, the promised reforms have been meager.

Nevertheless, with a view to maintaining pressure into the future, a wide-ranging set of globalization-from-below activists from labor rights, human rights, and religious groups, among others, have been struggling on behalf of the sporting goods manufacturing labor force for improved wages and working conditions. Campaign for Labor Rights, International Labor Organization, Press for Change, the Clean Clothes Campaign, and Labour Behind the Label are organizations in the forefront of these campaigns (Ballinger 2008, 2009). They vow to continue their work into the future and to end the present system of exploitation and abuse in the sportswear and athletic footwear industries.

Play Fair at the Olympics Campaign, an alliance of Oxfam, Global Unions, the Clean Clothes Campaign, and their constituent organizations worldwide, has pledged to undertake identifiable and concrete measures to pressure sporting goods and footwear corporations, the IOC and its national organizing committees, and national governments into taking action to eliminate the exploitation and abuse of workers in the global sporting goods industry. According to the Play Fair Alliance, "Sporting bodies such as the International Olympic Committee, through their licensing arrangements, and the totality of those companies which market or produce sportswear, athletic footwear and other sporting goods, can take far greater responsibility for the labor practices in this industry than they do now" (2008).

Future Technology and Sporting Goods and Equipment

One aspect of sporting goods and equipment on which there is almost universal agreement is that advances in technology will continue unabated and will account for improvements in sports performance in virtually every sport. Indeed, the rate of change in which everyday sporting goods are being redeveloped, refined, and redeployed is astounding. An example of things to come is a next-generation design-technology running shoe

Mizuno has introduced called Gender Engineering, which delivers a tailored and individually engineered shoe for both men and women, resulting in optimal fit, feel, and performance for faster and smoother running (SGMA 2009).

There will always be the danger that future technology will lead to a product that creates problems for a sport, as swimsuit technology has done in swimming. Nontextile, polyurethane swimsuits led to 108 world records in 2008 and 43 world records broken in 2009 at the Fédération Internationale de Natation (FINA) World Championships before FINA banned the swimsuit, claiming that it gave swimmers more speed and buoyancy. Swimsuit makers and other who oppose the ban argue that advances in sport technology will benefit a sport and that to deny access to these technologies will hold the sport back in popularity.

The Future of Media Sports

The prominent role that media sport has played in the growth and expansion of all commercial sports cannot be overemphasized. Global media is currently at the forefront of sports marketing and dispensing information about sports leagues, teams, athletes, and coaches, and there is little doubt that media sport will retain this significant role in the future. However, it will likely be driven by what is being called "new media" (Leonard 2009).

Television Coverage

TV is at the center of nearly every facet of major global sports events, both economically and culturally. Its coverage has expanded spectator access to sports contests, thus strengthened the market reach of global sports leagues and the fan base of teams. All of this has magnified the perceived importance of contemporary sports. Consequently, global sport organizations and television executives realize that if any of the professional sports lost television revenues, that industry would be devastated.

In the future, global sports leagues and teams will develop TV pipelines directly targeting their fans. This trend is already underway. Sports leagues worldwide are building their own networks. Sports properties are becoming their own media companies, thus interacting directly with their consumers without the go-between of traditional media. The NFL Network, which broadcasts all regular-season games and builds the legends of the league with its popular NFL Films content, the National Basketball Association's NBATV, the Baseball Network, CBS College Sports Network, and single-team-only channels are redefining sports television and transforming the once-reliable sports rights infrastructure (Rein, Kotler, and Shields 2007).

Television Technology and Sports Viewing

Broadcast sports at first entailed people listening to accounts of events on their radios while sitting in their living rooms. Today, many people have home-entertainment centers and watch sports events on their huge flat-screen high-definition television sets. But a key facet of the new media environment is interactivity, and with anticipated technological advances in computer-enhancement, TV viewers will be able to interact with the coverage and the game and customize the content of the broadcast sports coverage they receive. Viewers will have control over what aspects of events they watch; they will be able to direct camera angles and request regular and slow-motion replays of viewer-defined action; they will be able to call up certain cameras to focus on a single player, coach, or part of the field or court; and they will be able to ask for statistics and personal background on the players and coaches. In short, sports fans of the future will be able to view any number of games on a dizzying array of platforms.

Sports TV networks will also proliferate. As I noted above, it seems likely that all of the major global sport organizations will have their own networks, so viewers will be able to watch their favorite athletes and teams 24/7. This will include the ability to view broadcast games over the Internet, an initiative that is already underway. As teams and leagues take control, traditional networks like ABC's ESPN, CBS, and NBC may have to find a niche beyond live sport programming, such as providing information like statistics, analyses, and fantasy league communication.

In Chapter 5, I said that pay-per-view television is going to become a major factor in the next decade. There appears to be little doubt that within ten years sports fans will have to pay for many events they now see on free TV or basic cable. Some forecasters predict—and sports executives worry—that as the costs to attend sports events escalate and as television increasingly makes viewing of all important sports events available at low cost, actual attendance at sports venues will decline.

To make up for the lost revenue, some sports public relations firms predict teams will turn to in-game sponsorship dollars. This might take the form of an increase in technologically injected product placements in sports telecasts and patches on players uniforms, turning athletes into walking billboards for corporations like McDonald's and Toyota. Auto and cycle racing have been doing this for decades.

Internet Technology and Sports Spectatorship

The Internet is one of the most sophisticated and useful technological innovations in human history, and it is the fundamental component of the new media. Scientists who work at the cutting edge of this technology believe the Internet is still in the early stages of achieving what the future holds for it. The full integration of Internet, computer technology, and telecommunications is a prospect for the near future. Sports fans will not only command an incredible choice of sporting events but also have virtually unlimited control over what they watch and how they view the events.

MLB has an Internet infrastructure for streaming live video of its games throughout the season called MLB.TV Mosaic, a downloadable media player designed to give baseball fans a more interactive viewing experience. This is accomplished by providing the capabilities that let customers customize the games they are watching, adding in player tracker rosters of the players they are interested in, and providing TV-quality single-game streaming with integrated live stats alongside the video. Subscriber-fans can watch almost all MLB games throughout the season on their computers.

This is a model for the ways that other professional sport leagues and teams in the future will emulate sports broadcasting on the Internet while making a profit in the process. British Sky Broadcasting's Sky Player service allows Sky TV customers to access a broad collection of programming online, including sports (Sky Sports), on demand, on their computer. ESPN360 is a broadband network for live sports programming in Australia, Brazil, Chile, Europe (except Italy), the Middle East, and North America. In the United States the network can only be accessed through an Internet service provider that has paid ESPN for the service.

Video Technology and Sports Video Games

Another form of mediated sports "participation" is video games, which provide simulations of various kinds and are extremely popular with a broad spectrum of age groups, especially teenagers. Sports games, in particular, are plentiful. Some of the most popular are exhilarating simulations of professional and colleges football and basketball games, but racing games are also popular, as are extreme-sports videos.

With the increase in technological sophistication over the past decade, the best sport video games feature outstanding graphics and put players squarely in the middle of the action. In several video games, players have play-calling options that mirror actual coaches' playbooks, making for a seamlessly realistic experience. Incredibly photorealistic graphics make the virtual sports games mesmerizing.

Microsoft, Nintendo, and Sony, the major makers of video game systems, are working diligently to make the audio and video of these games more and more realistic and the control equipment more precise. Given the growth of all forms of mediated sports over the past decade, there is every reason to expect that the introduction of remarkable new video game systems will be an annual event in the foreseeable future.

A number of futurists have expressed concern that television, the Internet, and video technology will become so exciting, so mesmerizing, that it will have an isolating effect. They fear that masses of sports fans may choose to remain in the comfort of their homes with their TV sets, computers, and video game systems rather than actually opt to attend sports events. A number of futurists have been warning that the privatization of leisure, through the retreat into the home for entertainment, has the danger of bringing about a collapse of the civic ethic, the sense of belonging to a society. Sport studies researcher Darcy Plymire suggests that "immersion in sport video games creates a relationship to the body and the self that are categorically different from those created by televised sport" (2009, 17).

Sports Blogging

Not all computer users use the Internet, and not all Internet users are bloggers, so I use this paragraph to describe blogging briefly for the aforementioned persons. A blog is basically a website, like a forum or a social-bookmarking site, with frequent, periodic posts creating an ongoing narrative. Blogs are sustained by both individuals and groups, the former being the most common. But some newspapers have incorporated blogs to their main website to offer a new channel for their writers.

Blogs can focus on a wide variety of topics, ranging from the political to the personal, and many individuals have created a blog to share their expertise on specific topics. That is the purpose behind many sports blogs, and more and more sports fans—some refer to themselves as "sports junkies"—are migrating online to express sports-related knowledge, in-sights, opinions, videos, and rumors; consequently, the sports blogging niche is growing at a rapid pace.

In its short history, sports blogging has created a great deal of con-troversy, especially between bloggers and professional journalists. Sport journalist H. G. Bissinger, author of the well-known *Friday Night Lights,* is a self-professed critic of sports bloggers. On a Bob Costas HBO series, *Costas Now,* Bissinger complained that the sports blogosphere is over-flowing with unprofessional writing, outright hatred, and rumor (HBO 2008). He is not alone in his view. In a survey of journalists (television, newspaper, and radio), established professional journalists saw less value in blogging than a younger group of journalists. But almost every journalist who responded also said that blogging was not going away; it would only increase in the future.

Sport Politics and the Future

In Chapter 6, I described the ways in which sport is employed to advance national unity and international recognition and how throughout the latter twentieth century it was an instrument of international politics and diplomacy for many nations. Between 1950 and 1990 there was a prolonged state of political hostility, economic competition, and military threat between the United States and Western Europe and the Soviet Union and its Eastern European satellite countries in what was called the Cold War. This rivalry was most intense over which was the best eco-nomic system, capitalism or socialism, and which was the superior political system, democracy or communism. Although there was never an all-out military conflict between the two sides, they competed over a variety of matters with each side periodically claiming victory and thus to possess the superior social system.

In Chapter 6, I explained how each side built up a formidable na-tional sports system with the deliberate political purpose of using their sports teams and athletes to win in international sports events. Winning victories in international sport competition was touted as a confirma-tion of that side's superiority. The Soviet view was expressed by a Soviet scholar: "Successes achieved by Soviet sportsmen in sport has particular political significance.... Each new victory is a victory for the Soviet form of society.... It provides irrefutable proof of the superiority of socialist culture over the decaying culture of the capitalist state" (Riordan 1980,

364). The U.S. view was expressed by an American Olympic athlete, who asserted that international sports set the stage for "system versus system. And I believe we should show them that the capitalist system just beats the living hell out of the [socialist] system." Several sport-studies scholars have referred to this sports ideological struggle as a "war without weapons."

In 1991, after the stunning collapse of the Soviet Union, most of the Eastern Bloc countries renounced communism, and East and West Germany reunified as a democratic, capitalist state. As this mélange of countries began to cope with their new identities, collectively they realized the efficacy of using elite sport as a useful instrument for advancing national unity and gaining international recognition through the achievements of their national teams and athletes.

Currently, those countries have joined what has become the global pattern of nation-states using international sports competition for political purposes—national recognition and prestige. However, missing are the seriousness, intensity, and treatment of opponents from the opposite side as enemies, which characterized the Cold War era. Today, no major world powers oppose each other for global domination. International sports events are lively with national rivalries, and there's a special incentive to defeat teams and athletes from other countries for "bragging rights" and to instill compatriots with "national pride," but opponents from other countries tend to be treated with mutual respect, not treated with hostility and animosity.

Accompanying this more respectful, less "political" attitude toward international sport competition, along with the other facilitating conditions associated with globalization that I have described in this book, there is little doubt that international sports will proliferate in the future—and perhaps new GSOs will too. In Chapter 2, I cited Daniel Bell's *Encyclopedia of International Games* (2003) in which he reports that there were 502 international multisport competitions between 1990 and 1999, more than double the number between 1980 and 1989. Moreover, the number has increased every decade for the past one hundred years, and this spectacular growth has occurred simultaneously with the maturation of globalization processes.

More than just international multisport events have increased in recent years. It is estimated that over one hundred new international team-sport and solo-sport events have taken place in the first decade of the twenty-first century. It is likely that the trend in new multisport and team- and solo-sport competitions will continue in the coming decade.

Summary

Curiosity about the future is pervasive, and there exists a thriving group of futurists—scholars who study current issues and trends and formulate predictions about what the future might be like. Because there has been such rapid growth in international sport competitions and events in recent decades, there is a great deal of speculation about the future directions of global sport.

The transformation from folk games and casual sports to the current global sports leagues, teams, and events owes much to changes in population growth and composition, as well as in where people live. Sport prognosticators believe that continued growth in the world's population, as well as an increasingly aging and urban population, together support an expansion of global sports in the decades ahead.

The expansion of commercial sport over the past half century has brought about a fragmentation of GSOs. This has generated a great deal of criticism from national governments, players' unions, and even international governmental organizations, leading some sport analysts to suggest that GSO's continued existence is problematic. There have been calls for an umbrella or a global-level sport governing structure. The United Nations' assuming global leadership in sport in the future has been explored. In fact UNESCO has been involved in various activities in support of international sport for thirty years. In 2005 the United Nations General Assembly organized an International Year of Sport and Physical Education, and the United Nations sponsored conferences, seminars, workshops, and sports events.

The most prominent GSO, the IOC, has undertaken to find the solution to several persistent problems for the future, namely, eradicating gender and race inequality, holding future Olympic Games on African and South American continents, controlling gigantism, eliminating doping and other performance aids by Olympic athletes, and enforcing recently approved rules, regulations, and policies to which Olympic site-bid, selection, and local organizations must conform.

There is little doubt that the future will see elite sports workers migrating worldwide in search of employment opportunities. Most of the restrictions on the number of foreign players teams may employ have been removed by laws, allowing leagues and teams to field the best players money can buy.

The sporting goods and equipment industry will likely continue to manufacture in low-wage countries in the future. However, wide-ranging globalization-from-below groups will actively struggle for improved wages and working conditions in this industry, with the goal of eliminating sweatshops.

Media sport will have a prominent role in the future. Television will continue to be the dominant choice for sporting events, especially the major global sports events, but the so-called new media will continue to expand their place in media sport.

Nations will continue to use sport to promote national unity and international status, but the extreme, hostile nationalism of the Cold War will be absent. Competitors will be more respectful of each other.

References

Alexandrakis, Ambrose, and March L. Krotee. 1988. The dialectics of the International Olympic Committee. *International Review for the Sociology of Sport* 23: 334.

Ballinger, Jeff. 2008. No Sweat? Corporate social responsibility and the dilemma of anti-sweatshop activism. *New Labor Forum* 17, no. 2: 91–98.

———. 2009. Finding an anti-sweatshop strategy that works. *Dissent* 56, no. 3: 5–8.

Bell, Daniel. 2003. *Encyclopedia of international games.* Jefferson, NC: McFarland & Company.

Bourg, Jean-François, and Jean-Jacques Gouguet. 2006. Sport and globalization: Sport as a global public good. In *Handbook of the economics of sport,* ed. Wladimir Andreff and Stefan Szymanski, 744–754. Northampton, MA: Edward Elgar.

Chappelet, Jean-Loup, and Brenda Kübler-Mabbott. 2008. *The International Olympic Committee and the Olympic system: The governance of world sport.* New York: Routledge.

Clarey, Christopher. 2009. Women's boxing added for 2012 Olympics. *New York Times,* August 14, B8.

Ensor, Jim. 2006. *Future net: The essential guide to Internet and technology mega-trends.* Bloomington, IN: Trafford Publishing.

Fordyce, Tom. 2005. 10 years since Bosman. *BBC Sport,* December 14. http://news.bbc.co.uk/sport2/hi/football/4528732.stm.

Forster, John, and Nigel Pope. 2004. *The political economy of global sporting organizations.* New York: Routledge.

Haub, C. 2007. Population aging is occurring worldwide. World population data sheet. United Nations Population Division. www.prb.org/pdf07/07WPDS_ Eng.pdf.

HBO. 2008. Bissinger vs. Leitch. *Costas Now,* April 30. http://deadspin. com/385770/bissinger-vs-leitch.

International Olympic Committee (IOC). 1998. *The IOC directory.* Lausanne: IOC.

———. 2007. Olympic Charter. IOC, July 7. http://multimedia.olympic.org/ pdf/en_report_122.pdf.

———. 2008. Fact sheet: The sports on the Olympic programme. IOC, February. http://multimedia.olympic.org/pdf/en_report_1135.pdf.

———. 2009. Rules of conduct applicable to all cities wishing to organise the Olympic Games (as from the 2018 bid process onwards). IOC, March 25. http://multimedia.olympic.org/pdf/en_report_1424.pdf.

———. 2010. *The IOC directory.* Lausanne: IOC.

Katwala, Sunder. 2000. *Democratising global sport.* London: Central Books.

Lenskyj, Helen Jefferson. 2008. *Olympic industry resistance: Challenging Olympic power and propaganda.* Albany: State University of New York Press.

Leonard, David. 2009. New media and global sporting cultures: Moving beyond the clichés and binaries. *Sociology of Sport Journal* 26: 1–16.

Longman, Jere. 1999. Olympics; investigators cite cash payments in Salt Lake City bid for Olympics. *New York Times,* January 8, A1.

Penn, Mark, and E. Kinney Zalesne. 2009. *Microtrends: The small forces behind tomorrow's big changes.* Rpt. ed. New York: Twelve.

Piven, Frances Fox. 2006. *Challenging authority: How ordinary people change America.* New York: Rowman & Littlefield.

Play Fair Alliance. 2008. The Beijing Olympics: Play Fair 2008 campaign statement. PlayFair2008.org. www.playfair2008.org/templates/templateplayfair/ docs/PF_2008_campaign_statement.pdf.

Plymire, Darcy C. 2009. Premeditating football for the posthuman future: Embodiment and subjectivity in sport video games. *Sociology of Sport Journal* 26: 17–30.

Pound, Richard. 2004. *Inside the Olympics: A behind-the-scenes look at the politics, the scandals, and the glory of the games.* Etobicoke, Canada: John Wiley & Sons Canada.

Rein, Irving, Philip Kotler, and Ben Shields. 2007. The future of sports media. *The Futurist,* (January–February): 40–43.

Riordan, James. 1980. *Sport in Soviet society.* London: Cambridge University Press.

Sporting Goods Manufacturers Association (SGMA). 2008. U.S. sports industry: Nearly a $70 billion business. SGMA, June 9. www.sgma.com/press.

———. 2009. Mizuno introduces gender engineering technology in running shoes. SGMA, January 19. www.sgma.com/press.

Toohey, Kristine, and A. J. Veal. 2007. *The Olympic Games: A social science perspective.* 2nd ed. Wallingford, UK: CAB International.

United Nations. 2004. *World population prospects: The 2004 revision analytical report.* Vol. 3. UN Department of Economic and Social Affairs, Population Division. www.un.org/esa/population/publications/WPP2004/WPP2004_Volume3.htm.

———. 2006. *Sport for development and peace: The way forward. Report of the Secretary-General.* United Nations Sport 2005, September 22. www.un.org/sport2005/resources/statements/N0653114.pdf.

———. 2008. *World population prospects: The 2006 revision* and *World Urbanization Prospects: The 2007 Revision.* UN Department of Economic and Social Affairs, Population Division. www.un.org/esa/population/publications/wup2007/2007WUP_Highlights_web.pdf.

United States Census Bureau. 2009. World population: 1950–2050. U.S. Census Bureau. www.census.gov/ipc/www/idb/worldpopgraph.php.

INDEX

Abdesselam, Rhadi Ben, 197

Abel, Clarence "Taffy," 79

Adidas AG, 101; athlete endorsements, 126–127; corporate information, 109–110; history of, 112–113; Mizuno and, 117; production locations, 125; Reebok acquisition, 113, 115; team and event sponsorships, 132; *We Are Not Machines* report, 124–125

Advertising and marketing: global media sport complex, 148–149; individual athlete endorsements, 126–130; mass media bias, 142; Nike, 117–118, 120; pay-per-view television, 244–245. *See also* Media

Africa: FIFA's Eurocentric bias, 211–212; geographical residence of IOC members, 232 (table); motivation for migration, 90–91; politics of sports, 196–199; population composition, 222; racial inequity in the Olympic Movement, 232. *See also specific countries*

Africa Football and FIFA: Politics Colonialism and Resistance (Darby), 212

African Americans, 68, 213

Age: aging populations, 222–224; perception of globalization and, 4

Alien-student rule, 85

Allison, Lincoln, 198

Amateur rule, 42–44, 192

Amdur, Neil, 85

Amer Sports Corporation, 111–112, 116. *See also* Wilson Sporting Goods

American Basketball League (ABL), 178

American League of Professional Baseball Clubs, 81

Americanization of sport, 15–17, 21, 148–149

Americas: geographical residence of IOC members, 232 (table); media reach, 141–142; racial inequity in the Olympic Movement, 232. *See also specific countries*

Amos Tuck School of Business (Dartmouth College), 122

Ancient civilizations: doping athletes in ancient Greece, 236–237; historical development of globalization, 4–5; sports betting, 171

Andrews, David, 149

Annenberg Foundation study, 173–174

Annual Review of the European Football Players' Labour Market, 73

Anschutz, Philip, 156–157

Apartheid, 185, 201(box), 205–207

Appiah, Kwame Anthony, 64

Arbitration, 40

Armstrong, Lance, 130

Ashland Manufacturing, 111

Asia: future labor issues in sporting goods manufacturing, 241–242;

Asia (continued): geographical residence of
IOC members, 232(table); Nike's labor
exploitation, 119–123; racial inequity
in the Olympic Movement, 232. *See also*
China; Japan
Asian Games, 57, 208
Association of International Olympic
Winter Federations (AIOFW), 47
Association of Recognized IOC
International Sports Federations
(ARISF), 47
Association of Summer Olympic
Federations (ASOIF), 47
Association of Tennis Professionals (ATP),
54–55
Association of the National Olympic
Committees (ANOC), 38
Athletes. *See* Migration of sport labor;
specific sports
ATP World Tour, 55
Australia: Americanization of sport, 21;
global organizations and the mass
media, 143; hosting Olympic Games,
233; human migration, 64; political
dissent at the Olympic Games, 213;
politics of sports, 194–195
Australian Rugby League, 156
Australian Rules Football, 46
Austria: Euro 2008, 74
Authority: FIFA organization, 52(fig.);
GSO hierarchy, 30–32

Baca Zinn, Maxine, 3
Bagdikian, 146
Bahamas: medal standings, Beijing
Olympics, 196(table)
Bairner, Alan, 21
Bale, John, 85, 92
Barber, Benjamin, 19–20
Baseball: Americanization of sport,
21; athlete endorsement of sport
products, 127, 129; foreign-born
players in MLB, 82(table); global
participation, 2; Internet broadcast,
169; labor migration, 67–69, 81–83;
media ownership and sport coverage,
156; Mizuno Corporation, 115; older
athletes, 224; pay TV, 159; print media

coverage, 151; recruitment of sports
labor, 92; television enhancing revenue,
160; Wilson Sporting Goods, 111;
women's Olympic competition, 236
Basketball: Americanization of sport, 21;
athlete endorsement of sport products,
129–130; athletes' motivation for
migration, 91; intercollegiate, 85–86;
labor migration, 68, 76–79, 91, 239;
Olympic amateur rule, 44
Basque separatists, 213
Beckham, David, 2, 63, 129, 161(table)
Belgian Football Association, 239
Bell, Daniel, 33, 57–58, 248
Ben Abdesselam, Rhadi, 197–198
Betting, online, 171–175
BetUK.com, 174
Bikila, Abebe, 197–198
Bissinger, H. G., 247
Blatter, Joseph "Sepp," 211
Bleifuss, Joel, 8
The Blind Side (film), 153
Blogging, 246–247
Blue Ribbon Sports, 117–119
Bolton Wanderers Football Club, 132
Booth, Doug, 207
Bosman, Jean-Marc, 239
Bosman ruling, 72, 239
Boston Bruins, 79
Bowerman, Bill, 117
Boxing: global sport organizations,
55–57; international competition, 33;
Olympic amateur rule, 44; political ban
in Sweden, 187; women in the 2012
Olympic Games, 230, 236
Boycotts, 185, 199–200, 201(box), 206,
208, 214
Brailsford, Dennis, 33
Branding, 123
Brawn drain, 85, 93–94
*The Brawn Drain: Foreign Student-Athletes
in American Universities* (Bale), 85
Brazil, 132–133, 168(table), 199
Britain: amateur status of athletes,
42; broadcast rights, 161–162;
commercialization of sport, 105; early
print media, 150–152; export-processing
system, 107; global media sport

complex, 148–149; history of GSOs, 33–34; Industrial Revolution, 102–103; medal standings, Beijing Olympics, 196(table); percentage of foreign soccer players, 73; political intervention in sport, 187; radio coverage, 152–153; recruiting foreign athletes, 92; soccer development and global growth, 72; television enhancing sport revenue, 159–160. *See also* United Kingdom

British Open, 219

British Sky Broadcasting (BSkyB), 146, 154–156, 158–160, 162, 245

Brundage, Avery, 34, 166, 229

Bryant, Kobe, 129–130

Buga, Konstantin, 89

Bush, George W., 194

Business sector. *See* Corporate sector; Sport production; Transnational corporations

Business Week, 147

Cable television, 145, 148

Cambodia: Nike labor, 124

Campbell, Kim, 15

Canada: Americanization of hockey, 21; baseball, 83; foreign-born Olympic athletes, 89; hockey's global growth, 79–81; homogenization of sport, 16; intercollegiate basketball, 86; media reach, 141–142; media treatment of women, 177; migration, 64; NAIA institutions, 95(n2); political dissent at Olympic Games, 214; politics of sports, 194–195; racial and ethnic diversity, 222–223; recruiting foreign athletes, 92; soccer player migration, 73, 75; women's ski jumping, 230

Carlin, John, 207

Carlos, John, 213

Carter, David, 127

Castro, Fidel, 195

Central League (Japan), 83

Chadwick, Henry, 109

Chakvetadze, Anna, 129

Chanda, Nayan, 4

Chapplelet, Jean-Loup, 227

Chariots of Fire (film), 114, 153

Chenoweth, Neil, 156

Children: exploited labor, 108; population composition, 222; video technology, 245–246

China: export-processing system, 107; FIFA's Women's Invitational, 75; future labor issues in sporting goods manufacturing, 241; government control of mass media, 143; Internet use, 168; medal standings, Beijing Olympics, 197(table); media treatment of women, 177; Nike factories, 118–120, 122; Olympic boycott and protest, 201(box), 214; population growth, 221–222; Reebok and Adidas economic model, 125; Soviet sports model, 192; team and event sponsorships, 132; television coverage of the Olympic Games, 158. *See also* Olympic Games (2008 Beijing)

Chiropractic sports councils, 48

Christianity, 19–20

Cincinnati Red Stockings, 67

Civil War, American, 67

The Clash of Civilizations and the Remaking of World Order (Huntington), 19–20

Clean Clothes Campaign, 242

Clothing manufacture. *See* Sport production

CNN, 16, 159

Coaches: gender inequity, 203

Coakley, Jay, 6

Cobb, Ty, 127

Comcast, 145

Commercialization of sport, 104–105

Committee of Mediterranean Games, 48

Commonwealth Games Federation, 47

Communication and information technology: Americanization of sport culture, 16; articulations between sport and media, 149–154; globalization from above, 10–11; historical development of globalization, 4–5; social networking tools, 170–172, 172(box), 173, 173(box). *See also* Internet; Media

Communism, 190–192

Communist Bloc countries, 44. *See also* Soviet Union

Corporate sector: broadcast rights, 163; conglomerate media ownership, 143–147; event and team sponsorships, 130–133; global organizations and the mass media, 142–143; media ownership of sport organizations, 154–156; political economy of globalization, 8–13; sportification, 7–8. *See also* Sport production; Transnational corporations

Corruption: FIFA politics, 211–212; Olympic Games site selection, 210, 234–235; sports betting, 171

Costas Now (television show), 247

Cotswold Olympics, 33

Court, Mat, 152

Court of Arbitration for Sport (CAS), 40, 226–227

Craig, Roger, 116

Cricket: commercialization of, 105; early print media coverage, 150; international growth of, 33; politics of sport, 185

Croci, Osvaldo, 30, 32

Crosby, Sidney, 129

Crusades, 19

Cuba: baseball, 83; boxing ban, 187; medal standings, Beijing Olympics, 196(table)–197(table); Olympic boycott, 201(box); politics of sports, 195

Culcay-Keth, Jack, 89

Cultural globalization: homogenization (Americanization) perspective, 15–17, 21–22, 148–149; hybridization perspective, 18–19, 21–22; manifestations in sport, 22(table); polarization perspective, 19–22

Culture: defining, 14; motivation for migration, 90; post-19th century development of organized sport, 66; shaping globalization, 13–15; soccer development, 71–72; sport and the promotion of political ideology, 187–188; TNC growth in developing countries, 109

Curran, Jack, 115

Cycling: Adidas AG, 113; athlete endorsements, 130

da Silva, Marta Vieira, 76

Darby, Paul, 212

Dartmouth College, New Hampshire, 122

Dassler, Adolph "Adi," 112–113, 126–127

Dassler, Horst, 113

Dassler, Rudolf "Rudi," 112

de Coubertin, Pierre, 30, 34–35, 42, 59, 86, 202, 231

de Klerk, Frederik, 207

Death rate, 222

Defar, Meseret, 129

Deford, Frank, 210

DeFrantz, Anita L., 35, 204

della Porta, Donatella, 11, 13

Designated Player Rule, soccer, 75

Deskilling a nation, 93–94

Deterritorialization: of fans, 175; of politics, 11

Developing countries: clothing manufacture, 7–8; FIFA World Cup, 53; globalization from above, 9; homogenization/Americanization of culture, 16–17. *See also* Sport production; Transnational corporations

Dibaba, Tirunesh, 129

Diplomacy, sports, 189–195

Disabilities, athletes with: globalization from above and below, 13; Paralympics, 40, 44–45, 59, 195; Special Olympics, 45–46, 59

Discrimination: apartheid, 185, 205–207, 210(box); gender inequity, 200–204; Olympic amateur rule, 43; Paralympics reversing, 44–45; political dissent at Olympic Games, 213; racial inequity, 204–209; Special Olympics reversing, 45–46; Title IX, 187; US baseball, 68

Diversity: Americanization of sport culture, 14–17; IOC, 60(nn1,3), World Olympians Associations, 40

Dominican Republic, 82–83, 92

Donald, Luke, 129

Doping: East German Olympic athletes, 191; GSO agencies monitoring, 226–227; Olympic Games, 236–238; steroid use, 199; WADA, 40, 226–227

E-media, 151

Economic globalization: commercialization of sport, 104–105; human migration,

64; manifestation in sport, 22(table); manufacturing, 104–106; TNC growth in developing countries, 109
Ecuador, 89
Education and training: Canada, 195; China's Olympic training, 192; Dominican baseball, 92; Olympic training centers, 44; Soviet sport education, 190–191; sport and the promotion of political ideology, 188
Egan, Pierce, 151
Eitzen, D. Stanley, 3
Electronic devices, 240–241
Eligibility: IOC rules, 87–88, 94, 95(n3)
Elliott, Richard, 89, 93
Employment. *See* Sport production
Encyclopedia of International Games (Bell), 58, 248
Endorsements: individual athlete endorsements, 126–130; Nike, Inc., 117–118; television enhancing athletes' revenues, 160
England. *See* Britain; United Kingdom
English Premier League soccer, 152, 154–155, 158–162
Entertainment industry: homogenization of sport, 16–17; intercollegiate athlete migration, 85; post-19th century development of organized sport, 66; social role of media, 142; video games, 170
Environmental issues, 108
Ernst & Young, 122
ESPN, 159, 169
Estonia: medal standings, Beijing Olympics, 197(table)
Ethics: Olympic Games site selection, 234–235
Ethnicity: population composition, 222–223; Soviet promotion of communism through sport, 190–191
Euro (2008), 74, 152
Eurobasket.com, 78–79
Eurobet, 174
Europe: broadcast rights, 161–162; geographical residence of IOC members, 232(table); online gambling, 174; racial inequity in the Olympic Movement, 232. *See also specific countries*

European Broadcasting Union, 48, 162–163, 169
European Court of Justice (ECJ), 239
Eurosport, 148
Export-processing zones (EPZs), 106–108, 118–119

Facebook, 170, 173(box)
Fair play, 40, 242
Falk, Richard, 8, 11, 13
Fantasy leagues, 174–175
Fantasy Sports Trade Association (FSTA), 174
Fédération Internationale de Chiropratique du Sport, 48
Fédération Internationale de Football Associations (FIFA): apartheid protest, 207; broadcast rights, 163; corporate sponsorships, 165–166; function and structure of, 51–53; international sport federations, 59; online gambling, 174; politics within, 211–212; soccer development and global growth, 72; social networking tools, 172; team and event sponsorships, 132; Women's Invitational, 75. *See also* Soccer
Federer, Roger, 55, 130, 228
FIFA Sponsorship Programme, 165
Financial Times, 143
Finland: Amer Sports Corporation, 111–112
Firefighters World Games, 57
Fireman, Paul, 113–115
Flew, Terry, 147
Foer, Franklin, 7
Fonseca, Flor Isava, 35, 203–204
Football. *See* Football, American; Soccer
Football, American: broadcast rights, 162; cultural globalization, 21; expansion of TV coverage, 243–244; fantasy leagues, 174; global media sport complex, 148–149; media ownership and sport coverage, 156; motion pictures, 153; pay TV, 159; player migration, 68; Roosevelt's ban, 187
Football Association (England), 72
Ford, Gerald, 186, 192–193
Forecasters, 219–220
Foreign direct investment, 104

Formula One racing, 130
Foster, Joseph William, 114
Forster, John, 30, 32, 226
Fourteenth Amendment rights, 85
FOX Network, 156, 164
France: broadcast rights, 164; medal standings, Beijing Olympics, 196(table); percentage of foreign soccer players, 73; television-sport symbiosis, 157
French Football Federation (FFF), 133
Futurists, 219–220

G-20 Summit on Financial Markets and the World Economy (2009), 240
Galily, Yair, 21
Gambling, 171–175
Gannett Corporation, 141, 144(box)
Gay and lesbian rights, 13
Gay Games, 57
Gehrig, Lou, 127
General Association of International Sports Federations (AGFIS), 47
General Electric, 144–145
Georgia: medal standings, Beijing Olympics, 197(table)
Geran, George "Gerry," 79
German Democratic Republic, 191–192
Germany: Adidas AG, 112–113; broadcast rights, 162, 164; foreign-born Olympic athletes, 89, 91; foreign-born soccer players, 73; Internet use, 168(table); medal standings, Beijing Olympics, 196(table)–197(table); pay TV, 158–159; politics of sport, 248; promoting Nazism through sport, 190; soccer migration, 74; television coverage of the 1936 Olympics, 153
Gilmour, Steve, 152–153
Global: defined, 2
Global Alliance for Workers and Communities, 124
Global assembly line, 24
Global Exchange, 124
Global sport organizations (GSOs): authority hierarchy, 31(fig.); boxing, 55–57; characteristics and functions of, 29–32, 58–59; FIFA, 51–53; fragmentation of, 249; future of, 226–

228; gender inequity, 202; international games, 57–58; international sport federations, 46–50; international sport initiatives, 32–34; IOC, 34–37; National Olympic committees, 38–39; politics of sport, 248; solo sports, 53–57. See also Fédération Internationale de Football Associations (FIFA); International Olympic Committee
Global Unions, 242
Globalism, 19–20
Globalism: The New Market Ideology (Steger), 19
Globalization: cultural forces shaping, 13–15; defined, 2–3; historical development of, 4–5; human migration, 64; increase in the use of the word, 5(table); intra- and intercontinental migration of sport labor, 69; manifestations in sport, 22, 22(table); media industry role in, 147; political economy of, 8–13
Globalization, cultural. See Cultural globalization
Globalization: The Transformation of Social Worlds (Eitzen, Baca Zinn), 3
Globalization from above, 8–11, 13, 25, 103
Globalization from below, 8–9, 11–13, 25, 177, 242
Glocalization, 17, 22
Goldstein, Fred, 9
Golf: Adidas AG, 113; athlete endorsement of sport products, 127, 129–130; commercialization of, 105; event and team sponsorships, 131; foreign athletes in intercollegiate sports, 86(table); global growth of, 219, 225; Mizuno Corporation, 115–116; older athletes, 224; political intervention in sport, 187; Reebok, 114; women's Olympic competition, 41, 236
GoodWorks International, 122
Governance. See Global sport organizations
Government involvement in sport. See Politics of sport
Gratschow, Wilhelm, 89
Great Depression, 10(box)
The Great Olympic Swindle (Jennings), 210

Growing the Game: The Globalization of Major League Baseball (Klein), 81–82
Guest-worker programs, 69–71, 94
Guillen, Carlos, 129
Gutenberg, Johannes, 150–151
Gymnastics, 33

H-1B visas, U.S., 69–70
Hagen, Walter, 127
Hamm, Mia, 130
Hammon, Becky, 91
Harris, Michael, 150
Health care, 48
Hearst, William Randolph, 150–151
Hellenic Football Federation (HFF), 211
Heroes, 148
Hesmondhalgh, David, 14
High school sports, 46
Hill, Christopher, 206
Hillerich & Bradsby, 127
Hitler, Adolf, 190
Hockey: Americanization of, 21; athlete endorsement of sport products, 129; intercollegiate athlete migration, 86(table); NHL by nationality, 80(fig.); Olympic amateur rule, 44; pay TV, 159; player migration, 68, 79–81, 80(table), 239; recruiting foreign athletes, 92; Reebok, 114; women's Olympic competition, 203
Hoehn, Thomas, 30
Hoffman, Abby, 88
Holden, J.R., 91
Homogenization of culture, 15–19, 21–22, 148–149
Horse racing, 151
Houlihan, Barrie, 208
How Soccer Explains the World: An Unlikely Theory of Globalization (Foer), 7
Howard University, 85
Human rights violations, 119–120, 122
Human trafficking, 64
Hungarian soccer migrants, 90
Huntington, Samuel, 20
Hybridization perspective of cultural globalization, 18–19, 21–22

Ice hockey. *See* Hockey

Iceland: medal standings, Beijing Olympics, 196(table)
Identity, national: developing countries, 195–199; glocalization, 22; hockey rules limiting foreign-born players, 81; national unity, 188–189; Olympic athletes, 86–89, 94, 95(n3); politics of sports, 194–198
Ideology, 188–189. *See also* Politics of sport
Ietto-Gillies, Grazia, 3
Immigration: population trends, 222–223. *See also* Migration of sport labor
India: Internet use, 168(table); population growth, 221
Indonesia: Asian Games ban on Israel's participation, 208; Nike labor, 119–120, 122, 125
Industrial Revolution, 102–103
Industrialization: commercialization of sport, 104–105; export-processing system, 106–108; global urbanization, 225; history of, 102–103
Information society, 11
Initiative Worldwide, 158
Intercollegiate sports: IFs, 46; pay TV, 159; player migration, 84–86, 198–199; Roosevelt's football ban, 187; team and event sponsorships, 132
Interconnectedness, globalized, 3
International Association of Athletics Federations (IAAF), 88, 132, 238
International Charter on Physical Education and Sport, 227
International Committee for Fair Play (ICFP), 40
International Federation of Gymnastics (IFG), 33
International games, 57–58. *See also entries beginning with* Olympic; World Cup
International Institute of Forecasters, 220
International Labour Organization (ILO), 108
International Monetary Fund (IMF), 11–12
International Network on Cultural Policy, 15
International Olympic Committee (IOC): amateur rule, 192; apartheid protest, 206–207; Asian Games, 208;

International Olympic Committee (IOC) (continued): corporate sponsorships, 166; diversity of, 60(nn1,3); doping and performance aids, 236–238; eligibility rules, 87–88, 94, 95(n3); function of, 59; future opportunities and challenges, 249; gender inequity, 202–204; geographical residence of IOC members, 232(table); gigantism, 235–236; governance, 228–229; GSOs within, 46–50; history and function, 34–37; IOC as GSO, 30; membership structure, 229; politics within, 209–211; site selection, 210, 234–235; women's participation, 41–42. *See also entries beginning with* Olympic

International Paralympic Committee (IPC), 40

International sport federations (IFs), 37, 39, 44, 46–50, 229

International sport initiatives, 32–34

Internet: basketball coverage, 78–79; blogging, 246–247; conglomerate media ownership, 144(box); deterritorialization of fans, 175; fantasy leagues, 174–175; global explosion in utility and use, 168–169; global media sport complex, 148–149; online gambling, 171–175; reach of, 141–142; social networking tools, 170–171, 172(box)–173(box); television coverage expansion, 244–245; top five sports websites, 169(table); top seven world users, 168(table)

Invictus (film), 153, 207

Iran, 208

Iraq, 208–209, 213

Islam: European population trends, 223; religious wars, 19–20

Israel: Americanization of sport, 21; Arab rejection of Israeli sports, 208; death of Olympic athletes, 213

Italy: broadcast rights, 162, 164; pay TV, 158–159; percentage of foreign soccer players, 73; World Cup final, 158

Ivanovic, Ana, 129

Iverson, Allen, 129

Jackson, Steven, 149

Jamaica: medal standings, Beijing Olympics, 196(table)–197(table)

Jamal, Maryam Yusuf, 89

James, LaBron, 130, 161(table)

Japan: baseball, 83, 84(table); Internet use, 168(table); Mizuno Corporation, 115–116; Nike, Inc., 116–118; social networking tools, 172

Japanese Baseball League, 83

Jennings, Andrew, 210

Jihad, 19–20

Jihad vs. McWorld: How Globalism and Tribalism are Reshaping the World (Barber), 19–20

Jobs: guest-worker programs, 69–71; history of human migration, 64–66; Nike, Inc., 116–118. *See also* Migration of sport labor; Sport production

Jones, Chipper, 129

Jones, Marion, 199

Jordan, Michael, 117, 127–128, 130, 148

Justice movement, global, 11–13

J. W. Foster and Sons, 114

Kaman, Chris, 91

Katwala, Sunder, 226

Kazakhstan, 89

Kelly, William W., 81

King, Billie Jean, 55

King, Christopher, 177

Keino, Kip, 198

Kenya: sport labor migration, 89, 91

Kenya Football Federation (KFF), 211–212

Kenyatta, Jomo, 198

Kidd, Bruce, 21, 195

Killanin, Lord, 166

Klein, Alan, 21, 81–82, 92

Knight, Philip H., 116–117, 119–123, 241

Knight-Ridder, 144(box)

Korea, North, 187, 197(table), 201(box)

Korea, South, 118, 201(box)

Kraidy, Marwan, 18

Kroft, Steve, 171

Kübler-Mabbott, Brenda, 227

Labor. *See* Migration of sport labor; Sport production

Labor organizations, 12

Labor standards and conditions: EPZ exploitation, 108; future challenges, 241–242; Nike factories, 118–126; Nike's "New Labor Initiative," 123–126; sweatshops, 123–126, 134(n1), 241–242. *See also* Sport production
La Feber, Walter,
Lagat, Bernard, 89
Latin America: baseball, 83; future labor issues in sporting goods manufacturing, 241–242
Lee, Jung Woo, 22
Leonard, David, 168
Levin Institute, 17
Liberalism, 10(box)
Life in London journal, 151
Ling-Temco-Vought Corporation, 111
Lomong, Lopez, 89
Long-distance fans, 175
Los Angeles Dodgers, 156
Loughborough University, 204
Louisville Slugger, 127
Low-Wage Capitalism (Goldstein), 9
Loy, John W., 6, 22

MacAloon, John, 34
Macfarlane, John, 21
Maguire, Joseph, 6, 21-22, 89, 93
Major League Baseball (MLB): baseball equipment manufacture, 127; deterritorialization of fans, 175; Internet infrastructure, 245; Japanese players on MLB rosters, 84(table); older athletes, 224; percentage of foreign-born players on MLB rosters, 82(table); player migration, 67–69, 81–83; television enhancing revenue, 160
Major League Soccer (MLS), 73, 75
Mallon, Bill, 88, 91
Manchester United, 155–156
Mandela, Nelson, 207
Manufacture of sporting goods. *See* Sport production
Manufacturing, historical rise of, 102–103
Manzano, Leo, 89
Mao Tse-tung, 192
Marconi, Guglielmo, 152

Marketing. *See* Advertising and marketing; Sport promotion
Martin, Susan F., 64
Mass communication, 140–141. *See also* Media
Massachusetts Institute of Technology (MIT), 125
Master Card, 165
Masters Golf Tournament, 219
McChesney, Robert, 146
McClatchy Company, 144(box)
McDonald's restaurants, 16
McKay, Jim, 21
McWorld, 19–20
Media: articulations between sport and, 149–154; basketball coverage, 78–79; broadcast rights, 161–164; conglomerate ownership, 143–147; cultural homogenization, 15; deterritorialization of fans, 175; European Broadcasting Union, 48; fantasy leagues, 174; future opportunities and challenges, 243–247, 249; global media sport complex, 147–149; global organizations and, 142–143; globalization from above, 9; historical development of globalization, 5; homogenization of sport, 16; mass communication, mass media, and media sport, 140–141; media ownership of sport organizations, 154–156; motion pictures, 153; Nike factory scrutiny, 120, 122; as public relations tool, 167; radio, 152–153; social roles of, 141–142; sport revenue, 159–161; television, 153; television-sport symbiosis, 157–167; transnational corporate sport sponsorships, 164–167; treatment of women, 175–178; video games, 170; world's largest corporations, 2008, 145(table). *See also* Internet
Media sports, 141
Megacities, 224
Mémoires Olympiques (de Coubertin), 34
Mexico: baseball, 83, 89; export-processing system, 107
Microsoft, 145
Migration: history of human migration, 64–66

Migration of sport labor: baseball, 81–83; basketball, 76–79; consequences of, 93–94; future opportunities and challenges, 238–240; guest-worker programs, 69–71, 94; hockey, 79–81; hybridization of culture, 18; intercollegiate athletes, 84–86; intra- and intercontinental migration, 68–71; intranational, 67–68; manifestations of globalization in sport, 22(table); motivations for, 89–91; nature of, 66–67; Nike labor practices, 118–119; Olympic athletes, 86–89; recruitment of sports labor, 91–93; soccer, 71–76

Milanovic, Branko, 72

Miller, Toby, 21

Miresmaeli, Arash, 208

Mizuno, Masato, 116

Mizuno Corporation, 101; athlete endorsements, 129–130; corporate information, 109–110; Gender Engineering running shoe, 243; history of, 115–116; team and event sponsorships, 132

Mizuno, Rohachi, 115

MLB.TV Mosaic, 245

Mongolia: medal standings, Beijing Olympics, 197(table)

Monnington, Terry, 198

Montreal Wanders, 79

Motion pictures, 153

Mountaineering, 115

Multisport competitions, 33, 57–58

Murdoch, Rupert, 144(box), 146–147, 154–156, 179

MySpace, 170

Nadal, Rafael, 130

Naismith, James, 76

N stase, Ilie, 130

National Association for Intercollegiate Athletics (NAIA), 84, 95(n2)

National Association of Professional Base Ball Players, 81

National Basketball Association (NBA), 76–79, 77(fig.), 129, 172, 239

National Collegiate Athletic Association (NCAA), 46, 84–86, 132

National Federation of State High School Associations, 46

National Football League (NFL), 159, 162

National Hockey League (NHL), 79–81, 239

National Intercollegiate Athletic Association, 46

National League of Professional Baseball Clubs, 81, 169

National Olympic committees (NOCs), 36–39, 87–88, 209–210, 229

Nationality: IOC eligibility rules, 87–88, 94, 95(n3). See also Identity, national

Nazism, 190

NBC, 162–163

Neo-Olympics, 30

Neoliberalism, 9–11, 10(box), 12

New Labor Initiatives (Nike), 123–126

New York Rangers, 79

New York Times, 5(table)

New Zealand, 148, 197(table)

News Corp., 144(box), 146, 154–156

Newspapers, 150–152, 177. See also Media

Newsquest, 144(box)

NFL Network, 243–244

Nike, Inc., 101; Adidas acquisition of Reebok, 113; athlete endorsements, 128, 130; corporate information, 109–110; future labor issues, 241–242; history of, 116–118; labor exploitation in developing countries, 119–123; reform plans, 123–126; response to Social Movement, 121–123; subsidizing Olympic athletes, 192; team and event sponsorships, 132–133

Nike Social Movement, 120–123

Nordic-Scandinavian soccer migrants, 90

Norman, Greg, 114, 224

Norman, Peter, 213

North America. See Americas; Canada; Mexico; United States

Norway: medal standings, Beijing Olympics, 196(table)

Oil industry, 156–157

Okayo, Margaret, 228

Olympic Games (1896; Athens), 36

Olympic Games (1900; Paris), 52

Olympic Games (1904; St. Louis), 52
Olympic Games (1908; London), 41–42, 52
Olympic Games (1912; Stockholm), 42–43
Olympic Games (1920; Antwerp), 206
Olympic Games (1924; Paris), 42, 114
Olympic Games (1932; Los Angeles), 189–190, 235
Olympic Games (1936; Berlin), 112, 126–127, 153
Olympic Games (1948; London), 206
Olympic Games (1952; Helsinki), 112
Olympic Games (1956; Melbourne), 46, 200, 201(box)
Olympic Games (1960; Rome), 45, 197–198, 235
Olympic Games (1968; Mexico City), 206, 213
Olympic Games (1972; Munich), 22(table), 166, 185, 213
Olympic Games (1976; Montreal), 201(box)
Olympic Games (1980; Moscow), 185, 201(box)
Olympic Games (1984; Los Angeles), 112–113, 166, 185, 201(box)
Olympic Games (1988; Seoul), 45, 167, 201(box)
Olympic Games (1992; Barcelona), 45, 202, 213, 235
Olympic Games (1996; Atlanta), 192–193, 203, 210, 213
Olympic Games (1998; Nagano), 132
Olympic Games (2000; Sydney), 128–129, 199, 213, 235
Olympic Games (2004; Athens), 158, 167, 202–203, 208, 213
Olympic Games (2008; Beijing): boycotts, 201(box); China's dominance of global sport, 221–222; corporate sponsorships, 167; Flame relay protest, 213–214; foreign-born athletes, 89, 91; globalization of sport, 22(table); Internet broadcasting, 169; Iraq's ban on attending, 208–209; medal standings per country by GDP, 197(table); medal standings per country by population, 196(table); numbers of sports and events, 236; Paralympics, 45; participation numbers, 2, 36; politics of sport, 192; television coverage, 158; women athletes, 42, 59, 203, 229–230
Olympic Games (2012; London), 36, 215(n1), 236
Olympic Games (2016; Rio de Janeiro), 234, 236
Olympic Movement: amateur status, 42–44; apartheid in South Africa, 206; basketball, 77; boycotts, 200, 201(box); broadcast rights, 163(table); broadcasting revenues, 162–163; Canada's national training program, 195; corporate sponsorships, 165–166; cultural globalization, 22; eligibility issues, 87–88, 94, 95(n3); FIFA and, 52–53; first international competitions, 33–34; future of GSOs, 228–238; gender inequity, 229–231; geographical location of the Games, 232–234; international sport federations, 39; IOC function, 35–37; media treatment of women, 177; migration of athletes, 86–89; motto, 209–210; National Olympic Committees, 38–39; OM partners, 39–40; Organizing Committee of the Olympic Games, 37; pay TV, 159; political dissent, 212–213; politics and the Games, 185–186; racial inequity, 231–232; site selection, 210, 232–235; Soviet participation, 191; special needs athletes, 44–46; Special Olympics, 45–46; women in, 41–42, 75–76, 229–231. See also International Olympic Committee
Olympic Partner Program (TOP), 167
Olympic Training Centers, 192–193
Olympic Winter Games (1936; Garmisch-Partenkirchen), 43
Olympic Winter Games (1960; Squaw Valley), 235
Olympic Winter Games (1994; Lillehammer), 166, 202–203
Olympic Winter Games (1998; Nagano), 210
Olympic Winter Games (2002; Salt Lake City), 193, 210–211, 234–235

Olympic Winter Games (2006; Turin), 89
Olympic Winter Games (2010; Vancouver), 36, 45, 203, 214, 229–230, 235
O'Neal, Shaquille, 161(table)
Organization for Economic Cooperation and Development (OECD) countries: characteristics of, 95(n1); human migration, 64; manufacturing in the global economy, 104
Organizations. *See* Global sport organizations; International Olympic Committee
Owens, Jesse, 112, 126–127
Oxfam, 242

Pacific League (Japan), 83
Palestinians, 213
Palmer, Arnold, 128
Pan American Games, 195
Pan-Hellenic Games, 171
Paralympics, 40, 44–45, 59, 195
Patriotism, 188–189
Pay-per-view television, 157–159, 164, 244–245
Pelé, 127
Pepsico, 111
Performance. *See* Sport performance
Peru, 199
PGA Championship, 219
Pieterse, Jan Nederveen, 18
Pistorius, Oscar, 238
Pitts, Brenda, 23, 100, 126
Piven, Frances Fox, 241
Play Fair at the Olympics Campaign, 242
Playing the Enemy: Nelson Mandela and the Game That Changed a Nation (Carlin), 207
Plymire, Darcy, 246
Podium Canada, 195
Polarization perspective of cultural globalization, 19–22
The Political Economy of Global Sporting Organizations (Forster and Pope), 30, 226
Political economy of globalization, 8–13
Political globalization, 22(table)
Politics of sport: anti-Iraq movements, 208–209; anti-Israel movements, 208; censorship through boycotts, 199–200; developing countries, 195–199; dissent at global sports events, 212–214; within FIFA, 211–212; future opportunities and challenges, 247–248; gender inequity, 200–204; government intervention in sport, 186–187; inevitable link, 185–186; within the IOC, 209–211; motivation for migration, 90; national embarrassments, 199; national governments and GSO tensions, 226; national unity and recognition, 188–189; promotion of political ideology, 187–188; racial inequity, 204–209; sport as an instrument of international politics and diplomacy, 189–195; United States involvement, 192–194
Pop culture, 16–17
Pope, Nigel, 30, 226
Population characteristics and statistics, 220–226
Pound, Richard, 167, 209, 211, 237
Powell, Colin, 213
Prefontaine, Steve, 130
President's Commission on Olympic Sports, 186, 192–193
Print media, 150–152. *See also* Media
Process, globalization as, 3–4
Production of sporting goods. *See* Sport production
Promotion, sports. *See* Sport promotion
Prosthetics, 238
Public relations, media and, 167
Puerto Rico: baseball, 83
Puma, 112, 117
Puritans, 187

Qatar, 89

Racial inequity, 204–209, 231–232
Radio, 152–153
Rahimov, Rustam, 89
Rawlings Company, 127
Real, Michael, 173–175
Recruitment of sports labor, 91–93
Reebok International, 101; Adidas acquisition of, 113; athlete endorsements, 129–130; corporate information, 109–110; history of, 113–

115; Nike and, 117; race-to-the-bottom economic model, 125; subsidizing Olympic athletes, 192; team and event sponsorships, 132

Regulation: neoliberalism, 10(box)

Religion: population composition, 222–223; post-19th century development of organized sport, 66; religious wars, 19–20

Reserve clause, baseball, 68

Rights: globalization from below and, 11–13

Ripken, Cal, Jr., 194

Ritzer, George,

Robertson, Roland, 17, 22

Rocky (film), 153

Rogge, Jacques, 229, 237

Ronaldinho, 130

Roosevelt, Theodore, 187

Rugby: commercialization of, 105; motion pictures, 153; Olympic Games 2016, 236; South African victory, 207

Rugby World Cup, 207

Rules development: hockey rules limiting foreign-born players, 81; soccer, 72

Running: Adidas AG, 112; African achievements, 197–198; athlete endorsement of sport products, 129

Russia, 132; foreign-born Olympic athletes, 91; medal standings, Beijing Olympics, 196(table)–197(table)

Ruth, Babe, 127

Salaries: highest-earning athletes in the world, 161(table); soccer, 75; television enhancing, 160; women's soccer, 76

Salomon Worldwide Group, 113

Samaranch, Juan Antonio, 35, 40, 166, 229

Sambrook, Clare, 210

Sarazen, Gene, 127–128

Satellite television and radio, 146, 148, 152–153

Schiller, Dan, 146

Scholte, Jan Aart, 3

Schumacher, Michael, 130

Scotland, 187

Segmentation of the global sport industry, 23–24

Selassie, Haile, 198

Senior citizens, 222

Senior Olympics, 224

September 11, 2001, 142

Setanta, 160

Sharapova, Maria, 130

Sheard, Ken,

Shriver, Eunice Kennedy, 45

Simon Fraser University, Canada, 95(n2)

Simson, Vyv, 210

Single-sport competitions, 33

Sirius Satellite Radio, 152

Skiing events: foreign athletes in intercollegiate sports, 86(table); Mizuno Corporation, 115; ski-jumping, 230

Slavery, 22(table), 64

Sloan School of Management (MIT), 125

Slovenia: medal standings, Beijing Olympics, 196(table)

Smart, Barry, 7

Smith, Adam, 10(box)

Smith, Michael, 92

Smith, Tommie, 213

Soccer: Adidas AG, 112–113; African athletes' migration, 198–199; athlete endorsement of sport products, 127, 130; Beckham's US migration, 63; Bosman ruling, 72, 239; Brazil's poor showing, 199; broadcast rights, 163–164; commercialization of, 105; corporate sponsorships, 165–166; fantasy leagues, 174; FIFA, 51–53; foreign athletes in intercollegiate sports, 86(table); future of sports labor migration, 239; global participation, 2; immigration fostering popularity, 224; media ownership of sport organizations, 154–156; motivation for migration, 90; Olympic amateur rule, 44; pay-per-view television, 158–159; player migration, 68, 71–76; politics within FIFA, 211–212; satellite media, 152; sportification, 7–8; team and event sponsorships, 132–133; television enhancing revenue, 159–160; women in, 75–76. *See also* Fédération Internationale de Football Associations

Social change, 150–151

Social integration, 149

Social movements, 12–13

Social networking tools, 170–171, 172(box)–173(box)

Social sphere: articulations between sport and media, 149–154; motivation for migration, 90; post-19th century development of organized sport, 66; social roles of mass media, 141–142; sport and the promotion of political ideology, 187–188; TNC growth in developing countries, 109

Softball, 203, 215(n1), 236

Solo sports, 53–57

Somalia, 89

Sony Ericsson WTA Tour, 55

South Africa: apartheid, 205–207; Olympic boycott, 201(box); Olympic Games, 200; politics of sport, 185–186

Soviet Union: Cold War competition, 192–193; intracontinental sport labor migration, 69; Olympic boycott, 201(box); politics of sport, 185, 247–248; promoting communism through sport, 190–191

Spain: basketball, 78; pay TV, 158–159; percentage of foreign soccer players, 73

Special needs athletes, 44–46, 59. See also Disabilities, athletes with

Special Olympics, 45–46, 59

Spirit of the Times journal, 151

Sponsorship: event and team, 130–133; pay-per-view television, 244–245; TNC sponsorships, 164–167

Sport: defined, 2, 5–6; globalization from above and below, 13; historical development of, 6; post-19th century development of organized sport, 66

Sport Canada, 195

Sport labor. See Sport production

Sport media. See Media

Sport performance: individual athlete endorsements, 126; segmentation of the global sport industry, 24

Sport production: Adidas AG, 112–113; Americanization of sport, 15; future labor issues in sporting goods manufacture, 241–242; future opportunities and challenges, 240–243, 249; future technology, 242–243; global economy, 106–108; global media sport complex, 147–149; globalization from above and below, 13; growth of commercial sport, 104–106; human migration, 64–66; individual athlete endorsements, 126–128; Mizuno Corporation, 115–116; Nike's labor exploitation, 119–123; Nike's plan for reform, 123–126; Nike's response to the Nike Social Movement, 121–123; origins in developing countries, 7–8; Reebok International, 113–115; segmentation of the global sport industry, 23–24; sweatshops, 123–126, 134(n1), 241–242; TNC growth in developing countries, 100–102, 108–110; Wilson Sporting Goods, 111–112; world merchandise trade volume, 1960–2009, 65(fig.)

Sport promotion: event and team sponsorships, 130–133; individual athlete endorsements, 126–130; segmentation of the global sport industry, 24

Sportification, 7–8, 24

Sporting goods manufacture. See Sport production

Sporting Goods Manufacturers Association (SGMA), 101–102, 109, 240

Sporting News, 147

Sports and Pastimes of the People of England (Strutt), 151

Sports Illustrated, 151, 172

Sports Sponsor Fact Book, 131

SportsFanLive.com, 173(box)

STAR TV, 146

State Department, U.S., 194

Steger, Manfred, 3, 14–15, 19

Sterner, Ulf, 79

Steroid use, 199

Stotlar, David, 23, 100, 126

Strange, Susan, 57

Strikes, labor, 120, 125

Strutt, Joseph, 151

Students: gambling on sports events, 173–174; high school sports, 46; Nike Social Movement, 123; social movements, 12–13, 123. See also Intercollegiate sports

Sudan, 89, 213–214

Suleiman, Mohammed, 89

Super Bowl, 158
Suzuki, Ichiro, 129
Sweatshops, 123–126, 134(n1), 241–242
Sweden: boxing ban, 187
Swimming: advanced technology, 128–129, 243
Switzerland, 74
Swoosh, Nike, 117, 122–123, 130

Table tennis, 132
Taiwan, 118–119, 201(box), 208
Tajikistan, 89
Talk on Sport (radio program), 152
TaylorMade, 113
Technology: controlling doping, 238; expansion of television coverage, 244–245; future advances, 242–243; historical rise of manufacturing, 102–103; Internet expansion, 245; social networking tools, 172–173; sport production, 116; swimsuit technology, 128–129. *See also* Communication and information technology; Media
Tejada, Miguel, 129
Television, 153–154; broadcast rights, 161–164; enhancing sport revenue, 159–161; expansion of coverage, 243–245; sports television menu, 158(table); television-sport symbiosis, 157–167. *See also* Media
Tennis: Adidas AG, 112; athlete endorsement of sport products, 129–130; global growth of, 33, 225; global sport organizations, 54–55; media treatment of women, 177; older athletes, 224; Wilson Sporting Goods, 111; women's Olympic competition, 41
Tennis for Two video game, 170
Tenorio, Rafael, 56
Terrorism: death of Olympic athletes, 213; manifestations of globalization in sport, 22(table); polarization of cultural globalization, 19–20; politics of sport, 185; role of the media, 142
Textiles. *See* Sport production
TF1 Group, 148
Thailand: Nike labor, 119, 124–125
Thorpe, Ian, 128–129
Thorpe, Jim, 43
Tibet, 213–214

Title IX, 187
Toohey, Kristine, 209, 229
Totalization of sport, 7
Tourism, global, 22(table)
Track and field: athlete endorsement of sport products, 130; doping, 199; political dissent at the Olympic Games, 213
Translocal recruitment systems, 92–93
Transnational corporations (TNCs): conglomerate media ownership, 143–147; corporate sport sponsorships, 164–167; dominating sport production, 100–101; exploitation of foreign labor, 106–108; global media sport complex, 147–149; globalization from above, 9; growth in developing countries, 103, 108–110; GSOs and, 30; IOC as profit-making organization, 35; McDonald's as global force, 16; Olympic Movement, 36; stability of ownership, 241. *See also* Adidas AG; Corporate sector; Mizuno Corporation; Nike, Inc.; Reebok International; Sport production; Wilson Sporting Goods
Trends Research Institute, 220
Tribalism, 19–20
Tse-tung, Mao, 192
Turner Broadcasting System, 169
Twitter, 170, 172(box)

Union labor, 119–120
Union of European Football Associations (UEFA): Bosman ruling, 239; broadcast media, 163–164; satellite media, 152; team and event sponsorships, 132; Women's Euro, 75
Union of European Leagues of Basketball (ULEB), 78
United Kingdom: broadcast rights, 162, 164; conglomerate media ownership, 144(box); fantasy leagues, 174; global organizations and the mass media, 143; Internet use, 168(table); media ownership and sport organizations, 154–156; media reach, 141; media treatment of women, 177; online gambling, 174; population trends, 223; radio coverage, 152. *See also* Britain

United Nations: global sport governance, 226–228

United Nations Educational, Scientific, and Cultural Organization (UNESCO), 227–228, 249

United States: Americanization of sport, 15–17, 21, 148–149; basketball migration, 76–77; Beckham's US migration, 63; broadcast rights, 162; conglomerate media ownership, 146; fantasy leagues, 174; foreign-born Olympic athletes, 89; global media sport complex, 148–149; hockey's global growth, 79–81; human migration, 64; Internet use, 168(table); Iraq invasion, 208–209, 213; medal standings, Beijing Olympics, 196(table)–197(table); media reach, 141–142; media treatment of women, 177; Mizuno Corporation baseball equipment, 115–116; MLB player numbers, 82; Nike, Inc., 116–118; Olympic boycott, 201(box); Olympic training centers, 43–44; politics of sport, 187, 192–194, 248; racial and ethnic diversity, 222–223; rise of manufacturing, 102–103; soccer player migration, 73; soccer's global growth, 75–76; sport labor migration, 67–68; steroid use, 199; television-sport symbiosis, 157; women's basketball, 78

United States Olympic Committee (USOC), 159, 192–193, 203–204

United Students Against Sweatshops (USAS), 123

Urban Community Mission (Jakarta), 124

Urbanization, 104–105, 224–225

USA Today newspaper, 141, 144(box)

Uzbekistan, 89

Vaccaro, Sonny, 128

Values, 40

Vamplew, Wray, 105

Veal, A. J., 209, 229

Video games and technology, 170, 245–246

Vietnam: Nike labor, 119–120, 122, 124–125

Virgil, Ozzie Sr., 82

Visas, US, 69–70

Volleyball, 132, 199

Wagner, Honus, 127

Walker, Sam, 175

Walt Disney Corporation, 145

Watson, Tom, 224

We Are Not Machines report, 124–125

Whannel, Garry, 36, 157

Wii, 170

Williams, Serena, 130

Williams, Venus, 129

Wilson, Des, 185

Wilson, Thomas E., 111

Wilson Sporting Goods, 101; athlete endorsements, 128–129; corporate information, 109–110; event and team sponsorships, 131–132; history of, 111–112; pioneering golf wear and equipment, 127

Wimbledon Championships, 177

Winter Olympics. See Olympic Winter Games

Winter Olympics IFs, 47

Winn, Luke, 85

Wolff, Michael, 156

Women and Sport Commission (IOC), 231

Women and women's sports: athlete endorsement of products, 128–130; basketball, 78; development and spread of organized soccer, 75–76; exploited labor, 108; FIFA Women's World Cup, 53; foreign athletes in intercollegiate sports, 86(table); foreign-born Olympic athletes, 87, 89, 91; global gender inequity, 200–204; global population trends, 223; global urbanization, 225; IOC membership, 35, 59; media treatment of, 175–178; Nike's labor exploitation, 119; Olympic athletes, 41–42, 87, 89, 91, 224–231, 236; Olympic Movement gender inequity, 229–231; online gambling, 174; volleyball in Peru, 199

Women's Euro, 75

Women's National Basketball Association (WNBA), 78, 91, 178

Women's Professional Basketball League, 78

Women's Professional Soccer (WPS), 76

Women's Tennis Association (WTA), 54–55
Women's United Soccer Association (WUSA), 75–76
Woods, Tiger, 117, 130, 161(table)
World Anti-Doping Agency (WADA), 40, 226–227, 237
World Anti-Doping Code, 237
World Bank, 11–12
World Championship Tennis, 54
World Cup, 163, 163(table); Brazil's embarrassments, 199; corporate sponsorships, 165; FIFA function, 51–54; GSOs, 32; origins of, 72; viewing numbers, 2; Women's World Cup, 75–76
World Cup, Rugby (1995), 207
World Cup (1954), 113
World Cup (1966), 207
World Cup (1970), 207
World Cup (1974), 113
World Cup (2006), 163

World Cup (2010), 163, 186, 200
World Federation of the Sporting Goods Industry (WFSGI), 240
World Future Society, 220
World Games, 48
World Masters Games, 57
World Olympians Associations, 40
World Trade Organization (WTO), 11–12
World University Games, 186
Wrestling, 236
Wu, Ping, 177

Yachting: international growth of, 33
Young, Andrew, 122
YouTube, 170

Zaharias, Babe Didrikson, 128
Zinn, Maxine Baca, 3
Zen-Ruffinen, Michael, 211
Zimbabwe, 197(table), 200
Zuma, Jacob, 207

ABOUT THE AUTHOR

George H. Sage is professor emeritus of Sociology and Kinesiology at the University of Northern Colorado. He received B.A. and M.A. degrees from the University of Northern Colorado and a doctorate degree from UCLA. He was the head basketball coach at Pomona College for four years and head basketball coach at the University of Northern Colorado for five years, winning four conference championships and taking the UNC teams to three NCAA Regional Basketball Tournaments.

Dr. Sage has published more than fifty articles in the professional literature, authored or co-authored fifteen books (including multiple editions), and written several chapters in edited books. He is past president of the National Association for Kinesiology and Physical Education in Higher Education (NAKPEHE) and past president of the North American Society for the Sociology of Sport (NASSS); he holds Fellowship status in the American Academy of Kinesiology and Physical Education, as well as the Research Consortium of the American Alliance for Health, Physical Education, Recreation, and Dance (AAHPERD). He was selected as an Alliance Scholar by AAHPERD in 1985 and was inducted into the National Association for Sport & Physical Education Hall of Fame in 2006. At the University of Northern Colorado, Sage was selected for a UNC Distinguished Scholar Award, the Lucile Harrison Outstanding Teaching Award, and he was inducted into the UNC Athletic Hall of Fame, first as a individual and second as a member of the 1955 baseball team.